This is the first book-length study of popular culture in Islamic society. Dr Boaz Shoshan draws together a wealth of Arabic sources to explore literature, religious celebrations, and annual festivities in medieval Cairo and addresses questions of relevance throughout the Islamic world and beyond.

Dr Shoshan examines popular religion against the background of the growing influence of Sufism. In particular, he discusses the sermons of Ibn ʿAṭāʾ Allāh, a leading Cairene Sufi, which shed considerable light on the beliefs of ordinary Muslims. The author then analyses the importance of a biography of Muḥammad, which has been attributed to Abū'l-Ḥasan al-Bakrī and suppressed by the learned. He then traces the origins and popular practices of the annual Nawrūz festival. Finally he explores the political beliefs and economic expectations of the Cairene commoners and demonstrates the complex relationship between the culture of the Cairene elite and that of the people.

This book presents a stimulating discussion of a subject touched on only peripherally previously. The author tests his theories against similar phenomena in European society and with reference to several standard authorities in anthropology and social history. *Popular culture in medieval Cairo* will, therefore, be of interest to students and specialists in Middle Eastern studies and also to medieval historians.

Cambridge Studies in Islamic Civilization

Popular culture in medieval Cairo

Cambridge Studies in Islamic Civilization

Titles in the series

B. F. MUSALLAM. *Sex and society in Islam: birth control before the nineteenth century*
SURAIYA FAROQHI. *Towns and townsmen of Ottoman Anatolia: trade, crafts and food production in an urban setting, 1520–1650*
SURAIYA FAROQHI. *Men of modest substance: house owners and house property in seventeenth-century Ankara and Kayseri*
PATRICIA CRONE. *Roman, provincial and Islamic law: the origins of the Islamic patronate*
STEFAN SPERL. *Mannerism in Arabic poetry: a structural analysis of selected texts, 3rd century AH/9th century AD–5th century AH/11th century AD*
BEATRICE FORBES MANZ. *The rise and rule of Tamerlane*
AMNON COHEN. *Economic life in Ottoman Jerusalem*
PAUL E. WALKER. *Early philosophical Shiism: the Ismaili Neoplatonism of Abū Ya'qūb al-Sijistānī*

Popular culture in medieval Cairo

BOAZ SHOSHAN
Ben-Gurion University, Beer-Sheva

CAMBRIDGE
UNIVERSITY PRESS

Published by the Press Syndicate of the University of Cambridge
The Pitt Building, Trumpington Street, Cambridge CB2 1RP
40 West 20th Street, New York, NY 10011–4211, USA
10 Stamford Road, Oakleigh, Melbourne 3166, Australia

First published 1993

Printed in Great Britain at the University Press, Cambridge

A catalogue record for this book is available from the British Library

Library of Congress cataloguing in publication data

Shoshan, Boaz.
Popular culture in medieval Cairo / Boaz Shoshan.
p. cm. – (Cambridge studies in Islamic civilization)
Includes bibliographical references and index.
ISBN 0 521 43209 X
1. Cairo (Egypt) – Social life and customs. I. Title.
II. Series.
DT146.S54 1993
962'.1602–dc20 92–34084 CIP

ISBN 0 521 43209 X hardback

Contents

Preface

"La culture arabe médiévale est une culture d'élite, donc de classe", wrote a student of medieval Arabic literature in the late seventies. It was statements of this sort, or presumably more the general character of works written in the field of Islamic studies, which led Ernest Gellner, about the same time, to the observation that orientalists – as opposed to anthropologists – being at home with texts, naturally tend to see Islam "from above", not "from below". Almost twenty years later, and after a generation of scholars tracing histories "from below", Gellner's statement about orientalists still retains its validity. From the vantage point of the early nineties, two qualifications should be made, however.

First, there has been, at least since the turn of our century, an unsteady current even within orientalism of writing on topics related to popular culture. Already one hundred years ago the towering Ignaz Goldziher wrote on the "cult of saints" in Islam as an expression of popular religion. Of the works written in recent years one should mention Bosworth's painstaking study of the jargon of the medieval Islamic "underworld"; Memon's analysis of Ibn Taymiyya's critique of popular Islam; and parts of Langner's doctoral dissertation on folklore (*Volkskunde*) in Mamluk Egypt, especially her chapter on customs associated with Islamic holidays. These names certainly do not exhaust the important work which has been done by historians on the culture of "ordinary" Muslims.

Second, contrary to Gellner, the text, including the historical text, need not in itself be a hindrance to studying culture "from below". After all, texts are the main tool historians can work with, and in several excellent works historians have demonstrated that certain texts, if imaginatively utilized, can be found to be "thick" enough and invaluable for the study of popular culture.

It was in 1981 that I first read Peter Burke's *Popular Culture in Early Modern Europe*, fascinated by the subject, admiring the scholarship invested in that book, and also regretting that a similar work on the world of Islam would never be written. My basic reaction to Burke's achievement has not changed since. However, when I was teaching a seminar on the social bases of medieval Islamic culture in 1986 and 1987, I certainly "discovered" the "people" and the popular as a significant element in that culture. With the inspiration of Burke's book and other historical works, I gradually ventured to envisage a study on popular culture in medieval

Egypt, a region with the history of which I am to some extent familiar. This study is now complete: it is of limited scope, but I venture to think it is a pioneer of its kind, being entirely devoted to the popular culture of one medieval Islamic region.

This book consists of five chapters, each dealing with a separate phenomenon of popular culture in late medieval Cairo. It is actually a collection of studies, the only format, I suspect, for treating so wide and variegated a subject as culture yet on a limited basis of historical data. This is the reason why there can be no "conclusions" in the conventional sense to derive from the available material. Chapter 5, however, is an attempt to compensate for that by presenting popular culture in late medieval Cairo from a wider perspective.

I will postpone a brief discussion of the concept of popular culture and its use in this book to the Introduction. Here I wish to stress three points. First, despite a temptation to claim otherwise, this book is only about Cairo, not about Egypt. The material in it relates by and large to Egypt's largest city, and so it should be viewed. Only too often a case is made for a large region when the evidence in fact is much more limited. I think medieval Egypt is a case where one should avoid this bad habit, since there was a great divergence among cities in Egypt and naturally great differences between cities and villages, between the Delta and Upper Egypt, etc. My occasional forays in the book into provincial areas are made only when I have good reason to think that Cairo in one way or another was connected with the provinces through some particular phenomenon.

Second, I disclaim exhaustiveness of the topic: this is not a definitive study of popular culture in medieval Cairo, let alone Egypt. For one thing, it cannot be assumed that I am familiar with all the historical records that exist. Also, there are topics that have been studied by others. And I have deliberately not included in this book all that I came across and that could be associated with popular culture in medieval Cairo. One reason is that the book deals with a select number of themes. Another has to do with the problem of incorporating isolated reports as if they were representative. Can a single account for a given year be used to characterize a cultural trait in a study which treats a rather extended period? In more than one case my answer was in the negative. The question of generalization, not a particularly sophisticated question, seems to me still of much relevance and one which has to be confronted in a study based on fragmentary data, as this one certainly is. As a result I dropped into my waste-paper basket or saved for further research cards with information interesting in itself but of questionable value for making a case which will have validity for several past generations.

Which leads me to the last methodological point. Having a great deal of sympathy for the Braudelian vision of the *longue durée*, I certainly would not have liked to delimit the boundaries of a cultural study to the conventional periodization according to dynasties. Although most of what is in this book pertains to the Mamluk era (AD 1250–1517), this fact is more the result of the nature of the sources than anything else. As anyone familiar with medieval Islamic historiography will agree, there is nothing that can be compared to the records written under the Mamluks in terms of the variety of phenomena treated by the medieval writers. This is why we can write on popular culture in the Mamluk period at all. Yet I do not think for a moment that culture, or popular culture at least, had a peculiar nature in the Mamluk period. Some phenomena, perhaps, but not the cultural system as a whole. Whenever possible I have crossed the boundaries to earlier periods. Had I the knowledge, I would certainly look beyond the year 1517 as a terminus. Much that happened in the cultural domain after the Ottoman conquest of Egypt was not much different, I suspect, from what had been before. E. W. Lane's reports, written in the early nineteenth century, some of which I refer to when appropriate, occasionally make this point. A structural approach (in Fernand Braudel's sense) to the culture under consideration is therefore in order. I can only regret that I am forced to limit my study to about two and a half centuries.

Most of the research and a preliminary draft of this book were done and written during the academic years 1988–9, while I was an Alexander von Humboldt fellow. I am most grateful to the Alexander von Humboldt-Stiftung (AvH) for enabling me to work intensively on my typescript, free of the regular teaching load. The generosity of the AvH was manifest throughout my two-year fellowship as well as afterwards. The AvH also financed two short trips to libraries in (then) West Berlin and Paris to consult relevant material.

My research in the Federal Republic of Germany was done at the Orientalisches Seminar of Albert-Ludwigs Universität in Freiburg. I am thankful to Professor Werner Ende, the Seminar's co-director, for facilitating my work. Professor Ulrich Haarmann was in Freiburg a source of inspiration. I thank him for countless discussions about my project, numerous suggestions, and an attentive reading of at least two drafts of this book. A few scholars read a chapter each. Of these I would like to thank Dr H. T. Norris of the University of London for some useful bibliographical notes concerning Chapter 2, and Professor Michael Cook of Princeton University for suggesting some corrections in the same chapter. Others are acknowledged in the notes when appropriate. I should also like to thank an anonymous reader for Cambridge University Press whose query drew my attention to Ibn 'Aṭā' Allāh and produced the discussion of that Sufi scholar in Chapter 1. The Department of Oriental Manuscripts at the Staatsbibliothek Preussischer Kulturbesitz, Berlin-Tiergarten, the Vatican Library, the British Library, the India Office Library, and Hamburg University Library were kind enough to produce microfilms which were essential for my study.

The Basic Research Foundation administered by the Israel Academy of Sciences and Humanities was generous enough to support my research financially with a grant which met the costs of microfilming in various libraries. The School of Humanities and Social Sciences of Ben-Gurion University covered part of the costs involved in preparing the typescript of this book. Ms Catherine Logan carefully read my text, and her stylistic suggestions were most important. Mr Ari Sapojnic tirelessly typed many drafts of this book. Ms Pauline Marsh meticulously copy-edited the typescript for Cambridge University Press.

Abbreviations

AHR	*American Historical Review*
AI	*Annales islamologiques*
BEO	*Bulletin d'études orientales*
BSOAS	*Bulletin of the School of Oriental and African Studies*
EI[1]	*The Encyclopaedia of Islam* (1st edn, Leiden, 1913–34)
EI[2]	*The Encyclopaedia of Islam* (new edn, Leiden, 1960–)
GAL	Carl Brockelmann, *Geschichte der arabischen Litteratur* (2nd edn, 2 vols., Leiden, 1943–9)
GAL Suppl.	Carl Brockelmann, *Geschichte der arabischen Litteratur* (3 supplementary vols., Leiden, 1937–42)
IJMES	*International Journal of Middle East Studies*
JESHO	*Journal of the Economic and Social History of the Orient*
JSS	*Journal of Semitic Studies*
REI	*Revue des études islamiques*

List of short references to frequently cited works

(for further details see Select bibliography)

ʿAbd al-Bāsiṭ, *Ḥawādith*	ʿAbd al-Bāsiṭ, *Ḥawādith ad-duhūr fī maḍā'l-ayyām wash-shuhūr.*
Ahlwardt	W. Ahlwardt, *Die Handschriften-Verzeichnisse der königlichen Bibliothek zu Berlin, arabische Handschriften.*
Badā'iʿ	Ibn Iyās, *Badā'iʿ az-zuhūr fī waqā'iʿ ad-duhūr*, Cairo and Wiesbaden.
Bidāya	Ibn Kathīr, *al-Bidāya wa'n-nihāya fi't-ta'rīkh.*
Ḍaw'	as-Sakhāwī, *ad-Ḍaw' al-lāmiʿ.*
Dawādārī	Ibn ad-Dawādārī, *Kanz ad-durar wa-jāmiʿl-ghurar*, Vol. IX: *ad-Durr al-fākhir fī sīrat al-Malik an-Nāṣir.*
Dhayl	al-Yūnīnī, *Dhayl mir'āt az-zamān.*
Durar	Ibn Ḥajar al-ʿAsqalānī, *ad-Durar al-kāmina fī aʿyān al-mi'a ath-thāmina.*
Ḥawādith	Ibn Taghrī Birdī, *Ḥawādith ad-duhūr fī maḍā'l – ayyām wash-shuhūr.*
Ibn Furāt	Ibn Furāt, *Ta'rīkh Ibn al-Furāt.*
Ighātha	al-Maqrīzī, *Ighāthat al-'umma bi-kashf al-ghumma.*
IH	Ibn Hishām, *as-Sīra an-nabawiyya.*
Inbā'	Ibn Ḥajar al-ʿAsqalānī, *Inbā' al-ghumr bi-anbā' al-ʿumr.*
Inbā' al-haṣr	al-Jawharī, *Inbā' al-haṣr bi-abnā' al-ʿaṣr.*
Intiṣār	Ibn Duqmāq, *al-Intiṣār.*
ʿIqd	al-ʿAynī, *ʿIqd al-jumān fī ta'rīkh ahl az-zamān.*
IS	Ibn Saʿd, *aṭ-Ṭabaqāt al-kubrā.*
Ittiʿāẓ	al-Maqrīzī, *Ittiʿāẓ al-ḥunafā' bi-akhbār al-a'imma al-Fāṭimiyyīn al-khulafā'.*
Khiṭaṭ	al-Maqrīzī, *al-Mawāʿiẓ wa'l-iʿtibār bi-dhikr al-khiṭaṭ wa'l-āthār.*
Madkhal	Ibn al-Ḥājj al-ʿAbdarī, *al-Madkhal.*
Manhal	Ibn Taghrī Birdī, *al-Manhal aṣ-ṣāfī wa'l-mustawfī baʿda'l-wāfī.*

Nahj	Mufaḍḍal b. Abi'l-Faḍā'il, *an-Nahj as-sadīd wa'd-durr al-farīd fī mā ba'da ta'rīkh Ibn al-'Amīd.*
Nihāya	an-Nuwayrī, *Nihāyat al-arab fī funūn al-adab.*
Nujūm	Ibn Taghrī Birdī, *an-Nujūm az-zāhira fī mulūk Miṣr wa'l-Qāhira*; English trans., *History of Egypt 1382–1469 A.D.*
Nuzha	al-Jawharī, *Nuzhat an-nufūs wa'l-abdān fī tawārīkh az-zamān.*
Shujā'ī	ash-Shujā'ī, *Ta'rīkh al-Malik an-Nāṣir Muḥammad b. Qalāwūn aṣ-Ṣāliḥī wa-awlādihi.*
Ṣubḥ	al-Qalqashandī, *Ṣubḥ al-a'shā.*
Sulūk	al-Maqrīzī, *as-Sulūk li-ma'rifat duwal al-mulūk.*
Suyūṭī, *Ḥusn*	as-Suyūṭī, *Ḥusn al-muḥāḍara fī ta'rīkh Miṣr wa'l-Qāhira.*
Ṭabaqāt kubrā	ash-Sha'rānī, *aṭ-Ṭabaqāt al-kubrā.*
Ṭabaqāt ṣughrā	ash-Sha'rānī, *aṭ-Ṭabaqāt aṣ-ṣughrā.*
Ṭabarī	aṭ-Ṭabarī, *Ta'rīkh ar-rusul wa'l-mulūk.*
Tibr	as-Sakhāwī, *at-Tibr al-masbūk fī dhayl as-Sulūk.*
Tuḥfa	as-Sakhāwī, *Tuḥfat al-aḥbāb wa-bughyat aṭ-ṭullāb.*

Note on transcription and dates

For transcription of Arabic names and terms I have used a standard system of transcription which generally follows that of the Library of Congress (bulletin 91, September 1970), except for defining the so-called solar letters. To simplify the plural form of Arabic terms I have added the letter *s*, except where the collective noun is a standard term (e.g., *'ulamā'*). Familiar geographical names such as Cairo, Mecca, Medina, and Baghdad are given in their common form or spelling.

Dates are mostly given in Christian years; in case of ambiguity I have added AD. Hijri years are given only when required either by reference to an Islamic month of a particular year, or by paraphrasing an Arabic text which mentions a Hijri year. In that case the Christian equivalent follows, either in parentheses or after a solidus. Where a Hijri year only is given, AH has been added.

Introduction

"Mother of cities . . . mistress of broad provinces and fruitful lands, boundless in multitudes of buildings, peerless in beauty and splendor . . . she surges as the sea with her throngs of folk and can scarcely contain them for all the capacity of her situation and sustaining power." Thus Ibn Baṭṭūṭa, a Muslim globetrotter, described the city of Cairo in the 1320s.[1] Lest we think of his description as the report of a highly partisan Muslim, the enormous population of medieval Cairo is also described in several foreign accounts. In 1384, the Italian Frescobaldi claimed that "This city of Cairo has a population greater than all of Tuscany, and there is one street more populated than all of Florence."[2] At the end of the fifteenth century, Bernard von Breydenbach wrote: "I do not think that there exists another city in the world today as populous, as large, as rich, and as powerful as Cairo . . . Elbowing our way through masses of men, we saw one spot where the throng of people was beyond words."[3] Similarly, to Fabri (1483), Cairo was the largest town in the world, three times larger than Cologne and seven times larger than Paris.[4]

Statements of magnitude by medieval reporters, be they indigenous or foreign, should not be taken at face value. Cairo's population, by modern estimates, reached 250,000 to half a million by the mid fourteenth century,[5] and declined to between 150,000 and 300,000 by the fifteenth century, a result of the ravaging recurrences of the plague known as the Black Death.[6] The city was possibly larger, but certainly not many times larger than major European towns. Scholarly guesses put the population of medieval Paris, for example, the largest European town at the time, at 100,000 to 200,000.[7]

In any case, precise numbers of Cairo's population are not a major concern for us in the present study. Suffice it to state that, judging by medieval standards, Cairo was indeed a very large and densely inhabited town. It is in this regard that the travellers' accounts are of some value. Fusṭāṭ (Old Cairo) had houses of five, six, and even seven storeys – a Persian traveller wrote of no fewer than fourteen, which made Fusṭāṭ look like "a mountain" – occasionally up to two hundred people living in one house (houses were mostly built of unfired brick).[8] The commercial zone of fourteenth-century Cairo, according to a contemporary

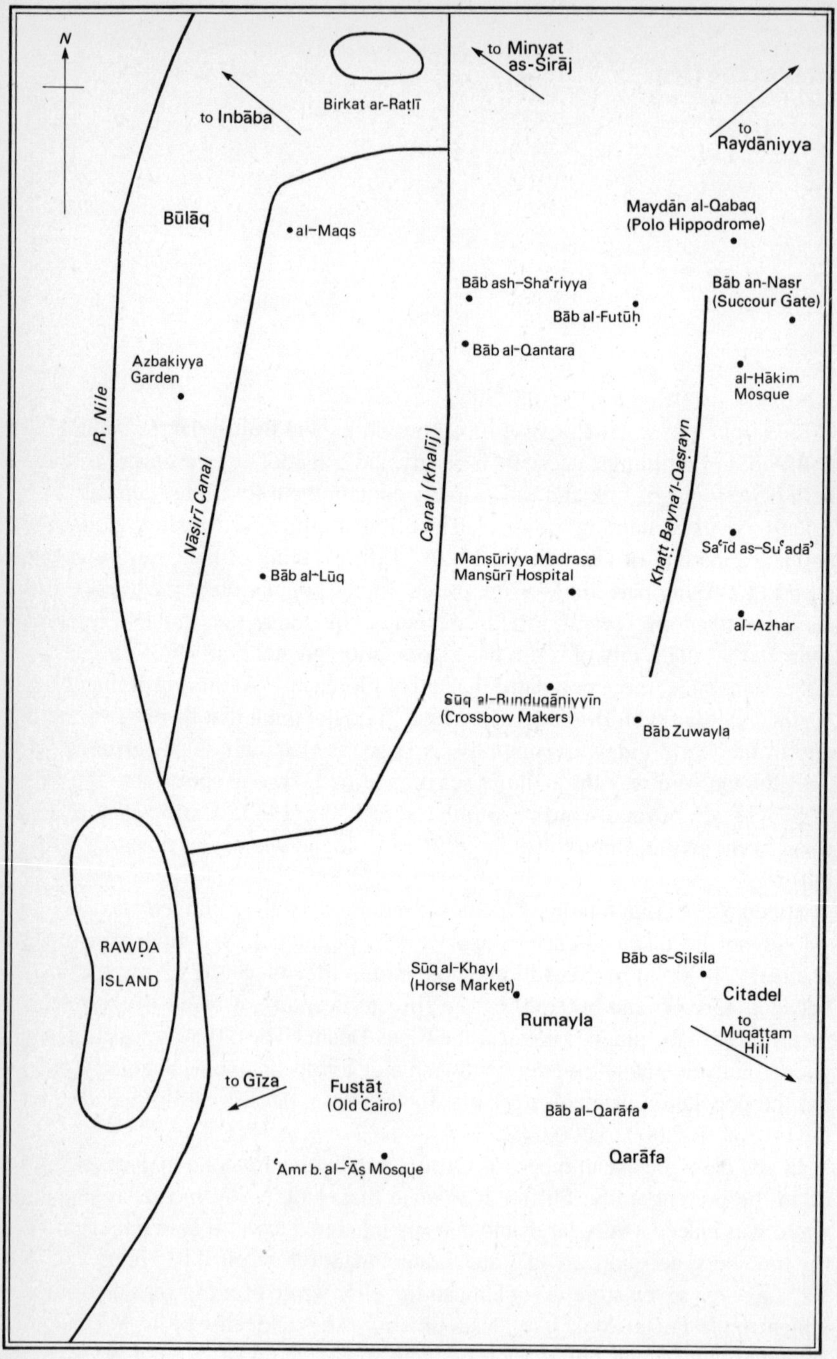

Map 1 Locations in Mamluk Cairo cited in this book

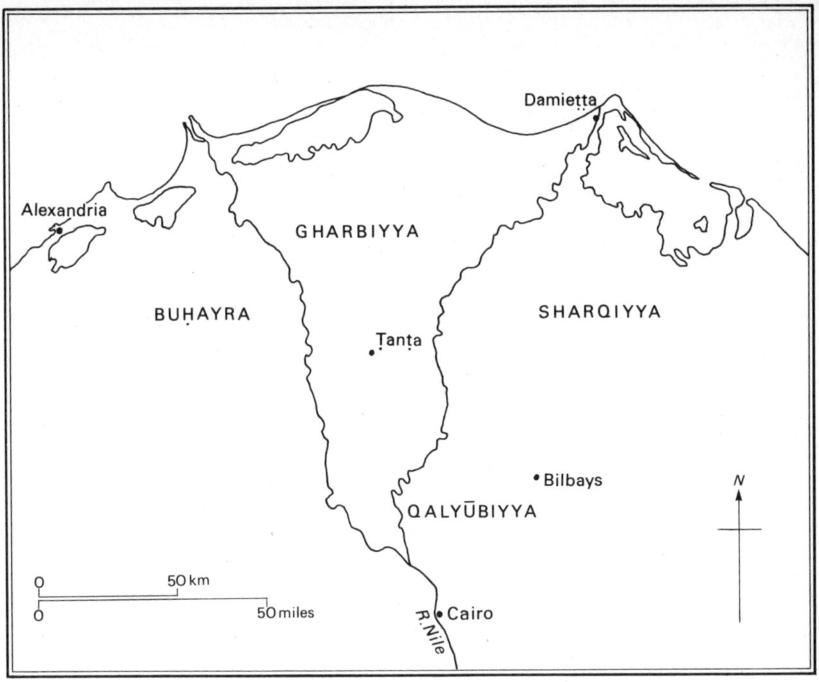

Map 2 Northern Egypt (after William Popper, *Egypt and Syria under the Circassian Sultans 1382–1468 A.D.: Systematic Notes to Ibn Taghrī Birdī's Chronicles of Egypt* (Berkeley, 1955)

account, bustled with 12,000 shops and numberless itinerant vendors, who blocked the public thoroughfares with their wares.[9]

Who were the inhabitants of late medieval Cairo? Standard descriptions of the social set-up of the city suggest that the Cairenes were divided into four social strata: the Mamluk elite, the scholars (*'ulamā'*), the economic bourgeoisie, and the commoners.[10] A modern writer, using a physiological image, described the Mamluks as the head of Cairo, the notables (*'ulamā'* and bureaucrats) as its nerves, the merchants as the circulatory system, and the commoners as the flesh and blood of the largest Egyptian city.[11]

At present we possess a reasonable body of knowledge about the social fabric and culture of three of the four strata. The Mamluk elite of slaves-turned-soldiers has been extensively studied, and the unique mechanism of its operation is now fairly clear.[12] The courtly culture of the Mamluks is also known to some extent: royal etiquette and ceremonies;[13] special pastimes – hunting, sport and games, and competitions;[14] patronage of literary works,[15] especially of equestrian treatises (*furūsiyya*) and manuals of military techniques;[16] and support of the visual arts.[17] The community of the Cairene *'ulamā'* of the fifteenth century has been recently studied with an emphasis on such questions as geographical origins, patterns of residence, and the distribution of occupations.[18] Its culture, however, still awaits a thorough study. The socio-economic profile of the bourgeoisie and the material aspects of their culture – mainly in the eleventh and twelfth centuries – are known to us thanks to Goitein's monumental research of the Geniza documents.[19] What about the "flesh and blood", the commoners, of medieval Cairo?

These were artisans – engaged in dozens of manual occupations, from glass-making through tannery to sawdusting[20] – retailers and shopkeepers, as well as men of a rich variety of other occupations, and their families. Very little was recorded about them in contemporary works, and even less has been stated about them by modern historians. Their private lives, unlike that of their social superiors, are therefore almost unknown,[21] and their professional realm is also largely obscure.[22] If one were to write a sketchy history of the commoners in medieval Cairo, it would be, by and large, a history of their misery: economic hardship caused by heavy taxation, monetary instability, and high prices;[23] and political oppression inflicted by the Mamluks and outside enemies.[24] Above all, it was Death, so it seems to me, which, ironically, was the prevailing factor in the life of the commoners in late medieval Cairo. It deserves a few words.[25]

The major cause of death in Mamluk Cairo was the so-called Black Death, which, between 1348 and 1517, struck the city more than fifty times[26] and decimated its population.[27] The thousands of funerals that crowded the streets of Cairo every third year on the average, creating a long "procession of death", thus turned death from a private event into a communal affair. At the outbreak of the Black Death in 1348, for example, the daily death toll was 300; then, according to one chronicler, it increased to 1,000. Funerals blocked roadways, but otherwise streets were empty.[28] In 1430, another occasion of a severe period of plague, an eye-witness compared the long lines of funerals to columns of white marble, probably in reference to the shrouds covering the corpses.[29] There were years in which coffins had to be placed in crowded cemeteries, one on top of the other.[30] Lamentations were heard everywhere, and no one could pass in front of a house without being upset by the plaintive cries coming from within. "Everyone imagined himself to be soon dead."[31] A contemporary chronicler reported that in the plague of 1468–9 wailings over the victims were heard "day and night" in every quarter of Cairo.[32]

The death of multitudes and the endless public funerals, too many to handle properly, surely had an enormous impact on the psychology of the people. One reaction, naturally enough, was of gloom, anxiety, and fear. An example of this reaction may be found in some lines by an anonymous poet, referring to the plague of 1348:

> The approaching funerals frighten us,
> And we are delighted when they have passed by.
> Like the gazelle (*jahma*), fearful of the assailing lion,
> Then returning to graze (*rāti'āt*) when the lion is gone.[33]

During that year people abstained from weddings and celebrations.[34] Of the year 881 (1476–7) the contemporary Ibn Iyās stated: "This year has elapsed leaving the people in a state of anxiety (*fī amr murīb*), as they lost their children and families. They have seen no good."[35]

There was also a sense of resignation, with people expecting their death any moment. In 1430 the inhabitants of Cairo would return home from Friday prayers, taking account of how many were present to compare with the number on the following Friday. Each man had resigned himself to death, having made his will and repented. Each of the young men carried a string of prayer beads in his hand and did little besides attending the prayers for the dead, performing the five daily prayers, weeping, directing his thoughts to God, and showing his humility.[36] In that year people started to wear labels with personal details (name, place of residence, etc.) so that they could be identified in case they died suddenly in the street.[37]

Panic, a necessary result of rumours hitting upon fragile souls, must have been a frequent visitor. In 1438, Ibn Taghrī Birdī tells us,

> The people had rumored that men were all to die on Friday, and the resurrection would come. Most of the populace feared this, and when the time for prayer arrived on this Friday, and the men went to prayers, I [Ibn Taghrī Birdī] too, rode to the Azhar Mosque, as men were crowding to the baths so that they might die in a state of complete purity. I arrived at the Mosque and took a seat in it. The muezzins chanted the call to prayer, then the preacher came out as usual, mounted the pulpit, preached, and explained traditions to the people; when he had finished his first address he sat down to rest before the second sermon . . . but before he had finished his address he sat down a second time and leaned against the side of the pulpit a long time, like one who had fainted. As a result, the crowd, because of the previous report that men were all to die on Friday, was agitated; they believed the rumor was confirmed, and that death had made the preacher the first victim. While men were in this condition someone called out, "The preacher is dead." The Mosque was thrown into confusion, people cried out in fear, wept with one another, and went up to the pulpit; there was much crowding against the preacher until he recovered.

This particular Friday prayer ended in total confusion.[38]

There were other circumstances besides plagues in which death became a communal event. Hardly a year passed in Mamluk Cairo without an execution being performed in public. Years with an especially high number of executions (e.g., five in 1341), or the execution of persons of high standing, or inflicting the death penalty on many at one time – all these must have left a grave impression on the people. This was probably the case in 1253, when as many as 2,600, the troops of the *sharīf* (a descendant of the Prophet) Ḥiṣn ad-dīn Thaʿlab, a rebellious bedouin chieftain, were hanged along the road leading from Bilbays (in the Sharqiyya province) to Cairo.[39] It could also have been the case in 1453, when a qadi's servant and his two companions were caught after they had habitually invited whores to their homes, murdered them and stolen their clothes. The criminals were executed and their corpses carried through the streets together with cages containing the bones of their victims.[40]

Gruesome punishments of this sort probably left their mark on people's minds. "The cruel excitement and coarse compassion raised by an execution formed an important item in the spiritual food of the common people. They were spectacular plays with a moral."[41] Take, for example, the execution scene in 1380 of Emir Ibn ʿArrām, governor of Alexandria. He was stripped naked, nailed to a camel, and thus sent from the Citadel down to the Horse Market (Sūq al-Khayl) to be hanged finally at Bāb Zuwayla. Ibn ʿArrām's fate became so well known that a saying spread: "God forbid the suffering of Ibn ʿArrām's sort."[42] There were possibly profound, hidden effects of capital punishment carried out in front of large crowds. A student of popular culture has recently suggested that "the spectacle of public execution most probably reassured men by projecting death from themselves onto the criminal". A different effect of executions could have been "aggressiveness and scorn for human life".[43]

It is against this (admittedly, poorly known) background of economic hardship, political oppression, frequent death, and their mental effect – the lot of ordinary people in medieval Cairo – that what follows in this book should be considered. A large part of what we shall encounter in the coming chapters – entertainment through literature, religious celebrations, or festivals – undoubtedly also served as a means of escaping the darker side of life. In fact these diversions, on occasion, caught the eyes of outside observers to the point of creating an illusion that life in Cairo was constant entertainment. Thus, to the Ottoman writer Muṣṭafā ʿAlī of Gallipoli (1599), it seemed that "in Cairo [contrary to other places] never a month passes without some festivity [taking place], without their flocking together saying today is the day of the excursion to such and such place, or today is the day when such and such [procession] goes around. Therefore most of their time passes in leisure."[44] Muṣṭafā ʿAlī probably exaggerated about the leisure of medieval Cairenes. Yet, his statement raises some little-studied questions. What did the people of Cairo do for leisure? What was their entertainment? How did they celebrate, and on what occasions? In a larger sense, what was their culture?

Some words should be said about "popular culture", for even recently it has been admitted to be an elusive concept, whose "boundaries shift in response to many kinds of circumstances".[45] One question: with whom should popular culture be associated? Was it the culture of the oppressed classes (as Marxist historians would claim)? Or was it rather the culture of the illiterate?[46] Of both, is the response of some, combining economic and educational criteria. For them popular culture is the culture of the poor, the rural, the subordinated, the laity, the illiterate, and so on.[47] A second question: was popular culture created *by* the people or *for* them?[48] The best answer seems to be that both possibilities apply.[49] But in that case the implication is that popular culture, at least to some extent, depends on a dominant culture. Popular culture thus suffers from the ideological imprint of a "higher", learned culture, and its existence as a separate entity is doubtful.

Indeed, not only is definition problematic,[50] but the very concept of popular culture has lately been under attack. Is it indeed possible to demonstrate exclusive relationships between specific cultural forms and particular social groups?[51] Chartier has been most critical in this regard. He has recently argued that "it is pointless to try to identify popular culture by some supposedly specific distribution of cultural objects". That is, identifying cultural sets (certain texts, for example) as popular is problematic. To Chartier, the historian's task is the search not for a specific culture but rather for "differentiated ways in which common material was used. What distinguishes cultural worlds is different kinds of use and different strategies of appropriation." Hence, a more meaningful approach is to look at "the relation of appropriation to texts or behavior in a given society", namely, observing the way in which cultural products are used. A good example of this approach is Ginzburg's study of the world-view of the sixteenth-century Menocchio of Montereale, by now perhaps the most famous miller in history.[52] The books Menocchio read were in no way designed for a popular audience. Still, he read them, but not in the way a learned man would.[53]

Popular culture as a concept thus raises crucial problems which, at this stage, can only be handled temporarily and arbitrarily. Certainly, Chartier's is an interesting and novel approach. But it seems not to contradict the historical existence of popular culture. Even Chartier finds it difficult to do away with classification ("cultural worlds"), and his main approach is to substitute the relation to the cultural object for the object itself. Here I concur with Le Goff that, though it is easy to criticize the method which postulates the existence of a popular culture – for which proof remains to be given – there are genres of "texts", both written and non-written (non-written including forms as diverse as an oath and a carnival), which, despite their unavoidably uncertain boundaries, provide safe bases for analysis as primarily popular. As Le Goff argues, "the very historical context that shapes us, and from which we have not yet extricated ourselves, obliges us to begin with the vocabulary [of which popular culture is part]". And despite being manipulated, popular culture has had plenty of scope for originality and freedom.[54]

As for definition, the culture treated in this book is of – what I can mainly assume, but in some cases more safely argue – those socially inferior to the bourgeoisie; hence, supposedly also illiterate, at least by and large. It is a culture some elements of which were created *by* them, and others *for* them. At any rate, I subscribe to the suggestion that, for the time being, and this is especially valid for the case considered here, it may be wiser to describe and analyse rather than futilely attempt an exact definition. "Theologians, after all, can worship together even if they disagree bitterly in the lecture halls."[55]

Some texts – both in the literal and the metaphorical sense – that can be confidently characterized as popular are my concern in what follows. The method implied in their study is that described by Le Goff as "demanding that the corpus itself explicate the nature and meaning of its culture, whether through structural analysis, or content analysis, or both simultaneously".[56] This method of examining cultural objects, as argued by Le Goff, also has the advantage of precipitating a hierarchically organized opposition between "learned" and "popular" cultures. It may lead us to some sort of solution to the problems just raised. I think this applies, at least to some extent, also to the case of medieval Cairo. How, I shall try to show in the concluding chapter of this book.

CHAPTER 1

Sufism and the people

Some time in 1343, near a heap of dung in the vicinity of the gate known as Bāb al-Lūq, a resident of Cairo unearthed what he claimed to be an old mosque. A "rowdy" (*baʿḍ shayāṭīn al-ʿāmma*) named Shuʿayb could not miss this golden opportunity. He claimed that an apparition revealed to him that the site was an ancient grave of a Companion of the Prophet.[1] He started to preach there, and many gathered to listen to his sermons. Excavations were begun by the commoners, including women, and indeed a "shrine" surfaced. That new discovery further increased the number of visitors, and industrious Shuʿayb organized "guided tours" for fees, in which wives of dignitaries also took part. He spread the rumour that the shrine was blessed with supernatural powers, by which the sick could be healed and the blind regain their eyesight. Indeed, Shuʿayb was credited with performing miracles. Every night celebrations were held at the site. Ultimately, the chief qadis and some of the emirs were alarmed and sent the prefect of Cairo to investigate what exactly was happening. At first the official had to retreat under a hail of stones and only additional force was able to disperse the crowd. In the mean time Shuʿayb disappeared with large sums of money in his pocket. Now it became clear that he was a mere swindler and that the shrine was his pure invention.[2]

Half a century or so later, in Ramaḍān of 819 (1416), a man inhabiting a desolate tomb in the vicinity of Bāb al-Qarāfa, by the large cemetery of the city of Cairo, was summoned to one of the sultan's tribunals to defend his claim of performing heavenly journeys.[3] In these, the man maintained, he used to see God "in person" and converse with Him. The man had followers among the people, who believed his stories. In his trial he proclaimed, as he probably used to do before his audiences, that God appeared to him "in the shape of a sultan". He was sentenced to confinement at the Manṣūrī Hospital.[4]

In 1419 the *muḥtasib* (market inspector) of Cairo forbade men to enter al-Ḥākim Mosque[5] wearing their shoes. He banned the attendance of women altogether. Thus sanctity was restored after sins and children's games had desecrated the mosque.[6]

In 1509 Sultan Qānṣawh al-Ghawrī called on Muslims to perform the five daily prayers in congregational mosques. Commenting on the people's response, a contemporary chronicler stated that the sultan's appeal "entered one ear and left through the other".[7]

It is only rarely that one glimpses in medieval Arabic sources religious beliefs and practices ascribed to ordinary Muslims. Only too often we conceive of Islam as a set of prescriptions in scholarly texts. Yet the "religion of the people" was certainly something else and should be taken account of. One ought to study the beliefs of those multitudes who were not normally of interest to contemporary writers except under special circumstances; those whose devotion took a different course from the scholarly and has left little trace upon the records of any given time.[8] That there existed a popular religion quite distinct from the religion of the learned, different from that expressed in sacred texts, has recently been pointed out in a Christian context by a number of scholars.[9] Thus, Thomas has masterfully demonstrated that the hold of orthodox Christianity upon the English people at the end of the Middle Ages was never more than partial; a considerable number of them remained throughout their lives utterly ignorant of the elementary tenets of Christian dogma.[10] Delumeau has argued that on the eve of the Reformation the average inhabitant of the European continent was but superficially Christianized.[11]

How, then, to study the religion of Muslims in late medieval Cairo or, for that matter, in any other Islamic place in the past? Narrative sources contain meagre information and are problematic in another respect. "Deprived of the oral communication of the past, we can only see the beliefs of the illiterate refracted through the writings of the literate, whose religious understanding was professedly of a different order."[12] Quantitative assessment of attendance at masses, or the study of parish records for reconstructing mores and attitudes of parishioners – two useful tools for studying medieval Christians[13] – are both irrelevant and impossible in the case of Islamic society. It is thus unknown how devout medieval Muslims were, although there are certainly indications that norms and practices did not necessarily go hand in glove.[14] And yet, the purpose of what follows is to substantiate the thesis that there was "another" Islam in medieval Cairo (as elsewhere) – an Islam practised and experienced by the commoners.[15]

The presentation of this thesis can only be sketchy and, on occasion, based on inference. Certainly it is impossible to tell what precisely was the Islam of an ordinary Muslim, let alone many medieval Muslims. I shall concentrate mainly on one theme which seems to me of primary importance in studying popular religion in late medieval Cairo, a phenomenon which rests on a solid body of documentation: the growing influence of Sufism on ordinary Muslims. My argument is that, whatever was the religious world of the medieval Cairenes, Sufism filled a significant part of it.

Once again let us start with a few reports. The blind Cairene *shaykh* Abū Zakariyyā' Yaḥyā b. 'Alī aṣ-Ṣanāfīrī (d. 1371) first resided in a domed shrine (*qubba*) in the large Qarāfa Cemetery. Frequently visited by many believers, he was forced to create a retreat for himself. When that was not enough to ensure his privacy, he started to deter visitors by pelting stones at them. But to no avail. Ultimately he left his shrine in Cairo and chose to settle in Ṣanāfīr (in the Qalyūbiyya province), whence his name. There an emir built a *zāwiya* for him.[16] When he died, over 50,000 persons, so we are told, attended his funeral.[17] Another Egyptian *shaykh*, Abū'l-Najā' al-Fūwwī (*fl.* second half of the fifteenth century and early sixteenth century), was also venerated by the Cairenes. Whenever they heard of his visit to their city, they used to come in great numbers to the dock of Būlāq to welcome him.[18] In the late fourteenth or early fifteenth century, we read in a third report, the residents of Fusṭāṭ (Old Cairo) would flock every Friday to view the Sufis of the Ṣalāḥiyya *khānqāh*,[19] also known as Sa'īd as-Su'adā' – the most important Sufi lodge in Egypt at the time – marching in procession to al-Ḥākim Mosque. The people believed that by viewing the Sufis' procession they would be blessed.[20]

These three reports, which could well be multiplied, exemplify what could be characterized as the most significant religious development in late medieval Egypt: the rise of Sufism to a prominent position in the country's socio-religious structure. Although it had been known in Egypt for centuries,[21] by the thirteenth century Sufism was no longer an abstract religious doctrine or the faith of reclusive mystics. It was increasingly penetrating congregational life. In this, Sufi orders played a major role: the Qalandāriyya, Shādhiliyya, its derivative the Wafā'iyya, and the Aḥmadiyya, held sway.[22] Other orders which had a presence in Mamluk Cairo were the Rifā'iyya, Burhāniyya, and Khalwatiyya.[23] What precisely was their role in the expansion of Sufism? How did they operate?

Here we certainly face a serious problem. For while we know to some extent the influence of Sufism on the Mamluk ruling elite and on the community of Cairene scholars on the one hand, and the support, both material and moral, which Sufism received from Mamluk authorities on the other hand,[24] its impact on the ordinary people is much less documented and has hardly been studied.[25] In this chapter I shall try to shed some light on two questions: what were the mechanisms by which Sufism influenced medieval Cairenes? What was the nature of the influence?

The usual link between Sufism and the common people was the *shaykh*. Either a recluse or, more often, accompanied by his disciples, a *shaykh* would normally reside in the Sufi lodge known as *zāwiya*, *khānqāh*, or *ribāṭ*.[26] In the mid fourteenth century the activities of *shaykh*s were also permitted in mosques and orthodox learning institutions (*madrasa*s).[27] The overall number of *shaykh*s who were active in Cairo and its vicinity in the Mamluk period reached at least several dozens (see Appendix).

Two circles of Sufi influence radiated from the *shaykh*s. The first and narrower probably consisted of young people and others who were attracted to the Sufi orders. In the second half of the fourteenth century, according to one report, many a man used to gather at the *zāwiya* on Rawḍa Island, known as al-Mushtahā, to receive spiritual guidance from Shaykh Bahā' ad-Dīn Muḥammad al-Kāzarūnī

(d. 1373). Those attracted to the Shaykh's circle "severed their ties with their families".[28] There was probably a purely religious side to the attraction. But there were other, non-religious reasons for joining the Sufi orders.[29] In the first half of the sixteenth century, Sīdī Abū Saʿūd al-Jāriḥī complained to the Sufi writer ash-Shaʿrānī: "All the people who have come to me have done so because of their troubles with their wives, neighbors, or masters. None of them desired to be brought closer to God."[30] This may have been too critical a view on the part of al-Jāriḥī, but it serves as a useful reminder of the social dimension of the Sufi role. We shall return to it later on.

It is impossible to know how many Egyptians actively joined Sufi orders. However, when we read that Abū'l-ʿAbbās al-Ḥārithī (d. 1538 or 1539) initiated ten thousand Sufi disciples (*murīd*),[31] the number, though probably much inflated, indicates that al-Ḥārithī made many "converts". Apparently, he was an exceptionally zealous missionary for the Sufi cause and an extraordinarily attractive figure. But there were many other *shaykh*s who presumably operated on a more modest scale, with the result that there was a constant movement of Muslims into Sufi ranks.

About the second, wider circle of Sufi influence, which penetrated the populace at large in a less structured form, one can only speculate. But if we assume that through sermons, for example, Sufi ideas could be filtered into people's minds, then Sufism in late medieval Cairo must have had a considerable impact. For we have the names of more than a dozen Sufi *shaykh*s, mostly of the Shādhiliyya order, who acted as popular preachers (*khaṭīb*, *wāʿiẓ*, *mudhakkir*) in mosques and Sufi institutions. Burhān ad-Dīn Ibrāhīm b. Miʿḍād al-Jaʿbarī (d. 1288) preached at the *zāwiya* named after him, which stood outside the Succour Gate. Many flocked to listen to him.[32] The sermons of the renowned Shādhilite Ibn ʿAṭā' Allāh (d. 1309) (see below) "had great influence on people's hearts and souls".[33] Shihāb ad-Dīn Abū'l-ʿAbbās b. Maylaq (d. 1348 or 1349)[34] and Ḥasan (or Ḥusayn) al-Khabbāz (d. 1389), formerly a baker,[35] were also Shādhilite preachers. Ḥusayn al-Jākī (d. 1337) preached at a mosque (or *zāwiya*) named after him. In a tribunal at the sultan's court he was accused of delivering Sufi instructions. According to an obviously hagiographic story, the Mamluk ruler was later punished for summoning him to court.[36] Aḥmad b. Muḥammad b. Sulaymān "The Ascetic" (*az-zāhid*) (d. 1416) preached at al-Azhar, and, in his last year, at his own mosque at al-Maqs. Also women were in his audience.[37] The Shādhilite Shihāb ad-Dīn Abū'l-ʿAbbās al-Anṣārī known as "the Repenting Youth" (*ash-shābb a-tā'ib*) (d. 1429), had a *zāwiya* by Zuwayla Gate, where he preached to the commoners (*ʿāmma*).[38] Shams ad-Dīn Muḥammad b. Badr ad-Dīn Ḥasan al-Ḥanafī (d. 1443) preached at his *zāwiya* and "his speeches had great influence". Even Sultan Ṭaṭar came to visit him.[39] Other popular preachers were the Shādhilite Shihāb ad-Dīn Aḥmad b. Muḥammad al-Wafā', known as Ibn Abī'l-Wafā' (d. 1453),[40] and Aḥmad b. ʿAbd Allāh, also known as Abū'l-ʿAbbās al-Qudsī(or al-Maqdisī) (d. 1466).[41] Shihāb ad-Dīn b. ʿAbd al-Ḥaqq as-Sunbāṭī (d. first half of the sixteenth century), a Sufi preacher at al-Azhar, was so admired that whenever he finished a sermon, people would quarrel to reach him; whoever did not succeed stretched his hand to rub his gown on as-Sunbāṭī's body and then wiped his face with it.[42] There were also women saints and preachers. One of them, the *shaykha* of the Sufi residence known as the Baghdadī *ribāṭ*,[43] was active in the latter part of the fourteenth century and, not surprisingly, used to preach mainly to women.[44]

In fact, a largely unknown aspect of the activity of *shaykh*s among the populace, but one which was there and certainly gave them an advantage over orthodox scholars, as far as religious leadership is concerned, was their appeal to and contact with women. Thus Aḥmad b. Muḥammad, known as az-Zāhid (d. 1416), one of the Sufi preachers to whom I have already referred, delivered sermons at his mosque in al-Maqs especially to women.[45] Another Sufi preacher who had women among his listeners was Ibn al-Ḥamawī. In 1489 he urged them to remove their "modish" headcovers (*ʿaṣā'ib*) of the type known as *al-miqraʿ* because, he claimed, they were forbidden by the Prophet. His call aroused some storm in scholarly circles, but in fact was heeded by a number of his female followers.[46]

To have been able to study the sermons of all the preachers just mentioned would have been invaluable for the student of popular religion, for scholars have argued that sermons perhaps come nearer to telling us what ordinary people believed in than most kinds of evidence. There are even those who claim that preachers of any period "are as necessarily bound to the preconceived notions, as to the language, of those whom they have to exhort. The pulpit does not mould the forms into which religious thought in any age runs; it simply accommodates itself to those that exist. For this very reason, because they must follow and cannot lead, sermons are the surest index of the prevailing religious feeling of their age."[47] One has to treat this one-sided argument with some reservation.[48] Still, there could hardly be a debate about the usefulness of sermons for the study of popular religion.

The study of sermons in the case under consideration is not easy, however. Information on sermons delivered in medieval Cairo is meagre, and some of it is certainly of a dubious nature. Thus, Shaykh Shams ad-Dīn Muḥammad b. Aḥmad b. al-Labbān (d. 1336 or 1337) is reported to have preached at a mosque in Fusṭāṭ that prostrating oneself before an idol was not prohibited, and that his mentor, Shaykh Yāqūt al-ʿArsh, was preferable to the Companions of the Prophet.[49] He was tried, called to repent, and banned from preaching.[50] The Shādhilite Ṣalāḥ ad-Dīn Muḥammad al-Kilā'ī (d. 1398), an associate of the previously mentioned Ḥusayn al-Khabbāz, allegedly preached abominations and blasphemies directed at the Qur'ān. The chief qadi had to ban his activity.[51]

If such reports of Sufi preachers are related by sources who may have been biased, not so the material about Ibn ʿAṭā' Allāh, the famous Sufi *shaykh*. Earlier we encountered his name among those preachers who exerted "great influence on people's hearts and souls". Ibn ʿAṭā' Allāh[52] was born in Alexandria sometime in the thirteenth century into a family of distinguished Mālikite scholars. The Alexandria of his youth was a meeting-place for Sufi teachers and the abode of many *zāwiya*s and, most notably, a centre of the Shādhilite order. In 1276, while still an opponent of Sufism, Ibn 'Aṭā' Allāh attended a public lecture delivered by Abū'l-'Abbās al-Mursī (d. 1288), the second of the early masters of the Shādhilites, and, as the story goes, was "converted". A few years later he migrated to Cairo, where he spent the rest of his life as both a Mālikite scholar and an honoured Sufi master. As a legal scholar, Ibn 'Aṭā' Allāh taught in various institutions such as al-Azhar and the Manṣūriyya Madrasa.[53] As a Shādhilite *shaykh* he established himself as the third great master of his order and the first to present its ideas in writing. Ibn 'Aṭā' Allāh died in Cairo in 1309. He left disciples, Shādhilite masters in their turn. After his death his tomb at the Qarāfa Cemetery was visited for centuries by the pious.

Ibn 'Aṭā' Allāh's works were certainly not intended to be read by or to ordinary Muslims.[54] His *Kitāb al-ḥikam* (*Book of Aphorisms*), for example, became an item in the scholarly curriculum at al-Azhar and was studied there for centuries following its author's death.[55] At one point in this book Ibn 'Aṭā' Allāh addresses "Those who are united with Him" and "Those who are voyaging towards Him",[56] hardly an address to the ordinary people. In the opinion of one modern student, Ibn 'Aṭā' Allāh's writings were directed toward "individuals for whom the ordinary interpretations of religion, in its dogmatic and obediential dress, are not sufficient to satisfy their intellectual and spiritual aspirations . . . [individuals who] seek that which is beyond all forms . . . because the Spirit moves them to search for liberation".[57] One can safely argue that the ideas expressed in Ibn 'Aṭā' Allāh's books are frequently too complex to be accessible to ordinary minds.[58]

We are fortunate, however, to have a book of Ibn 'Aṭā' Allāh's sermons, the *Tāj al-'arūs al-ḥāwī li-tahdhīb an-nufūs* (*The Encompassing Bride's Crown for the Discipline of Souls*), or, as simply entitled in one manuscript, *The Book of Sermons* (*Kitāb al-mawā'iẓ*).[59] Indeed, one scholar has characterized it as a book of "Sufi sermons" (*mawā'iẓ ṣūfiyya*) delivered to the general public (*'āmmat an-nās*).[60] As such, it is a unique source, for it allows us to glimpse the ideas that were preached to the ordinary people by a leading Sufi *shaykh*; hence, to return to an earlier argument, the religious notions current among ordinary believers.[61] That in the sermons collected in the *Tāj* Ibn 'Aṭā' Allāh in fact addressed ordinary Muslims can perhaps be gauged from phrases such as *yā akhī* ("O, my brother"),[62] *yā 'abd Allāh* ("O, servant of God"),[63] *yā hādhā* ("O, ye"),[64] and *ayyuhā al-mu'min* ("O, you believer").[65] All these phrases of address strike one as referring to common believers.

Most of the themes which recur in the *Tāj* are conventional: the importance of prayers;[66] the obligation to abstain from religious disobedience (*ma'ṣiya*);[67] the significance of repentance ("it is like the cleansing of a new pot which was burnt on the fire; if you cleanse it after each time you use it, the black will be removed; otherwise it will remain");[68] the insignificance of This World as opposed to the Hereafter ("he who favours This World is like one building a lavatory over a nice building");[69] the Devil (*shayṭān*, Iblīs) as the enemy of Muslims.[70] However, two features render Ibn 'Aṭā' Allāh's sermons an interesting document of popular Islam. One is that the author, to make his ideas comprehensible to ordinary believers, inserts in his sermons dozens of metaphors and illustrative stories (*mithāl*).[71] Another is that, being a Shādhilite master, Ibn ʿAṭā' Allāh introduces his audiences to some Sufi ideas.

Ibn ʿAṭā' Allāh tells his listeners that the heart of the believer is like a ceiling and a sinner is like one who frequently sets fires in his own house; at some point the ceiling will be blackened; likewise the heart of the sinner.[72] He who sins and then repents is like one who drinks poison and then takes medicine to recover; the danger is that one day the medicine may be slow to react.[73] An interesting set of illustrations in Ibn ʿAṭā' Allāh's *Tāj* derives from the sphere of family life, so dear to ordinary believers. The author compares the relationship between the Muslims and Allāh to that prevailing between a child and his mother.[74] Also in the same sphere, the soul is likened to a wife: whenever her feuds increase, her husband's feuds increase as well; so the believer and his soul.[75] A soul that deceives is like a wife who fornicates; just as a husband should divorce his unfaithful wife, so the believer should "divorce" his deceiving soul.[76] He who prefers This World to the Hereafter is like one who has two wives, one old and disloyal, one young and loyal, and in his foolishness he prefers the former.[77]

Another set of illustrations comes from the realm of economic activities, both in a rural and urban milieu, to which Ibn ʿAṭā' Allāh's listeners, as in the case of the family, could easily relate. Thus faith is compared to capital (*ra's māl*); whenever it is lost one should busy oneself, as in economics, regaining it, but in the case of lost faith one should busy oneself seeking it by letting one's tongue repeat invocations (*dhikr*; see below) and occupying one's heart with the love of God (*maḥabba*). The believer is called upon to "plough his existence" (*wujūd*) and wait for the seeds to come and sprout; he who exerts his heart like a peasant toiling in his field, his heart "will be ripe".[78] A soul that is attracted to passions should be restrained like a domestic animal which transgresses its owner's domain and should be blindfolded so that it stays within bounds.[79] He who considers This World as only leading to the next, and acts accordingly, is like the businessman who arranges his merchandise so that it can help him in case of need.[80] Thus religious notions and concepts are both couched in an allegorical mode and concretized so as to resemble everyday behaviour. In Ibn ʿAṭā' Allāh's sermons religion is brought down from an elevated sphere of abstraction to the level of the believer's daily routine.

Occasionally, there is a message which is clearly meant to appeal and give moral support to the underprivileged. The best example is the quotation of a saying attributed to Muḥammad, according to which "the poorest among the believers shall enter Paradise five hundred years before the rich". This would be so since in This World the poor were the first to perform the religious duties (*ʿibādāt*).[81]

There is, as one may expect, the special Sufi dimension which the Shādhilite master intended to reveal to, and encourage in, his ordinary listeners. The Sufi notions which feature in his sermons are simple yet appealing. Thus, Sufi saints (*walī*, pl. *awliyā'*) are repeatedly extolled. They, together with the prophets on the one hand and the pious (*ṣāliḥūn*) on the other, are depicted as a means of reaching God.[82] They are like brides, and just like brides should not be seen by evildoers.[83] The saints are many and their number must remain steady; if it drops, the "light of prophethood" is diminished.[84] An act of grace (*karāma*) performed by a *walī* is a testimony to the Prophet's truthfulness.[85] Saints can perform miracles (*kharq al-ʿādāt*) such as walking on water, flying in the air, and predicting the future.[86] Ibn ʿAṭāʾ Allāh relates a miracle story told by Shaykh Makīn ad-Dīn al-Asmar,[87] who in Alexandria met a youth from whom a light radiated, eclipsing the light of the sun. When al-Asmar asked the youth about his route the latter answered: I performed the morning prayer at al-Aqṣā (in Jerusalem), the noon prayer I shall pray with you (at Alexandria), and the evening prayer at Medina.[88] According to Ibn ʿAṭāʾ Allāh, there are privileged people who can recognize a *walī* when they see him by experiencing a sweet taste in their mouth.[89] He stresses to his listeners the importance of asking for blessings (*tabarruk*) from a saint. Even Heaven and Earth, like humans, are instructed (*tataʾaddab*) by saints.[90] The Shādhilite Shaykh also urges his audience to perform the *ziyāra*, that is, visit the tombs of the saints and the pious.[91]

The particularly important Sufi concept and ritual of Invocation (*dhikr*),[92] to which Ibn ʿAṭāʾ Allāh devoted a special, scholarly study,[93] recurs in his book of sermons, once again, in a form congenial to ordinary believers. Thus, *dhikr* is a means of repentance;[94] it is the most useful way to worship God (*ʿibāda*), since it can be performed also by the elderly and the sick; in short, by anyone who cannot perform the bodily movements which are part of the regular prayer.[95] Invocation, together with reciting the Qurʾān and abstaining from sin, is a veil protecting the heart.[96] Also, *dhikr* and seclusion "polish the mirror of the heart" and make one ready for the encounter with God.[97] Another Sufi concept recurring in the *Tāj* is the "love of God" (*ḥubb*, or *maḥabbat Allāh*).[98] Prayer, in the light of this notion, is a union between two lovers.[99]

So much for Ibn ʿAṭāʾ Allāh's sermons. One is left intrigued as regards a few important, contextual, questions that are crucial for comprehending the Shaykh's influence on, and response to, his medieval Cairene audiences. Foremost is the question how his sermons affected (and reflected) the listeners. Alas, we have to satisfy ourselves with meagre information. There is, let us recall, the laconic, stereotypic statement that Ibn ʿAṭāʾ Allāh's preaching exerted "great influence on people's hearts and souls".[100] An additional short report is, however, quite revealing. Accordingly, in 1307 or 1308, a crowd of over 500 commoners (*al-ʿāmma*) joined Ibn ʿAṭāʾ Allāh and the master of the Sufi *khānqāh* of Saʿīd as-Suʿadāʾ[101] in their march to the Citadel. Their aim was to protest against Ibn Taymiyya, the leading theologian of the age, because of his polemics directed against the Shādhilite Sufis.[102] This popular march can be interpreted as a testimony to the diffusion of Ibn ʿAṭāʾ Allāh's ideas among medieval Cairenes.[103]

Other than sermons, religious celebrations of various sorts were other occasions during which ordinary Muslims might fall under the spell of Sufi *shaykh*s. First and foremost of these events in Mamluk Cairo was the *mawlid* (*mūlid*, in the vernacular), the celebration of the Prophet's birthday on the twelfth day of Rabīʿ al-Awwal.[104] Muḥammad b. Aḥmad b. Manẓūr (d. 1277), who, together with his disciples, lived in a *zāwiya* in al-Maqs, performed a *mawlid* every year in the presence of a large crowd.[105] Abū'l-ʿAbbās al-Qudsī (d. 1466) conducted festive *mawlid*s.[106] Still, one wonders how much of the religious aspect remained in celebrations of this kind. Take, for example, the *mawlid* commemorated at the *zāwiya* of Shaykh Ismāʿīl at Inbāba, west of Cairo. In the nocturnal celebration that took place in 1388, a few months before Ismāʿīl's death, wine was consumed, and it was reported that on the next day 150 empty jugs were found near the *zāwiya*. Many women attended, and there were reports of sexual orgies.[107] A contemporary chronicler lamented the fact that many a man knew al-Inbābī's *zāwiya* only from its façade, coming to participate in the merriment year after year; other than that, they had no interest in the Shaykh's teaching.[108]

In addition to the Prophet's, there emerged *mawlid*s to honour various Sufi saints.[109] First on the list should be the *mawlid* at Ṭanṭā, in the Gharbiyya province, to commemorate Aḥmad al-Badawī (1200–76), the most popular Egyptian saint up to our own time.[110] Observers in the late Mamluk and early Ottoman periods remarked that al-Badawī's *mawlid* drew more people than the Prophet's, or even more than the Pilgrimage.[111] In 1447 the annual celebration was ordered to be discontinued because of the scandalous behaviour (*mafāsid*) involved. It was alleged that the Mamluk sultan was influenced in his decision by followers of another Sufi *shaykh*, Muḥammad al-Ghamrī. Under the pressure of al-Badawī's followers, the ban was lifted the following year.[112] Later, Shaykh Muḥammad ash-Shināwī (d. 1525) abolished some of the more frenzied practices during al-Badawī's *mawlid*, as well as a procession with musical instruments to the Shaykh's grave. Ash-Shināwī then organized *dhikr* sessions instead.[113]

In the fifteenth century, on the night before the twelfth of each month, the Cairenes commemorated the afore-mentioned Ismāʿīl al-Inbābī, who died in 1388.[114] When this nocturnal celebration (*waqt*, *layla*) was first initiated we do not know;[115] the earliest report refers to 1418. In that year the sultan ordered a huge bonfire (*waqda hā'ila*) to be built at Inbāba. The public were told to make simple torches and throw them in the Nile. Our source writes that this was "a night unheard of" as regards the pleasure and merriment that were generated. The river was full of boats packed with spectators.[116] In the latter part of the fifteenth and in the first half of the sixteenth centuries people used to arrive on boats at al-Inbābī's tomb, pitch tents in the hundreds, set up a fair, and enjoy themselves "to the utmost".[117] Immediately after the celebrations in 1507 crowds went on to Būlāq, to the *madrasa* known as Ibn az-Zamān, to observe the birthday of one Shaykh Suwaydān. They pitched tents, then fire broke out, but disaster was avoided "thanks to the grace of God and the *baraka* of the Shaykh".[118] Reporting on the Egyptians' customs on the occasion of *mawlid*s, ash-Shaʿrānī, in the first half of the sixteenth century, tells us that the participants would occasionally tire of the recitation of the Qur'ān and someone might cry out: "Enough of the Qur'ān! Let us hear something enjoyable! Let us have some singing and music!" The same writer also reports that the performance of shadow plays was part of the *mawlid* entertainment.[119]

A most important dimension of popular Sufism in the period under consideration was the reintroduction into Islam of the old association of religion with magic.[120] It "both stimulated and responded to the dark side of popular psychology which is always irresistibly drawn to the supernatural, to superstition and to a form of faith intelligible primarily through its own set of symbols and images".[121] Indeed, Muslims have generally accepted the existence of miracles: that is, extraordinary phenomena (*khawāriq*) that cannot be explained rationally, but whose occurrence cannot be doubted either. Miracles were seen primarily as a means toward establishing the truthfulness of prophets who were bearers of the divine message. Not only prophets, however, but also ordinary men could find themselves doing wholly unexpected and extraordinary things. But, whereas someone like al-Hujwīrī, the eleventh-century Iranian mystic, could maintain that a saint's miracles or graces (*karāmāt*) happen to him in spite of himself – he is not even aware of them and must therefore hide them – reverence of saints in the period under consideration was based on their capacity to affect at will the world of the phenomena, to do things ordinary mortals could not do. "Elaborate stories of their miracles were effectively circulated by their pupils, tightening their ever-increasing grip on the credulous masses."[122]

The impossibility on the part of Sufi masters of discussing the more abstruse truths of the faith with the people may have caused them to encourage popularly edifying tales of saints and their wondrous powers as valid as the dry legalism of the *'ulamā'*. "A general expectation of magic and miracle was sanctioned by those who could not expect the wider public to rise to the level of Truth . . . the expectation was increasingly focused not only on the dead saints and their tombs, but even the living adepts themselves . . . Magic was passed as miracle, and magic tricks as the gracious fruits of ascetic continence."[123] While no Sufi appears to have claimed performance of miracles in his writings, Sufis who had earned honour were soon ascribed all sorts of miracles, from simple acts of outstanding perceptiveness of others' mental states, through feats of healing and telepathy, to more imaginative deeds like flying from Delhi to Mecca for a nightly Pilgrimage. Such tales were subsequently accepted by the Sufis themselves.[124]

We find this pattern in force in medieval Cairo. Musallam al-Barqī al-Badawī (d. 1274), who resided in a *ribāṭ* by the Qarāfa Cemetery, was one whom the people visited (*ziyāra*) in order to be blessed (*tabarruk*).[125] His contemporary, Abū 'Abd Allāh Muḥammad b. 'Alī al-Mawṣilī, known as Ibn at-Ṭabbākh (d. 1271), a master of a *zāwiya*, was another *shaykh* known for the power of his blessings.[126] Another Sufi, a member of the Aḥmadiyya order (followers of Aḥmad al-Badawī),[127] sat one day in 1303 at the Horse Market (Sūq al-Khayl) and started a fast. Immediately he became an attraction; the people attributed all sorts of unusual abilities (*tawahhamū fīhi al-awhām*) to him. Consequently he was arrested, together with his ilk, for interfering with public order, and was instructed to leave Cairo.[128] The Cairenes who, upon his arrival from the Fayyūm in 1391 or 1392, flocked to the *ziyāra* of ʿAlī ar-Rūbī "the possessed" (*al-majdhūb*),[129] spread stories about his supernatural abilities (*khawāriq*), among them his correct prediction of an end to the plague.[130] As for Shams ad-Dīn al-Ḥanafī (d. 1443 or 1444), whenever he came to the public bath to have his hair cut, the people used to quarrel to get hold of a single hair to take home as a talisman.[131] Saʿdān (or Saʿd Allāh (*fl. ca* 1450), a slave (*ʿabd*) or a manumitted slave (*ʿatīq*), and apparently a member of the Aḥmadiyya order, was admired (*muʿtaqad*) and visited by large numbers because of a miracle which he had allegedly performed. Emirs, officials, scholars, and commoners, both men and women, among them sick people, began to extol him and came to seek his blessing (*baraka*). As the report goes, it was very difficult to reach the man because of the crowds surrounding him, and it was necessary to provide him with protection. Moreover, the quarter in which Saʿdān resided became a sort of a "picnic ground", and merchants came there to offer their goods for sale. The affair lasted ten days, until the sultan, who, according to one version, feared the "corruption of the people's faith", ordered the imprisonment of the man. Yet at first the ruler's messengers succumbed to the Shaykh's "spell" and to his adherents' resistance, and only in a second trial by more steadfast men was Saʿdān arrested and exiled to Damieṭṭa. Even there he was followed by some of his supporters, who crowded in front of the prison; only the use of force dispersed them.[132] Also to be mentioned in this context is Shaykh Shams ad-Dīn ad-Dīrūṭī (d. 1515), a preacher in al-Azhar. Whenever he walked in the streets of Cairo the commoners used to surround him and stretch out their hands to touch his garments and thus secure a *baraka*.[133]

Just how influential were stories of saints performing miracles may be gauged from the testimonies of their adversaries. Prominent among these was Ibn Taymiyya, who, in *fatwā*s (legal opinions) issued in the early fourteenth century, condemned Sufi doctrines and practices. One questionnaire, addressed to, or possibly initiated by, the famous theologian, runs as follows:

And is the tradition which is transmitted by many among the populace and which they claim to be emanating from the Prophet of God . . . viz.: "Any time people gather, there is bound to be among them a friend of God (*Walī Allāh*); he is not recognized by the people, nor does he himself know that he is a *walī*" – a true one? Is it a fact that the condition of God's friends (*auliyāʾ*) and their paths remain hidden from the learned and others? . . . Are the Substitutes (*abdāl*) found exclusively in Syria or in any place where Islamic rites are observed in consonance with the Book and the *Sunna*? Is it true that as a *walī* stands in the midst of a concourse his body disappears? . . . And what do you – our Learned Sir – say about these al-Qalandāriya[134] who shave off their beards? . . . What is your opinion about their claim that God's Messenger – may Divine blessings be upon him – fed grapes to their leader and conversed with him in non-Arabic? Is it lawful for a Muslim who believes in God – the Most High – to make rounds in markets and villages soliciting votive offerings for a given *shaikh* or his grave from anyone who may wish to make such an offering? Is it a sin to assist such a man? . . . So also about him who maintains that certain *shaikhs*, when they listen to spiritual concerts, are visited by *People from the Invisible* (*rijāl al-ghaib*), that walls and ceilings split open to allow angels to descend therefrom in order to dance with or above such *shaikhs*, and that, as some others believe, the Messenger of God – may he have God's blessings – himself comes to visit them? What is required of a man who has such a belief?[135]

Reports of miracles, obviously enough, were either meant to impress believers and convince them of the extraordinary powers of the *shaykh*, or reflected their belief in them. Yet some reports are more complex in function, for they associate miracles specifically with one *shaykh*'s social, communal role – to wit, improving the lot of ordinary Muslims – and thus portray Sufis as communal leaders. Rather than relating dazzling, fantastic performances of *shaykh*s, such reports reveal the ways by which Sufis solved problems, or, perhaps more precisely, were expected to solve problems.[136] We are told how one *shaykh* fed a large number of poor people during a period of starvation by performing a miracle, how another delivered an innocent man unjustly imprisoned, or even how some *shaykh*s used their supernatural powers to relieve people of catastrophes.[137] Take, for example, the report on Sīdī Muḥammad al-Wafā'ī, who, while staying in Cairo in 1362, a year of a low Nile, was requested by the people to perform an intercession and cause the river to water the land. Sure enough, his prayer was answered. Moreover, his very surname allegedly stemmed from his announcement on that particular occasion: "The Nile has reached its plenitude (*wafā*)!"[138] Ibrāhīm b. ʿAlī al-Matbūlī (d. 1472), of the Aḥmadiyya order, is believed to have fed five hundred believers at his *zāwiya* in Cairo in a year of famine, supposedly out of his own agricultural produce.[139] ʿAlī b. Shihāb ash-Shaʿrānī (d. 1486) – his grandson, the famous Sufi author, tells us – used to grind his wheat and leave the flour for the needy.[140] Muḥammad b. ʿInān (d. 1516) was able to feed 500 people miraculously with only a small measure of grain.[141] Sīdī Amīn ad-Dīn (d. 1522 or 1523), the *imām* of the Ghamrī Mosque,[142] shared his meals with the poor, the blind, orphans, and widows. He provided alms anonymously, a fact discovered only after his death.[143] Shaykh ʿAbd Allāh Shams ad-Dīn Damirdāsh (d. 1523), a former Mamluk of Sultan Qāyit Bāy, spent on the poor a third of his income from a huge orchard which he cultivated in Cairo.[144] Shaykh ʿAbd Allāh al-Miṣrī (d. 1530 or 1531) used to grind *ḥashīsh* in the Azbakiyya Garden and give it to people so that they would cease consuming it. In fact, it was reported that whoever took of the Shaykh's herb repented and never tried *ḥashīsh* again.[145] We should, of course, treat such reports not as historical facts, but as probable hagiographical stories. As such, however, they do not lack historical value, for they tell us what people believed in, and, in their turn, they probably reinforced popular belief. Here one can draw analogies with the world of medieval Christendom, where "the hagiographer's main contribution was to shape the received material according to the current, partly implicit, pressures of the saint-making process . . . and, not least, the expectations of local devotees". The hagiographer, and this is perfectly correct for the case under consideration, was an agent of the myth-making mechanism.[146]

Let us consider one more set of examples. In 1344 or 1345 Shaykh Aḥmad adh-Dharʿī petitioned the sultan to abolish illegal taxes. We are told that the sultan complied.[147] Abū'l-ʿAbbās Aḥmad b. Mūsā az-Zarʿī (d. 1360 or 1361), we read elsewhere, dared to stand up to the rulers of his time and to convince them to undo many wrongs (*abṭala maẓālim kathīra*).[148] Khalaf b. Ḥasan b. ʿAbd Allāh aṭ-Ṭūkhī (d. 1398) was admired by the people; he used to serve as an intermediary between them and their rulers.[149] Shaykh Muḥammad as-Safārī, who resided in ʿAmr b. al-ʿĀṣ Mosque, sent in 1451, a year of high grain prices,[150] two of his disciples, with chains on their necks, to the *muḥtasib* of Cairo. This was undoubtedly as-Safārī's peculiar way of protesting against the mismanagement which he associated with the market inspector. Yet his two men were arrested and he himself was summoned to the Citadel, a fact which prompted him to curse the sultan. Then a large crowd gathered at the gate of his *zāwiya* to hear as-Safārī's prediction about the imminent death of the ruler.[151] About half a century later another Sufi, Muḥammad ash-Shināwī (d. 1525),[152] was instrumental in abolishing heavy taxes on grain in the Gharbiyya province.[153]

There is a common motif in all these reports. As Fernandes has aptly suggested, thus revising earlier analyses, from the fourteenth century onwards any attempt to maintain an internal balance in Egypt between the military ruling group and the rest of the population had *a fortiori* to be based on Sufi institutions. In that respect, Sufis were at least as significant as orthodox scholars (*ʿulamāʾ*).[154] Thus we arrive from an initially religious message, via social performance, to the political role of Sufi *shaykh*s. Having established their communal authority as religious leaders, *shaykh*s felt responsible, perhaps were also expected, to mediate between Egyptian subjects and the Mamluk regime.

The veneration of *shaykh*s as portrayed in the above descriptions, certainly did not cease with the termination of their lives. The cult of dead Sufis was conceived of as a natural continuation of the worship of living saints. Already the funeral of a *shaykh* was an occasion for proving that veneration went on. Thus the funeral of Ḥusayn b. Ibrāhīm b. ʿAlī al-Jākī in 1337 was attended by large crowds. His coffin, placed at the Polo Hippodrome (Maydān al-Qabaq), was surrounded by crowds, and people fought their way to touch it; the line of mourners stretched from the Succour Gate to al-Jākī's *zawiya*, situated at the western bank of the Canal.[155] Aḥmad b. Ibrāhīm al-Burṣāwī, known as Ibn ʿArab, of Anatolian origin, a *shaykh* revered also by Mamluk officers, was honoured upon his death in 1426 with a "state funeral".[156] The coffin of ʿUmar b. Ibrāhīm al-Bābānī, a *shaykh* who settled in Cairo around 1436 and died there in 1463, had to be raised "on the finger tips" to save it from the enthusiastic crowd.[157] The property of deceased *shaykh*s was sometimes treated as relics. Ibn ʿArab's garments were sold for a high price as a means of blessing.[158] A similar case was that of Shaykh ʿAbd al-Ghaffār (d. 1308 or 1309).[159]

By the Mamluk period, dead Sufis were integrated into the cult of "visitation of graves" (*ziyārat al-qubūr*). This cult in its private manifestation had of course had a long history, which need not detain us here.[160] What is of more immediate concern to us is that in its collective, public, expression, tombs of *shaykh*s now featured along with tombs of allegedly pre-Islamic figures and graves of Shiite personages.[161] Several dozens of *shaykh*s' tombs that were "visited" are listed in our sources. They must be considered as only a fraction of a much larger number. Unfortunately, there is very little information on the customs that were part of the cult of dead Sufis;[162] only here and there does one come across a laconic statement concerning those customs. Thus we read that at gatherings which took place on the first day of Muḥarram of each year at the grave of Shaykh Abū Muḥammad ʿAbd Allāh b. Abī Jamra (d. 1296), literary material collected by the deceased *shaykh* himself, such as sayings (*ḥadīth*s) of the Prophet, was recited.[163] A *ziyāra* to the grave of the above-mentioned Ḥusayn b. Ibrāhīm b. ʿAlī al-Jākī (d. 1337), outside the Succour Gate, was performed each year for at least seventy or so years until the early fifteenth century. Vows (*nudhūr*) and offerings were made; it was claimed that requests at the grave were answered.[164] The tomb of Shaykh ʿAbd Allāh b. Muḥammad b. Sulaymān al-Manūfī al-Maghribī (d. 1348), a Sufi known for his miracles (*karāmāt khāriqa*), was visited on Saturdays.[165]

CHAPTER 2

Al-Bakrī's biography of Muḥammad

"Liar and swindler (*al-kadhdhāb, ad-dajjāl*) . . . inventor of stories (*wāḍiʿl-qiṣaṣ*)", whose books, however, were read (or sold) in bookshops. This is how Shams ad-Dīn adh-Dhahabī (1274–1348), a Damascene historian, characterized Abū'l-Ḥasan al-Bakrī.[1] He was not the only one to write about al-Bakrī in this manner. Other fourteenth- and fifteenth-century writers also evoked al-Bakrī's name in a clearly negative sense. Ibn Kathīr (*ca* 1300–73), a Damascene also, mentioned *Sīrat Dhī'l-himma wa'l-Baṭṭāl*,[2] *Sīrat ʿAntar*,[3] al-Bakrī's biography of the Prophet (*Sīrat al-Bakrī*), and *Sīrat ad-Danif*,[4] in one and the same stroke. He stressed that "the lies produced in al-Bakrī's *sīra* are an offence and a grave sin; their fabricator has fallen into the category of those warned by the Prophet: 'He who reports lies about me deliberately shall be condemned to Hell.'"[5] Ibn Ḥajar al-ʿAsqalānī (d. 1449), a leading Egyptian scholar, copied from adh-Dhahabī almost *verbatim*; to the works attributed to al-Bakrī he added what he considered al-Bakrī's most famous piece, the biography of the Prophet, already mentioned by Ibn Kathīr. Al-ʿAsqalānī also remarked that "there is not [by al-Bakrī] even one accurate description of a single one of Muḥammad's expeditions (*ma sāqa ghazwatan minhā ʿalā wajhihā*); whatever al-Bakrī related was full of falsification, corruption, or additions".[6] Another Egyptian, al-Qalqashandī (1355–1418), chose al-Bakrī as an archetype of liars in his chapter on historically famous (or infamous) characters.[7] Ibrāhīm b. Muḥammad Burhān ad-Dīn, known as Sibṭ b. al-ʿAjamī (d. 1438),[8] an Aleppin savant, warned emphatically against al-Bakrī and quoted adh-Dhahabī to that effect.[9] Other medieval writers followed suit.[10]

The repeated references to al-Bakrī suggest that his works made popular reading yet were condemned in scholarly circles of the late medieval period. The popularity of al-Bakrī in Egypt, specifically among the various Islamic regions, can be argued from a query addressed to Ibn Ḥajar al-Haytamī, a sixteenth-century scholar, most likely while he was in Cairo. Al-Haytamī was asked about the value of al-Bakrī's works; the scholar's legal opinion (*fatwā*) forbade their reading, since they mostly included "lies and falsehood, a hodgepodge of things". And "since the truth cannot be distinguished from the lies, the whole book is forbidden".[11]

Adh-Dhahabī listed six works by al-Bakrī.[12] Many more are scattered in libraries in the form of a few dozen manuscript fragments, all carrying an attribution to al-Bakrī.[13] Here I wish to examine in some detail al-Bakrī's biography of Muḥammad, entitled in most of its extant versions *al-Anwār wa-miṣbāḥ* [or *miftāḥ*] *as-surūr* [or *al-asrār*] *wa'l-afkār fī dhikr (sayyidinā) Muḥammad al-muṣṭafā al-mukhtār* (*The Lights and the Lamp* [or *Key*] *of Delight* [or *Secrets*] *and Thoughts concerning the Commemoration of* [*our Master*] *the Chosen*). It is the story of the Prophet's ancestors and his early life, up to the period in his career known as *al-mab'ath* ("the mission").[14] The *Anwār* has survived in more than a dozen manuscripts, most of which date to the seventeenth and eighteenth centuries. Fortunately, there is also one medieval manuscript, and thus we can examine a version to the like of which, presumably, the above-mentioned scholars referred.[15] Who al-Bakrī was is a question that I shall take up at the end of this chapter. In the mean time, to support an argument about the *Anwār* as a popular literary piece, a summary of its contents is offered.[16]

Muḥammad's primordiality and the *nūr Muḥammadī*[17]

Al-Bakrī's *sīra* begins with the early Islamic theme – also found in works of reputed Muslim scholars such as Ibn Sa'd (d. 845) and Ṭabarī (d. 923) – of Muḥammad's primordiality; namely, the existence of his spirit as part of the substance of his ancestors.[18] According to the *Anwār*, the Prophet's spirit was created in the following process. First, Gabriel was sent to fetch a handful of some unspecified white stuff (*qabḍa bayḍā'*).[19] Then the angel brought pure dust (*turāb*) from the Prophet's future grave at Medina. The dust was dipped first in the celestial spring Tansīm,[20] then each day in one of the springs of Paradise, until it became like a white, shining pearl (*durra bayḍā'*), which was then presented to the angels. It was welcomed by them and given great respect. After the creation of Adam, the special substance was transferred to him, and its light shone from his face.[21]

God ordered Adam to deposit the light only in a pure loin, which he did, thus keeping to "a pact and a covenant" (*'ahd wa-mīthāq*), which were later also binding on his descendants.[22] Adam's light was transferred to Eve when she was pregnant with Sheth, then to Sheth himself, then to his descendants.[23]

Hāshim

Hāshim is portrayed in the *Anwār* as a generous man who fed the hungry and covered the naked; his door was open to the needy and his table always set for visitors.[24] He preached to the Qurayshites the importance of cordial treatment of pilgrims arriving at Mecca, and himself led the effort to supply food and drink to them.[25] On one occasion, when there was famine in Mecca, he sent men to Syria(?) (Shām) for supplies.[26] In honour of his leadership the Meccans entrusted him with the "Keys of the Ka'ba", and awarded him the supervision of their Assembly House (*dār an-nadwa*) and the posts of *siqāya* and *rifāda*.[27] Furthermore, Hāshim was given a number of prestigious emblems: Sheth's Shoes, Ibrāhīm's Gown, Ismā'īl's Bow, and Niẓār's[28] Flag (*liwā'*).

Special stories illustrate the importance of Hāshim's divine light. It illuminated the Ka'ba, it shone on dark nights, and it allowed him to see clearly behind his back. Hāshim, of course, was bound by the special "pact" imposed upon Adam and therefore refused to be married into royal courts. He rejected offers of marriage from the Abyssinian and the Byzantine rulers (*qayṣar*), who both desired him as a husband for their daughters because of his light (*nūr rasūl Allāh*), recognized by their clerics (*aḥbār*, *ruhbān*, *kuhhān*). The *Anwār* then proceeds to the story of Hāshim's marriage.

While in standard medieval *sīra*s such as Ibn Kathīr's, Hāshim's engagement to Salma is told in a matter-of-fact manner and is incidental to one of his business trips,[29] in al-Bakrī's *sīra* Hashim is told in a dream to marry Salma, the daughter of 'Amr of the Banū Najjār of Yathrib (later Medina). There is an extended description of Hāshim's journey to Yathrib, in the company of forty "dignitaries" (*sayyid*) of the Banū 'Abd Manāf and other clans,[30] to ask for Salma's hand. Hāshim himself carried one of his sacred emblems, Niẓār's Flag, on the journey. Before he departed the Meccans gathered to say farewell to him.[31] When the party approached Yathrib, the blazing light (*ghurra*) shone from Hāshim's forehead and lit up the town; women climbed up on fences to see it. In the first meeting between the Meccans and 'Amr, Salma's father, the latter described his daughter as absolutely independent and entitled to her own decision (*amrī dūna amrihā*).[32]

The scene then shifts to the market of the Jewish tribe of Qaynuqā', where a huge tent was set up in honour of Hāshim. This site as well was illuminated by Hāshim's special light. People left their businesses and rushed to see the phenomenon. All were overwhelmed by Hāshim's beauty.[33] Those merchants who went to look at Hāshim suffered heavy losses on that day, as their unprotected merchandise was stolen. Salma, known for her excellent qualities and herself proud of her own beauty, was also struck by Hāshim's good looks and realized how inferior to him she was.[34] In the course of a dialogue she has with her father, the latter tells her about the merits of her would-be husband. Salma, however, is less than enthusiastic, reminding her father of her earlier, now dissolved, marriage.[35] Then the Devil (Iblīs) appears to Salma repeatedly, disguised once as an elderly man (*shaykh*), then as one of Hāshim's party, and initially dissuades her from the marriage plan. He describes Hāshim as a "Casanova" with whom a woman would not cohabit more than one month. He also depicts him as a coward. As a result Salma declares to her father that the engagement should not take place, yet 'Amr tries to convince her otherwise. The next day Salma and Hāshim have an "accidental" encounter, during which the woman, who sees the light on Hāshim's face, expresses her desire for him.[36] This leads to the engagement ceremony.[37]

Iblīs, once again in disguise, participates in the negotiations about the dowry and repeatedly signals to Salma's father to raise his bid. Finally, 'Amr tires of the obnoxious "shaykh" and his advice,[38] at which point the latter nods to a Jewish party, present at the meeting, to attack the Meccans. In the course of the clash,

Hāshim is able to get hold of Iblīs and hit him; the latter begs for mercy. The Jewish leader, Armūn(?),[39] is split in two by al-Muṭṭalib's (Hāshim's brother) sword, while Hāshim and his men kill seventy-two[40] Jews.[41] After that incident, Hāshim marries Salma, and when she is pregnant with the future ʿAbd al-Muṭṭalib, the light (*nūr Muḥammadī*) is transferred to her, and then to her son upon his birth.[42] Prior to his business journey to Gaza, where he would meet his death, Hāshim instructs Salma to hide their future offspring until his return. As Hāshim dies, the leadership of Mecca, together with all his titles, according to his own will, are entrusted to his brother al-Muṭṭalib.

ʿAbd al-Muṭṭalib

ʿAbd al-Muṭṭalib,[43] Hāshim's son, came into this world with the special light shining on his forehead and a smile on his face. His mother saw a white hair on his head, hence his original name Shayba.[44] For some time Salma was able to conceal the news of his birth. Then, as it spread, the people of Medina came to see his beauty. When Shayba reached the age of seven, he was so strong that parents used to complain about him "breaking their children's ribs and spilling their children's blood". One day, a Meccan of the Banū Ḥārith, while visiting Medina, saw the boy, interrogated him about his identity, and brought back to Mecca the news that Hāshim's son was alive.[45] Al-Muṭṭalib then went to see his "lost" nephew and took him home without asking the mother's permission.[46]

On their way to Mecca the two were ambushed by Jewish warriors who claimed their coming was to protect the boy. There is an extensive recounting of the dialogue between the two parties. In the clash which follows al-Muṭṭalib shoots some Jews with arrows and causes panic in the enemy's camp.[47] Consequently, there is some bargaining and a duel between one Jew and al-Muṭṭalib; the latter kills his opponent. Then follows another duel between al-Muṭṭalib and the leader of the Jewish camp. Again al-Muṭṭalib is able to overcome his adversary and "split" his body. A massacre of the Jewish party follows. At this point there appear on the scene 400 Medinan warriors,[48] Salma and her family amongst them. Following an emotional dialogue between Salma and her son, the latter expresses his desire to continue to Mecca.[49] After the arrival of the two men in the town[50] ʿAbd al-Muṭṭalib, through his special light, helps the Meccans whenever they are in need.[51]

Abraha's siege of Mecca[52]

Al-Bakrī's report of Abraha's expedition diverges in many details from all standard versions, mainly as regards the reasons for the expedition.[53] Accordingly, Abraha b. Ṣabbāḥ,[54] the Christian "king" of the Yemen,[55] had constructed a golden church in Najrān where, once a year, a festival lasting three days was celebrated in his presence. On the eve of one of the annual celebrations, a group of Meccan merchants happened to pass by the church, and, as one of its guards approached them, a dispute arose about which was better, the church of Najrān or the Ka'ba of Mecca. The dispute resulted in the killing of some Christians; the church itself was ransacked.[56] As Abraha arrived in Najrān to celebrate, the bad news reached him and he vowed to destroy the Ka'ba "without leaving a trace". He wrote about the affair to his subjects in the Yemen and young men gathered to his call.[57] His elephant, named Madhmūm,[58] was also dispatched to him. This elephant was tame and used to prostrate itself before its master.

At the vanguard of Abraha's expeditionary force was Shamīr b. Maqṣūd with an army of 20,000.[59] He took as a guide the chieftain of the Khath'am tribe.[60] On their way, other Arabs from the vicinity of Ṭā'if joined them.[61] Upon discovering that the people of Mecca had fled, the troops put their animals out to graze, and seized 200 red she-camels,[62] which happened to be the property of 'Abd al-Muṭṭalib. 'Abd al-Muṭṭalib himself was invited to Abraha's audience.[63] The troops at the Yemeni camp were astonished to see light shining from his forehead, and marvelled at his beauty. 'Abd al-Muṭṭalib, who passed by Abraha's elephant on his way to the audience, whispered some word in its ear, and the beast prostrated itself. Abraha, like his servants, was struck by the Meccan's handsome appearance. At their meeting,[64] 'Abd al-Muṭṭalib only asked for the return of his 100 (*sic*) confiscated camels, a request which surprised Abraha, who had expected him to beg for an end to the siege of his town.[65] Yet the Meccan declared that, as regards that matter, he put his trust in God. Abraha's reaction was sheer anger; he decided to enter Mecca.

During the Yemenite attack, 'Abd al-Muṭṭalib uttered a prayer and, consequently, Abraha's elephant, which was in the lead, stopped and went down on its knees.[66] All the troops stood frozen. Abraha ordered them to proceed, but then the famous miracle of the birds happened, on which al-Bakrī's report is more elaborate than any other source.[67] We also learn that Abraha himself was fatefully afflicted. During his attempt to evade disaster his limbs fell off one after the other; as he was carried into his kingdom, his head rolled down.[68]

'Abd Allāh[69]

When Fāṭima bt. 'Amr was pregnant with 'Abd Allāh, she received the special light which had been given earlier to 'Abd al-Muṭṭalib, and the light was then transferred to 'Abd Allāh upon his birth.[70] The child matured very rapidly, growing in one day as much as other children grow in one month, and in one month as much as other boys do in one year.[71] All the people (*al-bādiya wa'l-ḥāḍira*) were astonished at his beauty. Then one day, 'Abd al-Muṭṭalib, by then the father of eleven sons, decided to fulfil an earlier vow – to sacrifice a son if he ever begot one – a vow he had made when still heirless as a reaction to a challenge posed to him by 'Adī b. Nawfal, his opponent within Quraysh ('Adī had once mocked 'Abd al-Muṭṭalib for his lack of male children).[72] Now 'Abd al-Muṭṭalib gathered his sons, told them about his commitment, and asked for their opinion. All but 'Abd Allāh remained silent. Aged ten and the tenth in line (Ḥārith, the youngest, was absent), ʿAbd Allāh encouraged his father to go ahead with his vow. Hearing him, ʿAbd al-Muṭṭalib burst into tears; the rest agreed with ʿAbd Allāh's opinion.

On the day of the sacrifice, ʿAbd al-Muṭṭalib neither ate nor drank. All his sons gathered, dressed in their best garments, except for ʿAbd Allāh, whom Fāṭima tried to keep from going. There follows a scene in which ʿAbd al-Muṭṭalib tries to pull the boy out of his mother's grip and the mother resists, ʿAbd Allāh himself shouting that he would rather join his father so that the vow could be enacted. The boy says: "If God chooses me, we have to abide; if he chooses someone else, I shall return." In a dialogue between Fāṭima and ʿAbd al-Muṭṭalib, the shocked mother admonishes her husband for his intention to sacrifice her son.[73] Yet ʿAbd al-Muṭṭalib, determined, marches to the Kaʿba, accompanied by the people of Mecca. At the shrine he delivers a sermon in rhymed prose (*sajʿ*).[74] Then the soothsayer secludes himself in the Kaʿba to draw the lot by arrows, and thus inform the people who is the youth to be sacrificed.

ʿAbd al-Muṭṭalib, the distraught father, is roaming around restless; his wives are weeping. ʿAbd Allāh's lot is drawn, and ʿAbd al-Muṭṭalib faints; Fāṭima puts dust on her head; all the Meccans mourn.[75] The draw is repeated with the same result, and ʿAbd al-Muṭṭalib now takes his son to be slaughtered. The sacrifice is averted by a miracle: the three archangels cry for God's mercy and God replies that all was done to test ʿAbd al-Muṭṭalib's faith (*ablaytu ʿabdī*). Then the party turn to a woman soothsayer (*kāhina*), who, to conclude the affair, advises them to draw the lot several times until it falls on camels; these will replace ʿAbd Allāh as an offering. In the end, 100 camels are slaughtered.[76] Al-Bakrī's version of the sacrifice story contains the interesting observation that ʿAbd Allāh experienced what the biblical Joseph had before him; it is not clear, however, whether what is meant is general trials that both withstood, or just the sexual temptation they resisted.[77]

ʿAbd Allāh's marriage[78]

ʿAbd Allāh was desired for marriage by many, who were willing to reward him generously. Thus a Jewish soothsayer tried to seduce him, yet he resisted the temptation and married Āmina. When the Jewess learnt about it during a second encounter with ʿAbd Allāh, she stated that her desire for him was only for his light.[79] The *Anwār* draws here an analogy between ʿAbd Allāh and Joseph, who, according to the biblical story, had been seduced by Potiphar's (Arabic Qaṭfīr or Iṭfīr) wife. Both resisted carnal temptation.[80] A second example of ʿAbd Allāh's reputation occurs in the context of his (and his father's) trip to Yamāma in Central Arabia. Zarqāʾ, the local *kāhina*, tried to seduce the lad by promising him a large sum.[81]

The reason for ʿAbd Allāh's engagement to Āmina is peculiarly presented. Wahb, Āmina's father, witnessed ʿAbd Allāh's single-handed combat against the Jews (see below), and he summoned ʿAbd Allāh's clan for assistance. Wahb, much impressed by the lad's bravery, then suggested to his wife that their daughter and the young Qurayshi would make a good match. Wahb's wife, though initially sceptical, takes it upon herself to discuss the matter with ʿAbd al-Muṭṭalib. Following the discussion, ʿAbd al-Muṭṭalib turns to ʿAbd Allāh himself to ask his opinion. The young man's silence is interpreted by the father as a sign of consent and the engagement is concluded. The earthly wedding ceremony is reflected in a heavenly celebration by the angels.[82]

ʿAbd Allāh dies while on his way to Yathrib to fetch provisions for a *fête* that should have taken place following the birth of his child. According to another version, ʿAbd Allāh's death occurred only after the birth of Muḥammad.[83]

The birth of Muḥammad[84]

In the Vatican version of the *Anwār* Āmina herself is the narrator of mysterious occurrences which precede and follow the birth of Muḥammad. She sees the wing of a white bird rubbing against her heart.[85] Thus her labour pains are removed. Suddenly she observes a white liquid[86] and, being thirsty, she drinks it. As she does so, light radiates from her. Then tall women appear, spreading perfumes around. Surprised at their appearance, Āmina wonders how they were able to enter her house, since she had locked the door. Then each of the women announces in a particular phrase the good tidings of the imminent birth of Muḥammad. Later on, Āmina sees "human beings with wings", holding cups full of an unknown liquid. A voice is booming: "Take him away lest demons (*jinn*) and humans see him." At this point Āmina wishes that ʿAbd al-Muṭṭalib, the grandfather, who is at the Kaʿba making a vow, had been present.[87] The vision is then concluded by the appearance of a group of birds with white wings, green legs, and red beaks, all uttering the praise of God. Then follows the birth. As soon as Muḥammad comes into this world he prostrates in the direction of the Kaʿba, then raises his finger towards Heaven.[88]

Āmina's house is filled with strange noises. Then a white cloud covers both the mother and the new-born child, and the latter is taken away.[89] Āmina hears Allāh's command: "Perform the circumambulation (*ṭūfū*) with Muḥammad to the West, South, and North, enter the sea . . . " After a very brief disappearance, the child is returned to his mother, wrapped in white wool, three keys made of pearls in his hand. Again a voice booms: "These are the keys of Victory, the *qibla*, and light."[90] A second cloud, larger than the first, descends, and again the infant is taken away, now for a longer time, and once more a voice exclaims that this time Muḥammad will be presented before all earlier Messengers and be given a quality of each of them.[91] When Muḥammad is returned to Āmina, the voice states that the child was given hold of the entire world. Then three men enter, their faces shining like the sun, one holding a silver jug, another a basin of precious stones, the third a piece of silk,[92] and again a voice commands that Muḥammad must be presented to all ends of this world. Then Riḍwān, the Keeper of Paradise, stamps upon the baby's shoulder the special Seal of Prophecy (*khatam*).

So much for Āmina's report. The *Anwār* goes on to tell us that ʿAbd al-Muṭṭalib was at the Kaʿba at the time of the birth and witnessed there the destruction of idols (*aṣnām*) and other occurrences which astonished him.[93] As he hurries to Āmina's dwelling, a dark cloud suddenly comes out. ʿAbd al-Muṭṭalib enters and finds out that the special light is no longer on Āmina's face; thus he learns that the birth has already taken place. He wants to see the baby and, upon Āmina's reply that he should wait three days, angrily pulls out his sword to clear his way. But then he is confronted by an awesome man who commands him to stay away for three days during which Muḥammad is to be visited (*ziyāra*) only by the angels. At the end of this period the Meccans come to greet Āmina; they smell a special perfume emanating from her. She explains that this is due to Muḥammad.

It should be noted that missing in al-Bakrī's account are details which appear in the standard biographies of Muḥammad, such as the light shining from "Buṣrā" (= Bostra, in the Syrian desert) to Āmina during her pregnancy, the reaction of the Jewish community in Yathrib to Muḥammad's birth, and the quaking of the Iranian palace (*irtijās al-īwān*) following the birth of the Prophet.[94]

The suckling of Muḥammad[95]

A few days after Muḥammad's birth Āmina hears a voice (*hātif*) commanding her to hire Ḥalīma of the Banū Saʿd as a wetnurse. Ḥalīma hears a voice as well, telling her to go to Mecca and fetch a particular infant.[96] Then, despite the famine prevailing in the region, and to the surprise of her fellow nurses, she regains an excellent physical condition. Later, a voice addresses Ḥalīma's clan, promising them blessings as a reward for the suckling of the special infant of Mecca.

As Ḥalīma comes to town to take the baby – that is, Muḥammad – she enters an extended dialogue with ʿAbd al-Muṭṭalib, from whom she learns that the child is fatherless. She then goes to consult her husband, who is very disappointed to hear that fact. Nevertheless, Ḥalīma, struck by the baby's beauty, and tempted by ʿAbd al-Muṭṭalib's promise to reward her generously, is determined to take Muḥammad with her. As she holds him, his special light is reflected in her own face; she thinks that a lantern was placed near the boy, but is told by Āmina that the light comes directly from him.

Ḥalīma takes Muḥammad with her and receives, now against her will, money for his maintenance. On her way back to her clan she and her companions encounter forty monks (*rāhib*) of Najrān,[97] who already know about the birth of Muḥammad and what will follow it – their own destruction. As they pull out their swords to attack, the baby lifts his head, utters some words, and fire comes out of Heaven and exterminates them.[98] Ḥalīma's clan see great blessings thanks to the presence of Muḥammad amongst them. With his thaumaturgic touch he is able to heal wounds and remove illness.

Sharḥ aṣ-ṣadr

The famous episode of *sharḥ aṣ-ṣadr* ("opening of the breast")[99] is foreseen by Ḥalīma in a dream, and she wishes, as a result, to return Muḥammad to his family. Some time later Muḥammad's foster brothers return from grazing their herds and with horror they tell that two giants seized Muḥammad, who had joined them against Ḥalīma's will. The boy is later found unharmed. He relates that the giants took a black drop out of his heart and informed him: "This is the Devil's part (*ḥaẓẓ ash-shayṭān*)."[100] The event prompts Ḥalīma to carry out her earlier wish, and thus Muḥammad is returned to Mecca. This episode too involves a bizarre occurrence: the boy disappears at the Kaʿba, only to be found later lying under a tree.[101]

The Vatican (medieval) manuscript of al-Bakrī's *Anwār* terminates abruptly with the beginning of the story of Muḥammad, now a young man, voyaging to Syria to sell merchandise for the rich woman Khadīja.[102] If one is curious to know how al-Bakrī treated that event, and Muḥammad's marriage to Khadīja, one can rely on the less old, more complete versions of the *Anwār*.[103] Although it is far from certain that these tally with the part missing in our earliest manuscript, the approximation, to this point in the story, of the Vatican to the later versions provides a possible basis for completing the story.[104] It goes as follows.

On his journey to Syria, Muḥammad demonstrates on several occasions his unique ability to predict future events. At the same time he is confronted by Abū Jahl, his jealous relative, who also makes an abortive attempt on his life. The standard stories of the two monks Baḥīrā and Nasṭūr (or Nasṭūrā), who recognized the gift of prophecy in Muḥammad,[105] are united in the *Anwār* and are unfolded differently. According to al-Bakrī the caravan, while passing through ʿAqaba, by the Red Sea, comes upon the monk Faylāq(?) b. al-Yūnān b. ʿAbd aṣ-Ṣalīb, known as Abū Khabīr, who for some time had expected the visit of the Messenger (*al-bashīr an-nadhīr*) from the Ḥijāz.[106] Abū Jahl's plot to leave Muḥammad as a guard of the merchandise fails, and the monk recognizes in the boy the future prophet. Another peculiar experience which befalls Muḥammad on the same voyage is an escape from yet another attempt on his life, this time by a Jew of the Banū Qurayẓa in Syria(?) (Shām).

Muḥammad is able to sell all of Khadīja's merchandise profitably and returns to Mecca to report his success to his patroness.[107] Then follows the episode of their engagement, which is much elaborated when compared with standard versions.[108] According to the *Anwār*, it is Khadīja who offers, to the surprise of Hāshim's clan, to marry Muḥammad despite his social inferiority.[109] As Khuwaylid, her father, who is not sober, refuses to approve the engagement, Khadīja contacts Waraqa, her uncle, to arrange the marriage.[110] A ceremony then takes place in Khadīja's spacious dwelling, during which Khuwaylid receives a large sum of money from Abū Ṭālib (no other than Khadīja herself is the donor). A generous marriage gift demanded by both Khuwaylid and Waraqa is also provided by Khadīja herself! The wedding is celebrated in great splendour.[111]

Thus far a summary of al-Bakrī's *sīra*. It should have given the reader an idea of the popular character of the work. Detailed and unique descriptions, and an obvious mythical treatment, envelop the circumstances leading to Salma's marriage to Hāshim, ʿAbd Allāh's sacrifice (averted at the last moment), the birth of the Prophet, and so on. I now turn to a brief discussion of the main motifs of the *Anwār*. These should shed further light on the popular element in al-Bakrī's work.

Hāshim's clan and the Jews

We have already had an occasion to glimpse the special role of the Jews in the *Anwār*. Let us consider further information about it. Armūn b. Fayṭūn(?), one of the leaders (*aḥbār*) of the Jews of Yathrib, had allegedly known about Hāshim prior to his coming to the town to search for Salma. Upon Hāshim's arrival, as the Jews go out with the rest to see him, Armūn bursts into tears, saying: "This man will beget a child who will bring destruction upon us; he will be the blood spiller (*saffāk*), the destroyer (*hattāk*); angels fight at his side; his name in the scriptures is the exterminator (*māḥī*); the light shining out of Hāshim is the light of that future enemy of the Jews." The Jewish party then decide to kill Hāshim, to "extinguish the light", and thus to avoid the coming disaster. Armūn, however, replies that this is impossible, since Heaven is on Hāshim's side; he has even defeated the angels.[112] The Jews, disarmed by the response, conceal their hatred to Hāshim. On that day there also emerged their animosity to the Messenger of God. Exactly the same phrase is repeated in the context of their defeat by Hāshim and his party during his wedding to Salma.[113] On another occasion, in the wedding story, the Jews are referred to as "a treacherous party" (*ʿaṣaba ghādira*).[114]

The Jews were instigated by Iblīs against Hāshim, and 400 of them[115] were persuaded to attack the Meccans.[116] A large number of them, however, were killed in the attack, a fact which enhanced the hatred felt by the survivors.[117] Later, when Salma was pregnant, Hāshim instructed her to hide their future son from the Jews, "his worst enemies".[118] Indeed, the Jews much detested the infant ʿAbd al-Muṭṭalib, since they had his description in their books as the one who would destroy their homes. Salma and the child therefore needed the protection of the warriors of the two Medinan tribes, Aws and Khazraj.[119] The Jews followed the track of al-Muṭṭalib and ʿAbd al-Muṭṭalib on their way from Medina to Mecca.[120] Their leader at that point, Lāṭiya b. Dalja(?),[121] is described as a "Devil" (*shayṭān*) and "an enemy of God".[122]

The Jewish rabbis (*aḥbār*, *aḥbār isrāʾīliyya*) had in their possession a white woollen gown, worn by Yaḥyā b. Zakariyyāʾ (John the Baptist) at the time of his martyrdom. It was stated in their scriptures that should the traces of blood on the gown become fresh once again, an attack upon the Jews would soon follow (*khurūj as-sayf al-maslūl*). After the birth of ʿAbd Allāh the blood spots indeed turned fresh, so the Jews hired assassins to murder the infant; to no avail.[123] The rabbis also tried to kill ʿAbd Allāh after his escape from the sacrifice and ambushed him as he went hunting alone.[124] He was able to withstand their attack single-handedly and was finally saved by his clan. His courage prompted Wahb, as we saw above, to offer his daughter, Āmina, to the youth. Another Jewish plot was to poison ʿAbd al-Muṭṭalib's family.[125] The Jews, prisoners at the house of Wahb, Āmina's father, also made an attempt on the lives of ʿAbd al-Muṭṭalib and ʿAbd Allāh. Their plan was discovered and they were massacred.[126]

Dreams

Dreams and their interpretation (*ta'wīl ar-ru'yā*) recur in al-Bakrī's *sīra*. Their role is at least two-fold: to enhance the element of mystery, and to lend the character who dreams a special quality. Let us consider a few examples.

On the night preceding the ceremony of his engagement to Salma, Hāshim dreams of a pack of dogs, led by one special dog with a twisted tail, staring at him. In his dream, Hāshim rushes to his sword. When he wakes up in horror, he recounts the dream to his party. He himself interprets it as a sign of a plot, obviously planned by the Jews against the Meccan party in Medina. Hāshim advises his kinsmen to be on the alert and carry their swords.[127]

ʿAbd al-Muṭṭalib as well tells about a dream he had at the Kaʿba. In that dream, a white chain, the glitter of which strikes the eye, has four edges: one reaching to the far East, one to the far West, one to Heaven, and the fourth piercing through the Earth. Then the chain suddenly turns into a tree, beneath which are lying two giant, awesome men. ʿAbd al-Muṭṭalib asks them who they are, and they say they are Noah and Abraham. ʿAbd al-Muṭṭalib wakes up in horror. The *kāhina* whom he approaches interprets the dream as a good omen: one of his descendants will be called "the ruler of the East, West, the Sea, and the Earth".[128]

ʿAbd Allāh also has a dream in which he is confronted by screaming apes (= Jews), swords in their hands. He barely escapes, and then fire comes and destroys his enemies. Ironically, his father, ʿAbd al-Muṭṭalib, asks Jews visiting from Syria to interpret the dream. The Jewish leader deceitfully answers that there is no reason for concern.[129]

Together with dreams, one should mention the role played in the *Anwār* by the "invisible speaker" (*hātif*). The latter, also to be found in scholarly works,[130] acts time and again, directing the heroes to the right decision or action. Thus Hāshim is commanded to marry Salma so that he can beget his children from a "pure loin".[131] Salma is told by the *hātif* about her pregnancy with ʿAbd al-Muṭṭalib,[132] and after giving birth, is directed to hide the infant.[133] The *hātif* admonishes the Jews who come to Mecca with the aim of killing ʿAbd Allāh.[134] It conveys to Āmina the imminent birth of Muḥammad,[135] tells her to hire Ḥalīma as a wetnurse,[136] and orders Ḥalīma to fetch Muḥammad the infant for suckling.[137]

The devil (Iblīs, *shayṭān*)

In contrast to scholarly discussions of the nature of Iblīs – whether angel or demon (*jinn*)[138] – the Devil in the *Anwār* features quite frequently in the guise of a human being. Thus he appears to Salma twice, the first time disguised as an old man, the second as a young man, and warns her of Hāshim.[139] At the engagement ceremony, again in disguise, he urges Salma's father to ask for a more generous gift of marriage.[140] As one would expect in a popular piece, Iblīs's role in the *Anwār* is quite significant, unlike his absence or only minor appearance in the standard biographies of the Prophet.[141] Thus, prior to the birth of Sheth, the angel Gabriel veils Eve with a screen of light to prevent Iblīs from approaching her.[142] After the birth of ʿAbd al-Muṭṭalib as well, a screen of light is sent from Heaven to protect Salma from the Devil.[143] The Devil's hatred of Hāshim stemmed from his knowledge that, with the coming of the latter, the idols would be eliminated.[144]

A systematic comparison between the *Anwār* and standard *sīra*s seems to me superfluous for the purpose of this chapter. It is instructive, however, to point out some differences between al-Bakrī's and scholarly biographies of Muḥammad. I shall use here Ibn Kathīr's *sīra*, which is part of his large historical work known as *al-Bidāya wan-nihāya* and is, so to speak, a medieval work, having been compiled in the fourteenth century. It therefore fits the chronological boundaries of this study.[145]

While al-Bakrī's *Anwār* does not contain some familiar accounts such as *ḥarb al-fijār*,[146] *ḥilf al-fuḍūl*,[147] or the building of the Kaʿba,[148] it offers material otherwise unknown on the primordial existence of Muḥammad and the creation of his and his ancestors' light (see p. 24 above), Hāshim's marriage to Salma (pp. 25–6 above), ʿAbd al-Muṭṭalib's combat against the Jews (p. 26 above), and, of course, the legends about the birth of Muḥammad (pp. 29–30 above). Structurally, there are some significant differences between al-Bakrī's and Ibn Kathīr's works. First, the narrative of the *Anwār* is built around the story of the Prophet's immediate ancestors in a sequence: Hāshim, then ʿAbd al-Muṭṭalib, then ʿAbd Allāh – this, unlike Ibn Kathīr's *sīra*, which moves back and forth to points in Muḥammad's career in quite an associative manner; on occasion the Prophet himself testifies about events in his early life.[149] Also, Ibn Kathīr's narrative is frequently lost among long chains of transmitters (*isnād*). It often juxtaposes slightly different versions and commentaries, as required by medieval scholarly standards, and occasionally, after relating information, rejects it for various reasons.[150]

Ibn Kathīr's prose was presumably not meant to entertain the reader; certainly his *sīra* cannot be viewed as literary nourishment for ordinary Muslims. For one thing, it clearly conveys a didactic message, as is fitting when the subject is the most celebrated *exemplum* in Islam. In this, it contrasts strongly with the entertaining character of the *Anwār*. The contrast is obvious also at the level of detail. Take, for example, the story of the birth of Muḥammad. Ibn Kathīr prefers to open it with a tedious discussion of the exact day in the week and month on which the Prophet was believed to be born.[151] Then, the short references to the standard miracles are complemented with a discussion of the pre-natal circumcision of the Prophet.[152] In another instance, the story of Abraha's expedition, Ibn Kathīr's *sīra* is a testimony to how medieval scholars could occasionally be deadly serious, to the point of absurdity, concerning details – undoubtedly as a result of their critical approach, yet "killing" a good story in the process. While in al-Bakrī we read as a matter of fact that Abraha's elephant, which was in the lead, miraculously went down on its knees to avert the conquest of Mecca (see p. 27 above), Ibn Kathīr, who also has the report of the kneeling elephant, questions the ability of an elephant to kneel.[153]

Still, it is difficult to understand fully why the *Anwār* was vehemently attacked by medieval scholars. After all, a close examination of a standard *sīra* of the kind reproduced by Ibn Kathīr reveals the insertion, at times, of material which is no less legendary than that found in the *Anwār*. Thus, in Ibn Kathīr's chapter dealing with the proofs (*āyāt*) of the birth of the Prophet, there is the "evidence" (copied from Ibn Isḥāq), provided by a Jewish merchant, of the birth of "the Prophet of this nation" (*nabī hādhihi'l-umma*) who carries a sign (*'alāma*) between his shoulders. We also find in Ibn Kathīr that the new-born baby would not suckle for two nights, since a demon (*'ifrīt*) put its finger in his mouth.[154] Another well-known legend featuring in the *Bidāya* is the quaking of the Iranian palace (*irtijās al-īwān*) on the night of Muḥammad's birth. Accordingly, things happened in the Persian kingdom (e.g., the Tigris stopped flowing) as a result of which the king was forced to consult his sages and thus learnt of the birth of Muḥammad.[155]

What was it, then, that made the stories copied into the *Bidāya* and its preceding, scholarly *sīras*, legitimate, as opposed to al-Bakrī's condemned material? This is an extremely difficult question, to which I shall return briefly later.

Having now a fair impression of al-Bakrī's *Anwār* and its characteristics as a popular piece, I should like at this point to turn to the question of al-Bakrī's identity. As we shall see, it is no trivial matter, and has been the subject of uncertainties and confusion.

Who Abū'l-Ḥasan Aḥmad b. 'Abd Allāh b. Muḥammad al-Bakrī[156] was and when he lived have both been unclear to scholars, both Muslim and orientalist, for quite some time. Al-Majlisī, the famous Shiite author (1627–98), identified al-Bakrī as a sixteenth-century scholar.[157] Wüstenfeld, about the middle of the nineteenth century, did not know al-Bakrī's dates and characterized the *Anwār* as "offenbar ein sehr spätes Machwerk"; its variants, when compared with Ibn Hishām's early *sīra*, were, in the German scholar's view, "ganz entbehrlich".[158] Somewhat later, it was suggested that al-Bakrī died as early as the middle of the ninth century.[159] More recently, scholars maintained that al-Bakrī wrote in the last years of the thirteenth or in the first half of the fourteenth century.[160]

The recent publication of Abū Rifā'a 'Umāra b. Wathīma al-Fārisī's *Kitāb bad' al-khalq wa-qiṣaṣ al-anbiyāʾ* now clearly demands the placing of al-Bakrī's *terminus ante quem* a number of centuries earlier, indeed as early as the ninth century, as suggested about 100 years ago.[161] Al-Fārisī, an Egyptian who died in 902, inserted at the end of his book an extended passage (four pages in the printed edition) from "Abū'l-Ḥasan ʿAbd Allāh [*sic*] al-Bakrī".[162] It bears a very close approximation to the medieval text of al-Bakrī's *Anwār* at our disposal. The inevitable conclusion is that the *Anwār*, or at least parts of it, were in circulation by the latter part of the ninth century at the latest.[163] Even allowing for the possibility that al-Bakrī's text was inserted not by al-Fārisī himself but by the copyist of the unique manuscript of his book, a rather unlikely supposition, a *terminus* of the eleventh century could still be suggested.[164]

According to Rosenthal, "there exists no cogent reason for doubting the historicity of al-Bakrī's elusive personality".[165] Yet mysteriously enough, the name is missing from all biographical encyclopaedias, beginning with early lists of Muslim transmitters.[166] It is laconically mentioned only in late medieval sources, as seen at the beginning of this chapter. Why is this so? One possibility, which goes against Rosenthal's conjecture, is that al-Bakrī was a quite early *literary invention*; the man did not actually exist apart from his appearance in certain texts, hence facts about him were unknown to authors of biographical collections. A second possible answer, this time supporting Rosenthal, is that here is another case of a neglected author, like the oft-quoted transmitter ʿUbayd b. Sharya, an enigmatic figure of the first Islamic century or al-Kisāʾī, the compiler of *Qiṣaṣ al-anbiyāʾ*. Their identities have been neglected by Muslim scholars (or was al-Kisāʾī another invented figure?).[167]

Be that as it may, was one single author, Abū'l-Ḥasan al-Bakrī (if we opt for the historicity of the man), the source (or transmitter) of the many pieces attributed to him?[168] Paret, for one, did not doubt that the author of the *Anwār* was also the author of several *maghāzī* works.[169] Rosenthal, however, suggested that there is no certainty that all the works attributed to al-Bakrī in fact stemmed from the same man; while in the biography of the Prophet actual books and authors are quoted, "the other works are vague and confused in their references to sources and prefer fictitious names in the rare cases where transmitters are mentioned".[170] I am inclined to support Rosenthal's doubts concerning al-Bakrī's authorship of the many works, but for a different reason. It is the fancy titles which al-Bakrī's *maghāzī* fragments carry. They seem to me to reflect a rather late sense of imagination.[171] In sum, if indeed a man named Abū'l-Ḥasan al-Bakrī ever ("ever" meaning early Islamic time) existed and was the author or transmitter of a *sīra*, his name was deliberately cited – so it appears – as the source of much later, popular stories.

What could have been al-Bakrī's, or to be more cautious now, the *Anwār*'s sources and the cultural milieu of its production? There are some statements (how reliable, it is impossible to judge) in this regard. The Companion ʿAmmār b. Yāsir[172] was allegedly "al-Bakrī's" source for *Ghazwat Biʾr Dhāt al-ʿAlam*.[173] Another of "al-Bakrī's" alleged sources is Salmān al-Fārisī.[174] "Al-Bakrī" is also mentioned in the same breath with the early Muslim historian al-Wāqidī (d. *ca* 822), and with Najd b. Hishām, as "transmitters of the Prophet's biography" (*ruwāt sīrat an-nabī*),[175] and again with al-Wāqidī, both as "transmitters of this marvellous biography".[176] "Al-Bakrī" is linked to Abū Mikhnaf (d. 775)[177] as a source of *Maqtal banī Umayya*(?).[178]

There are good reasons in my opinion to associate "al-Bakrī", or at any rate the creation of the *Anwār*, with early Muslim storytellers or compilers of *qiṣaṣ al-anbiyā'* ("Stories of the Prophets") books. This is suggested by al-Fārisī's quotation from the *Anwār* in his *Kitāb bad' al-khalq wa-qiṣaṣ al-anbiyā'*. Also, in the chain of transmitters, provided at the beginning of the *Anwār*, Ka'b al-Aḥbār appears as "al-Bakrī's" earliest source.[179] Now Ka'b, perhaps himself a *topos* rather than an historical figure, is known as the alleged generator of *qiṣaṣ* material.[180] Thus in Tha'labī's book of the *qiṣaṣ al-anbiyā'* genre (see below), there are thirty-five traditions attributed to Ka'b.[181] He is also quoted in medieval popular romances such as *Sīrat 'Antar*.[182] Another of "al-Bakrī's" sources is Wahb b. Munabbih, yet another alleged author of a book entitled *Qiṣaṣ al-anbiyā'*,[183] who in his *Mubtada' al-khalq* and in his narratives on the history of the Yemen included folktales and legends as if they were history.[184] Also among "al-Bakrī's" sources is 'Abd Allāh b. 'Abbās, often cited in works of the *qiṣaṣ* genre.[185] Another reason for connecting "al-Bakrī" with the milieu of storytellers is passages in the *Anwār* which are identical with material collected by Tha'labī (d. 1036), a known author of a *qiṣaṣ al-anbiyā'* book.[186] Finally, it is noteworthy that some of the works attributed to "al-Bakrī" are contained in eighteenth-century manuscripts of various *qiṣaṣ* works.[187]

To hypothesize, then, about "al-Bakrī's" milieu: he could have belonged to the body of storytellers who, in the period preceding the emergence of the early *sīra*s, were responsible for the elaboration of Qur'ānic allusions into complete stories, to make them more easily impressed on the minds of simple Muslims, or for the embellishment of legends about the Prophet. These tellers/preachers performed an important function in disseminating Qur'ānic ideas among the rank and file of the early Muslims. "Their primary motive must have been the spread of the Islamic religion, but in the course of their activity they were doubtless affected by the desire to assimilate the conception of Muḥammad to current conceptions of what a religious leader should be."[188] In fact the early storytellers (of "al-Bakrī's" type?) played, according to a recent argument, a major role in the formation of the standard sources on the rise of Islam: Ibn Isḥāq's *Sīra*, al-Wāqidī's *Maghāzī*, and Ibn Sa'd's *Ṭabaqāt*, to mention the most important ones.[189] After all, we had occasion to see that at least in one respect – namely, the spasmodic recourse to legends – there is no substantial difference between the *Anwār* and "scholarly" *sīra*s. The difference seems to be one of measure, not of principle. Let us also note that "al-Bakrī" is referred to in some works which carry his attribution as the "Baṣran Preacher" (*al-wā'iẓ al-Baṣrī*).[190] Now Baṣra, as we know, served as a centre for disseminating anecdotal material in the early centuries of Islam.[191] Why, then, was the storyteller "al-Bakrī" rejected by medieval scholars while other storytellers were accepted and their material used? The information before us does not suggest an answer. It would seem, at any rate, that the issue at stake was the personalities involved much more than the nature of the material itself.

Contrary to the negative Sunni approach to "al-Bakrī", it is worthy of note that al-Majlisī, the seventeenth-century Shiite writer, incorporated the *Anwār* in its complete form in his famous opus *Biḥār*,[192] praised its reliability, and presented it to Shiite *'ulamā'* as a worthy reading material in the Prophet's *mawlid* sessions of Rabīʿ al-Awwal.[193] Al-Majlisī, as we had occasion to observe, erroneously identified "our" al-Bakrī with a sixteenth-century namesake, an alleged teacher of the Shiite scholar known as ash-Shahīd ath-Thānī. Al-Bakrī's Shiism has been postulated also by modern writers.[194]

Al-Majlisī's error apart, why was the *Anwār* popular among the Shiites? One reason could be its insistence on the *nūr Muḥammadī*, a concept possibly developed in the circle of the Shiite seventh *imām*, Mūsā b. Jaʿfar as-Ṣādiq (d. 799); it is mentioned by famous tenth-century Shiite writers such as Kulaynī and Ibn Bābawayh.[195] Another reason could be ʿAlī's dominant role in six of al-Bakrī's alleged works.[196] Also, in the *Anwār* Abū Ṭālib, ʿAlī's father, has an important role to play. Thus in the episode of ʿAbd Allāh's sacrifice he confronts ʿAbd al-Muṭṭalib in an attempt to prevent the act.[197] Abū Ṭālib's part in that episode should be contrasted with standard *sīra*s, where al-ʿAbbās is the one who tries to rescue ʿAbd Allāh.[198] Abū Ṭālib is also credited with the idea of repeating the draw,[199] and is appointed by his father as the betrother (*khaṭīb*) in ʿAbd Allāh's marriage.[200]

One further note on the question of al-Bakrī's "Shiite connection": there is an interesting similarity between passages in the *Anwār* and passages in *Ithbāt al-waṣiyya li'l-imām 'Alī b. Abī Ṭālib*, a work usually attributed to al-Masʿūdī. The latter is undoubtedly a Shiite tract, regardless of whether its attribution to al-Masʿūdī is correct[201] and whether al-Masʿūdī was indeed a Shiite.[202] I am inclined to think that the *Ithbāt* was written at a time when a version of the *Anwār* was already in circulation. Thus similarities in content and phrasing between the two works could be explained either by direct borrowing from the *Anwār* or by the use, by the author of the *Ithbāt*, of an intermediary text. A direct borrowing on the latter's part, it should be emphasized, does not necessarily suggest a particular Shiite point of view in the *Anwār*: most of the passages which are similar in the two works do not appear to be of special Shiite significance.[203]

Popular culture, as we shall have occasion to see in some detail, never remains isolated from other cultural layers within the same system. The fate of the *Anwār* serves to illustrate this point. Some five hundred years after its initial circulation, the *Anwār* was utilized in *Siyer-i nabi*, a Turkish compilation made by Muṣṭafā b. Yūsuf Ḍarīr ("the Blindman") of Erzerum. According to one report, Ḍarīr began this work in 1377 for the Qarāmānid ʿAlā' ad-Dīn Khalīl. According to another, Ḍarīr, during a journey to Egypt, was asked by Emir (later Sultan) Barqūq to translate "into our Turkish language" the classical works on Muḥammad. Ḍarīr then consulted Shaykh Eçmelüddin, the mentor of leading Anatolian scholars, who in turn advised him to take al-Bakrī's *sīra* as his main source; Ibn Hishām's was considered more difficult to interpret.[204] Ḍarīr's *Siyer* was completed in 1388. It is a combined verse and prose work in both archaic and popular language, and contains many mystical and popular poems and miraculous and picturesque details. It treats the adventures of secondary heroes at great length.[205] An illuminated copy (814 miniatures) of Ḍarīr's book, in six volumes, was produced in 1594–5 for Sultan Murat III and presented to his son Mehmet III. Parts of it have survived in a number of libraries.[206]

About the time of Murat III, at the other end of the Mediterranean, in Spain, the *Anwār* became popular among the Morisco population and was translated into the Morisco dialect, the Aljamiado, as *Libro de las luces*.[207] Muhammad Rabadan, the leading Morisco poet, composed the *Discourse of Light* on the basis of al-Bakrī's *sīra*.[208]

In more recent times, after its continual rejection in medieval days, the *Anwār* gained currency, it seems, also in Sunni circles. Thus in the introduction to a Cairo (printed) edition of this century, based (so it appears) on a seventeenth- or eighteenth-century manuscript,[209] it is said that the book is intended to be read in the assemblies (*majālis*) set up in the "days and nights" of the month of Rabīʿ al-Awwal, namely, the celebration of the Prophet's *mawlid*. Its stated purpose is "to entertain (*wa-yutību awqāt*) Muslim believers, both the elite and the common people (*al-khāṣṣ wa'l-ʿāmm*), men and women".[210]

CHAPTER 3

The festival of Nawrūz: a world turned upside down

"Nowadays the people have neither the leisure which they need nor the comfort and vivaciousness that are necessary [in order to celebrate]." Thus al-Maqrīzī, a fifteenth-century Egyptian chronicler, concluded his report of the Nawrūz celebrations in Islamic Egypt.[1] If what he tells us of the fate of Nawrūz is indeed true, then a fascinating element of popular culture of his time disappeared. What precisely were the celebrations of Nawrūz? What was popular about them? What was their role in the society of medieval Cairo? Why did they disappear by the fifteenth century – or did they? These are some of the questions that will occupy us in this chapter. As it turns out, we must first look outside of Egypt for answers. Our story begins, so it appears, in ancient Iran.

Nō Rōz, "new day" in Middle Persian, the Arabic Nawrūz (or Nayrūz), is the day of the spring equinox on 21 March, a festival still celebrated in modern Iran. Though possibly in its origins a pagan pastoral festival marking the transition from winter to summer – primeval rites of fertility and renewal can be easily recognized in some of its customs – it must have been consecrated by Zoroaster. It completed a series of seven feasts which were linked with Zoroaster's fundamental teachings concerning the seven great "Holy Immortals" (Ameshaspands) and the Seven Creations. As a spring festival invested with special religious significance, Nō Rōz was the occasion to bring back Rapithwin, the "Spirit of Noon", who was also the personification of summer, the ideal season.[2]

Medieval Islamic sources gave various explanations of the origins of Nawrūz. One, apparently relying on an old Iranian tradition, was that Nawrūz had first commemorated the ascent of the mythical Jamshīd,[3] the great hero of Iranian tradition, into the skies in a chariot built by the demons whom he had subdued and forced into the service of mortals. According to another explanation, fire was created and the movement of the celestial sphere (*dawarān al-falak*) commenced on that day.[4] There was also a "biblical explanation" with a number of different versions. One was that Nawrūz was associated with an alleged event in the life of Abraham, as referred to in Qur'ān XXI/68–9; that is, the attempt by the idolaters to throw him into the fire and his escape by means of a divine miracle: the fire lost its heat and the idolaters jumped over it and were enveloped in its smoke.[5] According to a second version, the contest between Moses and the Egyptian sorcerers (*saḥara*) at Pharaoh's court took place on that day.[6] A third "biblical" story has it that King Solomon – incidentally, in Arabic literature sometimes identified with Jamshīd[7] – was the first to have established Nawrūz, for on that day his ring (*khatam*), stolen from him by a *jinn*, was recovered. It is noteworthy that two elements which were part of the ancient and medieval Nawrūz celebrations (see below) are mentioned in that story: giving presents – the "devils" (*shayāṭīn*) gave presents to Solomon; and the spraying of water – swallows (*khaṭāṭīf*) brought water in their beaks and sprayed it before the king.[8] A fourth "biblical" version has to do with Job (Ayyūb), who, according to Qur'ān XXXVIII/41, when summoning God one day to protect him from his enemies, was answered: "Strike thy riding beast with thy heels; here is cool water to wash with and drink." That day became Nawrūz and the people commemorated Job's acts by spraying water.[9] A fifth "biblical" explanation speaks of a tribe of 4,000 Israelites who were struck by the plague in Syria(?) (Shām) and were forced to emigrate to Iraq. When the king of Iran heard about that, he ordered the sick to be put into quarantine, where they subsequently perished. Then God revealed to the contemporary prophet that he should use the assistance of the perished tribe, soon to be resurrected, against his enemies. Indeed, one night God caused rain to fall on the quarantine and the dead tribe was restored to life. Informed of this miraculous event the Iranian king commanded: "Today [Nawrūz] ask for blessing (*tabarrakū*) and let each of you spray water on his fellow man." The custom survived.[10]

Indeed, various customs have been associated with Nō Rōz. Medieval Muslim writers tell us that it was the day to wear new clothes and serve food of the new (spring) season. Jāḥiẓ, the renowned ninth-century belletrist, wrote that "it was thought propitious to begin this day with . . . a mouthful of pure fresh milk and fresh cheese; all the kings of Persia took it as a blessing". Sowing seven kinds of seeds in small containers to emerge in time fresh for the holy day, a custom still observed in Zoroastrian villages in modern Iran, was an act emphasizing the number seven, Nō Rōz being the seventh holiday of the year. People exchanged gifts in token of friendship. They also rose early in the morning to go to wells or streams, draw water in vases, and pour it over themselves; or else sprinkle water over each other. Explanations for this custom varied: some said it was a good omen and a means of warding off harm; according to others, it was a way to cleanse the air; still others claimed that the water was meant to wash off the smoke which had stuck to the bodies of those attending the "Ritual of the Fire" the night before,[11] a ritual intended to clear the air of the putridity (*'ufūnāt*) left after winter. According to yet another version, people sprayed water on their bodies following the first rain that ended seven years of drought in the reign of King Fayrūz (Pērōz) in the fifth century. Their act on that occasion became a custom.[12]

Under the Sasanians, Nō Rōz signalled the beginning of the fiscal year and the time at which administrative appointments took place. It was also the occasion for minting new coins, issuing proclamations, and purifying the fire temples by ceremonial ablutions and sacrifices.[13]

After the Arab conquest of Iran, Nō Rōz, now in the Arabicized form of

Nawrūz, survived. It is for the early ʿAbbāsid period, especially the days of Caliph al-Mutawakkil (847–61), that we first find substantial information about its celebration. On one of the Nawrūz days, he was visited by a group of masked actors.[14] Masquerades of Nawrūz feature in a hemistich written by the Iraqi poet Ibn al-Muʿtazz (d. 908):

> The demons appeared to us during the day [of Nawrūz],
> Some in lines and some holding hand in hand.
> In their dance their bodies swaying
> As Cypresses swaying in the wind.
> Ugliness was installed upon their beauty
> Yet in their masks (*samājāt*) there is beauty.[15]

Around the year 900, people in Baghdad dared to sprinkle water on the police in an apparent extension of the Iranian custom of spraying water.[16] The contemporary poet Buḥturī reported that Nawrūz now resembled the holiday as celebrated under the Sasanian Ardashir.[17]

But it is with the Egyptian, the "Coptic" Nawrūz (*an-Nawrūz al-qibṭī*), as it came to be known, that we are here concerned. Contrary to the Iranian case, Nawrūz in Egypt was celebrated not in the spring but on the first day of the Coptic month of Thōt (or Thout), marking the beginning of the Coptic, that is, the agricultural, year. It coincided with 11 September in the Gregorian calendar, about the time when the Nile flood was expected to reach its peak. This was the time when vintages were completed and dates were picked.[18] As late as the Mamluk period, Nawrūz was the appropriate time for exacting the agricultural taxes (*kharāj*).[19]

We first learn of the Nawrūz celebrations in Islamic Egypt *sub anno* 300 (912). As is often the case with our medieval sources, it is impossible to tell how long before that date, if at all, annual festivities started to recur. This point leads us to the question of the obscure origins of Nawrūz in Egypt, to which I shall soon return. Be that as it may, when we first encounter Nawrūz in our sources it is celebrated by both the elite and the ordinary people.

Some of the customs associated with the Egyptian elite remind one of those noted for ancient Iran: the exchange of gifts,[20] eating special food,[21] and wearing new garments. For the celebration in 1123, a special *kiswa* (cover for the Kaʿba in Mecca)[22] and other luxurious fabrics were produced at the Alexandrian textile workshop (*ṭirāz*). The Fāṭimid court also distributed costly robes and gave money on that occasion.[23]

It is about the Nawrūz of the people, however, that we have most of our information. Like the dignitaries, the common people ate special food on that day. More interestingly, wine and beer were consumed in public, and occasionally one drunkard would kill another.[24]

Violence played a part in the proceedings; there were commoners who used to ambush travellers on roads and spray them with filthy water or wine. Others threw eggs or headgear on one another. There were those who, in what appears to be a remnant of a pagan ritual, slapped one another with boots (*akhfāf*) or leather mats (*anṭā'*) over the neck; they did it in public: on the main roads, in the market places, or on the banks of the Nile.[25] The "riffraff" (*sifla*) would use this "game" to take revenge on adversaries by attaching to the leather mat a stone or other object that was hard enough to cause death. Hence, what would start as play (*'ala jihat al-li'b*) could have tragic consequences. Curiously enough, in a case of murder, the suspect would not stand trial, and the prefect (*wālī*) of Cairo would let him escape unharmed. Gangsters used to commit highway robbery, and in the havoc they wrought prevented the public from conducting their normal business. Anyone who was caught in their hands was exposed to ridicule. Even emirs and other dignitaries would be sprayed with dirty water or pelted with eggs. To rescuc themselves, they would have to pay "ransom".[26]

Other characteristics of the Egyptian Nawrūz were sexual overtones and transvestism. In many a home, both young and old, men and women, used to play water games, causing one another to become wet so that naked bodies could be seen through clothes. On occasion people would strip naked except for the loin-cloth (*mi'zar*) or other kind of abbreviated cover.[27] In 1188 transvestites[28] and prostitutes (*fāsiqāt*) gathered under the Pearl Palace, carrying musical instruments and raising their voices so that they could be seen and heard by the Egyptian ruler.[29]

There were also masks and masquerades. In 975, in celebrations which lasted three days, crowds marched in the streets of Cairo; masquerades (or masks),[30] theatrical performances,[31] and man-made imitations of elephants, possibly a means of mocking two (real) elephants which had featured in a procession presided over by the Fāṭimid caliph al-Mu'izz two years earlier,[32] all were present. A medieval critic of Nawrūz lamented the adverse effect of the holiday not only on the common people (*'āmmat an-nās*) but on the learned as well. On that day, he tells us, schools were shut down and turned into playgrounds; teachers were attacked, insulted, and, unless they paid "ransom", even thrown into fountains.[33]

The high mark of Nawrūz in medieval Egypt appears to have been the procession of the "Emir of Nawrūz" (*amīr an-nawrūz*).[34] Elected by the Cairene crowd,[35] this "emir" had to be a wanton,[36] *'ābir al-'ayn*,[37] and "of firm nature".[38] Naked, or, in another version, dressed in yellow or red, his face besmeared with lime or flour, a beard of fur or some other material attached to his face, on his head a special cap made of palm leaves (*khūṣ*) and known as *ṭarṭūr*, he used to ride a small and ugly(?) donkey,[39] perhaps another survival of a pagan rite.[40] A sort of register (*daftar*) in his hand, at the head of a crowd, he "visited" homes of dignitaries and officials, and handed to each of them a statement about a "debt". Anyone who refused to pay, be he even "the most important man in Cairo", was scorned, cursed, and hard pressed until willing to clear the "debt". Some were sprayed with water, occasionally with mud, and verbally abused, or even beaten. Privacy was violated. Those who locked their homes to prevent the intruders from entering could not escape their lot: gates were broken and water poured on doorsteps.

Although of secondary importance in this context, the question of the origins of the Coptic Nawrūz is certainly intriguing. I shall briefly suggest three possible answers. However, given the deficiencies in the available information, each of the three suffers from uncertainties.

Some medieval reporters and modern scholars have suggested that Nawrūz was a cultural effect of the Achaemenid conquest of Egypt, which began in 525 BC and lasted for about 200 years.[41] One has to admit that some features are presented as common to both the ancient Iranian and the medieval Egyptian *fêtes*: wearing new costumes, serving special food, exchanging presents, lighting bonfires on the night before Nawrūz, and sprinkling water on the day itself.[42] The Egyptian procession of the "emir" finds a parallel in an Iranian procession which used to take place on the first day of Ādur, the Hurmūz spring festival, known as Bahār Jesm (or Jashn), and, at least in the late Sasanian period, identical with Nō Rōz.[43] This procession celebrated the departure of winter, and featured "the ride of the thinly-bearded man", rendered in Arabic sources as *rukūb al-kawsaj*.[44] We have a report of the Iranian procession, and although it is impossible to determine to which period it refers, whether the Sasanian or the Islamic, it is worth quoting in full:

> A beardless and, if possible, one-eyed buffoon was set naked [according to Qazwīnī's version: wearing tattered garments (*aṭmār*), his body smeared with some fluid[45]] on an ass, a horse, or a mule, and conducted in a sort of mock triumph through the streets of the city. In one hand he held a crow and in the other a fan, with which he fanned himself, complaining of the heat, while the people pelted him with ice and snow and drenched him with cold water. He was supposed to drive away the cold, and to aid him perhaps in discharging this useful function he was fed with hot food, and hot stuffs were smeared on his body. Riding on his ass and attended by all the king's household, if the city happened to be the capital, or, if it was not, by all the retainers of the governor, who were also mounted, he paraded the streets and extorted contributions. He stopped at the doors of the rich, and if they did not give him what he asked for, he befouled their garments with mud or a mixture of red ochre and water, which he carried in an earthenware pot. If a shopkeeper hesitated a moment to respond to his demands, the importunate beggar had the right to confiscate all the goods in the shop; so the tradesmen who saw him bearing down on them, not unnaturally hastened to anticipate his wants by contributing of their substance before he could board them. Everything that he thus collected from break of day to the time of morning prayers belonged to the king or governor of the city; but everything that he laid hands on between the first and the second hour of prayers he kept for himself. After the second prayers he disappeared, and if the people caught him later in the day they were free to beat him to their heart's content.[46]

The total absence of Nawrūz in pre-Islamic Egyptian sources is, of course, puzzling.[47] In any case, if the Egyptian Nawrūz had actually been an Iranian import, as the name would seem to suggest, at some point it was adapted to specifically local needs. As in ancient Iran, it retained in pre-Islamic Egypt its role as the beginning of the agricultural year. Yet the Egyptian New Year was determined by the cycle of the Nile, and thus Nawrūz in Egypt was transferred from March to September, the time of the river's flood.

A second hypothesis is that the Egyptian Nawrūz was a successor of Saturnalia, which many scholars consider to be the ancient forerunner of the medieval Carnival.[48] A December festival commemorating the "golden age" of Saturn, the god of sowing, an age when, so it was believed, slavery and private property were alike unknown, Saturnalia in the Roman empire was a time of general jollity, in which gambling in public was allowed, and in which masters waited at meal-time on their servants, who were briefly treated as equals. Within the family, a mock king, *Saturnalicius princeps*, was chosen as a Master of Revels.[49] The influence of Saturnalia, as well as of the Kalends (that is, the first day) of January, the Roman New Year festival,[50] has indeed been suggested by Westermarck on a late nineteenth- and early twentieth-century carnival in Moroccan Fez. In the carnival of Fez, which, like the Kalends, used to take place in the first month, but of the Muslim year (Muḥarram), a fat qadi, wearing a ridiculous cupola-shaped headdress, accompanied by two or three scribes and three or four men disguised as female prostitutes, would address dignitaries and highly respected men, accusing them of not paying their debts.[51] Some elements in this description bear a striking similarity to the Egyptian procession of the Emir of Nawrūz.

Is it possible to combine the two hypotheses and argue that in Roman Egypt Saturnalia overlaid the earlier layer of the Iranian (originally) Nawrūz? The problem (and this seems to be the case with the fairly modern festival of Fez also) is the significant documentary gap between the last mention of Saturnalia in ancient Egyptian records and the earliest mention of Nawrūz in medieval sources, a gap of several hundred years.[52] This chronological gap has recently been stressed also in the medieval European context and has produced a categorical denial of any continuity between Saturnalia and Carnival.[53]

A third possibility, which seems less likely, is that Nawrūz was a survival of ancient Egyptian customs. Medieval Muslim writers tell us that it was first celebrated during the reign of the ancient Egyptian king Manāwush(?), son of Manqāwush(?), as a festival honouring the stars.[54] Although accepted by some modern scholars,[55] this should be dismissed as mythical.[56] Also insufficiently substantiated is one Egyptologist's opinion that the procession of the "emir" could have been a late evolution of a ritual which had originated in the time of the XIIth dynasty, the "New Year King of All the Nobles", apparently an elective king of the old hereditary nobles.[57] Furthermore, the supposition of Pharaonic origins of Nawrūz raises two questions. First, there seems to be no record of a New Year celebration in ancient Egypt similar to the medieval Nawrūz. The celebrations at Dendera, in honour of the goddess Hathor, or at Edfu, in honour of Horus, were exclusively reserved for kings and priests and do not suggest any similarities with the people's revelries on Nawrūz.[58] The second question has to do with the name itself. If Nawrūz was of local, Egyptian origin, why was the Iranian name borrowed? Its use for an indigenous phenomenon over many centuries is certainly puzzling.[59]

Having raised some possibilities about the origins of the Egyptian Nawrūz, but, because of the nature of our data, being forced to leave the issue unresolved, let us move to the level of interpretation. What was the meaning of the Nawrūz festival in medieval Cairo? What was its socio-cultural role? We look in vain for an answer in contemporary sources, which, as we had occasion to see, fall back on much earlier, legendary stories of the origins of Nawrūz in *Iran* (not in Egypt). These, their intrinsic value notwithstanding, are obviously irrelevant to our main concern. They have nothing to do with the meaning of the festival in the context of Muslim Egypt. Much closer to the truth seems to me the medieval scholar al-Bīrūnī (973–1048), who, reporting on the "thinly bearded" procession – as we have seen above, analogous to the Nawrūz procession – commented that, in his own days, the festival no longer signified the change of seasons from winter to spring, but functioned as *farce only*.[60] The argument I should like to introduce at this stage is that the Egyptian Nawrūz could be characterized as a carnival, an argument laconically suggested long ago by the orientalist Mez and, most recently, by the Arabist Molan.[61]

By "carnival" I do not mean Carnival as a specifically Christian festival, opposed to Lent and possibly defying Christian spirituality.[62] "Carnival" here means a festival characterized by status reversal and riotous revelry.[63] Now one can identify in the available descriptions of the Egyptian Nawrūz several features that would justify its classification as carnival in the latter sense: the lighting of bonfires and the spraying of water, originally common symbols of purification; maskers, often licensed to burst into private houses; the throwing of eggs; inordinate consumption of food and excess in general; pupils beating their teachers, and the performance of transvestites.[64] The latter has been interpreted as a sign of sexual inversion, in its turn a widespread theme in medieval European literature, art, and festivals. It more often involved the male taking on the role or garb of the unruly female, the man being disguised as a grotesque, cavorting woman. This is implied also in the Arabic term *mu'annath* ("effeminate"). Did transvestism suggest the blurring of social boundaries or the reversal of roles in Egypt as well?[65] Be that as it may, the behaviour of Egyptians on the occasion of the Nawrūz celebrations clearly evokes the licence given in carnival to disorderly conduct or "misrule", the inversion of prevailing norms, the reversal of status within the social structure, the "turning" of the universe "upside down".[66] Drawing an analogy between festivals such as Nawrūz and carnival is clearly implied in the theory which goes back to James Frazer at the beginning of our century and, more recently, to Bakhtin, Turner, and others, who all argued that carnival and "misrule" are present in all cultures, that there are universal ways by which people "turn their classifications upside down or disintegrate them entirely".[67]

It is obviously the procession of the Emir of Nawrūz, with its analogy to medieval and early modern Christian feasts, which is the most intriguing. Once again it was Frazer who first recognized in the analogous Iranian procession of the "thinly bearded" man the feature of the mock or temporary king, who is invested, for a short time, with the pomp and privileges of royalty.[68] I myself am struck by the similarity between the "thinly bearded" man and the Emir of Nawrūz on the one hand, and the Christian King of Fools, *prince des sots*, Boy Bishop, Lord of Misrule, and the three "kings" of the German *Dreikönigstag* on the other.[69] Although most of these featured in Christian holidays, which were celebrated in the days between Christmas and Epiphany and involved extreme satire of the mannerisms and mores of the court and the high church, a radical mockery of ecclesiastical structure and religious doctrine, we also find in them the carnivalesque elements enumerated above: masks, men dressing up as women,[70] violence,[71] and collecting contributions.[72] The King of Fools and the Emir of Nawrūz both presided over ephemeral commonwealths complete with the paraphernalia of serious kingship, but dedicated to satire and clowning. They were, in their capacity, regulators of a world temporarily turned upside down.[73]

Once we recognize Nawrūz as a carnival we can draw on the available socio-historical interpretations in an attempt to capture its socio-cultural function. Carnivals, of course, can be seen as providing entertainment, a welcome respite from a routine of misery and hardship which was prevalent in the life of ordinary people in past societies.[74] But there is perhaps more to the carnival than just that, as scholars from different disciplines have argued in recent decades. For how, in the first place, could the carnival, with its unlicensed reversal and mockery, be legitimized? Why should conduct that seems to fly in the face of order and propriety be tolerated by the authorities?[75] As regards Nawrūz, how did it come about that, according to one of its contemporary critics, "its participants [were able] to commit all kinds of evil . . . there was no interdiction [to any sort of behaviour] and no authority imposed"?[76]

We may first turn to the concept of "safety-valve", known since medieval times, as an explanation for the festive inversion of roles and categories. Accordingly, festivals which involve such inversion serve to release social tension which tends to build up between one festival and the next.[77] In the same vein, the functionalist argument, put forward since the middle of the twentieth century, has been that "rites of reversal" were a "symbolic expression of underlying and normally suppressed conflicts within the society". They "constitute a mechanism by which the pressures engendered by social conflict may be vented without allowing the conflict to become fully overt and threaten the survival of the society". The rites of reversal, in other words, "lay bare the conflicts and allow for the expression of the hostilities they engender, but in a symbolic, encapsulated, and thus neutralized way". As such, understandably enough, rites of reversal could be tolerated by the authorities.[78] It is important to stress at this point that, although carnival was an uninhibited time of licence and permitted anarchy – a ceremony which openly expressed social tensions, enabled subjects to state their resentment, and even allowed a ritual overturning of authority – it was contained within its own time and space.[79] "Whatever the case . . . seasonal misrule involved, not simple riot or confusion, but conventional styles of ritual and symbol, associated with inversion-recognized forms of 'uncivil rule'."[80]

The anthropologist Max Gluckman suggested a somewhat different interpretation of carnival. As a rite of reversal and a ritual of rebellion, it was an act of expressive behaviour which inverted, contradicted, abrogated, or in some fashion presented an alternative to commonly held cultural codes, values, and norms, whether they were linguistic, literary, or artistic, religious, social, or political. Yet the role of carnival was not in the least the overthrowing of an established order.[81] It was actually intended to preserve and strengthen that order. Furthermore, rebellious rituals occurred only because the social order was well established and unchallenged, and were effective only so long as there was no querying of the order within which the ritual of protest was set.[82] The symbolic enactment of conflicts thus emphasized the social cohesion of the system.[83]

A third interpretation of carnival is that of Bakhtin, who regarded festivities of a carnivalesque nature as rituals of equality. These parodied the stratification of power and provided a symbolic suspension of norms and privileges; they contrasted official and ecclesiastical ceremonies of ordered society, the very rituals of inequality which reinforced the dominant order. The carnival, according to Bakhtin, revealed a world in which a playful mutability was possible and provided an experience, at once symbolic and concrete, of the suspension of social barriers. By dramatizing the comic and relative side of absolute truths and supreme authorities, it highlighted the ambivalence of reality.[84]

Obviously, there is no such thing as "true" or "correct" meaning in decoding the different expressions of the "ritual of rebellion". In recent studies it has been argued that rites of reversal can be used to make a variety of statements about the social order: "to affirm it, attack it, suspend it, redefine it, oppose it, buttress it, emphasize one part of it at the cost of another, and so forth".[85] Thus, in her study of "rites of misrule" in sixteenth-century France, Davis attempts some synthesis of interpretations. While rejecting the "safety-valve" explanation as inadequate, she maintains that festive acts can, on the one hand, perpetuate certain values of the community – even guarantee its survival – and on the other hand criticize the political order. In other words, "the structure of the carnival form can evolve so that it can act both to reinforce order and to suggest alternatives to the existing order". What rites and ceremonies of reversal do not do is question the basic order of society. "They can renew the system, but they cannot change it."[86]

Armed with these interdisciplinary interpretations, let us now return for a moment to the medieval Egyptian scene. Though less formally structured than contemporary Western societies, and not *ordered* in a manner resembling the "three-orders society" of the medieval European type, Egyptian society was still very hierarchic. Barriers against social mobility, although, once again, not as rigid as in medieval Christendom, nevertheless existed, and any mobility usually took place within the middle strata, and less frequently from the lower classes upward. Hence, the ordinary people probably enjoyed no socio-economic improvement generation after generation, struggling with daily routine and hardship, and on occasion subject to repression. In such dismal circumstances, what *communal* means were available for them to convey their anxiety? What were their channels for demonstrating dissatisfaction, and what were their methods of confronting the authorities? One of these, as regards the problem of basic needs, was the grain riot, a subject to be discussed in the following chapter. Another, on a specific day in the year, was the annual festival of Nawrūz. What was the role of the Emir of Nawrūz and his fellow merry-makers on that particular day? Simple mockery and enjoyment? Did they convey a controversial message? Did they comment on the structure of their society?[87] Or did they in their "games" rather confirm the existing order? Perhaps a mixture of all these? As with the European carnival, a definitive answer is impossible. One thing seems clear, however: in medieval Cairo, at least for one day every year, ordinary people "turned" their universe "upside down".

A threat to the public order, carnivals were viewed by theologians and the authorities with disfavour and, on occasion, they were repressed. One could mention Erasmus' criticism of a carnival he witnessed in Sienna in 1509 as un-Christian, containing "traces of ancient paganism", an occasion for indulging in licence.[88] The Islamic Nawrūz fared no better.[89] In medieval Cairo it was repeatedly banned. Thus in 913, on both Nawrūz and the festival of Mihrajān,[90] the ʿAbbāsid governor of Egypt ordered transvestites (*mu'annathūn*), who were dressed in "their special costume" (i.e., women's garb?) and playing their musical instruments, to march around the major mosque in Old Cairo. They were ridiculed (*shahharahum*).[91] In 946 the custom of spraying water was banned.[92] In 974 the Fāṭimid al-Muʿizz forbade the lighting of bonfires on the eve of Nawrūz and spraying water on the day itself.[93] The following year, as celebrations continued unabashed, the edict was repeated; this time a few persons were arrested and made to ride camels, disgraced, through the streets of Cairo.[94] In 1023 the "play with water" (*laʿb bi'l-mā'*) was banned once again.[95] Some time prior to 1198 celebrations were interdicted.[96] In 1380 the play with water was banned, and threats of corporal punishment and confiscation of property were announced. Indeed, four men were punished in public.[97] In 1385 Sultan Barqūq ordered the celebrations to be abolished altogether. Officials inspected the amusement places and arrested those found feasting there. Some of the revellers were clubbed, hands were chopped off, and further threats were made. Gallows were constructed for transgressors. From that time onwards, so we are told, people stopped celebrating Nawrūz – but not quite, since some features of the festival survived in pools of water, the main canal of the Nile, and "places of this sort".[98] According to another source, until 1389 (it is unclear how long before that date: is it 1385?) only the sprinkling of water and beating with leather (*taṣāfuʿ*) were allowed; the lighting of bonfires was restricted to the dwellings of the Copts.[99] During the Nawrūz of 1435 no games were seen because of the sultan's ban.[100] About that time al-Maqrīzī, as we noted at the beginning of this chapter, remarked on the disappearance of the festival altogether.

Popular festivals, despite their repression, appear to die hard. If Nawrūz indeed disappeared from the Egyptian capital in the year 1400 or thereabouts,[101] it certainly survived in one form or another in Egyptian provinces. Was it more difficult to repress there, far from the eyes of the central bureaucracy? Was it kept going clandestinely? At any rate, I have been able to find four accounts about the celebration of Nawrūz in Upper Egyptian villages in the nineteenth and early twentieth century.

The earliest is an illustration which presents Nawrūz as an agricultural festival. It was done by Rifaud, a French sculptor and excavator, who documented his experience in Egypt in the years 1805 to 1827. The illustration has as its theme the collecting of dates,[102] and features in its centre what clearly seems to be the Emir of Nawrūz riding a horse, an exceptionally long (artificial?) moustache under his nose, wearing an unusually tall headdress. The emir holds "royal" insignia in one hand and what appears to be a written scroll in the other. He is preceded by a band of musicians. Behind him are men, women, and children, carrying bundles of dates.[103]

Another account is by the Egyptologist Murray, who, at the beginning of our century, witnessed celebrations of Nawrūz in the small Coptic town of Reqāda in Upper Egypt. Both Copts and Muslims, according to her report, came to celebrate. In what strikes one as a reminiscence of the medieval "play with water", women stood knee-deep in the Nile and drank nine times, or dipped themselves in the water the same number of times.[104]

The most striking piece of information about the survival of Nawrūz in modern Egypt undoubtedly belongs to the German physician Klunzinger, who spent eight years, both in the 1860s and the 1870s, in Egypt as medical advisor to the Khedive's government.[105] His report is particularly noteworthy as it describes in great detail the procession of the Emir of Nawrūz in Upper Egyptian villages. It deserves to be quoted in full:

> On the 10th September, the first day of the Coptic solar year, the river has reached to about its highest point, and on this day – the *nerûs*, the people give themselves up to the pleasures of the carnival. For three days it is all up with the rule of the Turks; every little town chooses for itself in its own way, and from its own midst, a ruler (*abu nerûs*), who has a towering fool's cap set upon his head, and a long spectral beard of flax fastened to his chin, and is clothed in a peculiar garment. With a long sceptre in his hand, and followed by a crowd of correspondingly-dressed bailiffs, hangmen, and scribes, he promenades the streets and turns his steps straight to the hall of the chief magistrate.[106] Every one bends before him, the guards at the door make way, the governor of the province or of the town has the humour to let himself be ousted, while the new dignitary seats himself on his throne and holds a most rigorous criminal investigation, from which even the displaced functionary and his abettors do not escape. The hangman's assistant of yesterday is sentenced to be hanged, the bastinadoer to be beaten, the *bashkatib* or chief secretary to imprisonment, immense taxes are imposed, and all decisions are set down on a sheet of paper. There is no

pardon for the condemned unless on the payment of a few piasters as backshish. Thus they move from house to house, the taxes being levied in the form of backshish. Three days does the capricious rule of the ephemeral tyrant last; at length he, that is his dress, is condemned to death by burning, and from the ashes creeps out the slavish Fellah. In the times of good-natured Mohammed Ali the *abu nerûs* is said to have ventured even to approach his throne, but the harmless jest has now fallen a good deal out of practice.[107]

Klunzinger's fascinating report is repeated in similar language by Leeder, who toured Egypt about half a century later, in the year 1914. Here is his account of the celebration of the first day of the Coptic month of Tūt (or Thout), namely the day of Nawrūz:

Cairo has its own river festival, but there are still a few of the villages which keep revels entirely of their own for three days. The people first choose a ruler from their midst, whom they call *Abu Nerus*. He is clothed in a robe of brilliant colour, a towering fool's cap is set upon his head, with a long caricature of a beard of flax, and a sceptre in his hand; and, followed by a crowd of quaintly dressed attendants, some of them hangmen and scribes, he sets off direct to the hall of the chief magistrate. Here every one humorously bows to his rule; he takes the chair of authority, and proceeds to hold a stern assize, arraigning more particularly the magistrate himself and all his functionaries. The hangman is to be hanged, the jailor to be thrust into the lowest dungeon (in the old days the jailor whose duty was to whip the prisoners had an awful verdict of lashes given against him); on the rich, fabulous taxes are assessed. Everything is done with mock pomposity; and every judgment is punctiliously written out. The procession again sets out, to enforce its will; the only chance of pardon is to offer a few small coins in *backsheesh*. When the jest is exhausted, a bonfire is lighted, and a pretence is made of burning the tyrant himself. In these days it is only possible to meet *Abu Nerus* by travelling to the distant villages.[108]

The details of the nineteenth-century procession are strikingly similar to those of the medieval one. There is one item, however, which features only in the "modern" Nawrūz as reported by Klunzinger: the Egyptian Emir of Nawrūz has to die at the end of his three-day rule, and, as a substitute, his dress "is condemned to death by burning, and from the ashes creeps out the slavish Fellah". The analogy of the nineteenth-century Nawrūz to the custom of burning effigies in ancient and modern carnivals is perfect![109]

CHAPTER 4

The politics and "moral economy" of the Cairene crowd

The early years of the fourteenth century witnessed a power struggle between the young sultan an-Nāṣir Muḥammad, son of Qalāwūn, now in his early twenties and reigning for the second time, and two leading emirs, Baybars al-Jashnikīr and Sayf ad-Dīn Salār.[1] In this conflict, we read in our sources, "the people's hearts were with the sultan". In 1308, when an-Nāṣir's plot to rid himself of his two rivals was uncovered and rumours of revenge were in the air, the people of Cairo marched toward the Citadel. In a matter of a few hours the crowd swelled, and as the word came that an-Nāṣir was planning to abdicate, the commoners expressed their discontent. The reason for that, we are informed, was two-fold. First, as already noted, they simply felt an attachment to their ruler. Second, and this is quite revealing, they desired to see the Qalāwūnid dynasty, namely, the descendants of Sultan Qalāwūn (r. 1279–90) – two of whom they had already cheered for as rulers – stay in power. They were opposed to the possibility that an "ordinary Mamluk" (*aḥad min al-mamālīk*) would ascend to the throne. The crowd gathered in the streets of Cairo, shouting slogans in favour of the sultan (*yā nāṣir, yā manṣūr*).[2] As troops were sent by the two rebelling emirs to disperse the demonstrators, more slogans were heard, this time condemning the "traitors" (*Allāh yakhūnu'l-khā'in, Allāh yakhūn man yakhūn ibn Qalāwūn*). The troops were pelted with stones and their commander returned to his masters and reported the people's commitment (*ta'aṣṣub*) to the cause of an-Nāṣir Muḥammad. A few months later, however, in 1309, the sultan found himself losing ground and decided to leave for Kerak (in today's Jordan). This was the occasion for another show of support staged by the people. As their ruler was descending from the Citadel, the commoners surrounded him, separated him from his entourage, wept for his departure, and bade him farewell.[3]

The popular support of the Qalāwūnid sultan did not vanish with the accession of Baybars al-Jashnikīr, better known to modern historians as Baybars II, who, in a move to solidify his position, solicited a letter of investiture from the caliph,[4] to be read from the pulpits of Cairene mosques. In the letter, which was obviously intended to influence the people, the former sultan was referred to negatively ("he failed to protect his Muslim subjects"), and the listeners were called on to pay respect to Baybars. However, they did not do this. Instead, whenever an-Nāṣir

Muḥammad's name was mentioned in the Friday sermons, they cheered ("may God give him victory!"); whenever they heard Baybars's name, they booed.

The reign of Baybars lasted about one year. Brief as it was, it was dogged by various problems. First came the plague, then the Nile was slow to rise. Furthermore, in Kerak an-Nāṣir Muḥammad was already plotting his return to the throne. Baybars then probably found himself under considerable pressure, and this is, perhaps, why, contrary to an almost sacred custom in Egypt, he ordered the opening of the dam on the Nile and thus let the water flood, although the river did not reach a level which would have justified such an act.[5] In reaction, the people of Cairo composed the following lines,[6] set to a popular tune, which were sung in places of amusement (*amākin al-muftarajāt*):

> Our sultan is only partly firm,[7]
> While his viceroy [Salār] is beardless,[8]
> Where shall we get water from?
> Bring us the lame! [an-Nāṣir Muḥammad]
> The water will then come.[9]
>
> (*sulṭānunā rukayn*
> *wa-nā'ibunā duqayn*
> *yajīna'l-mā' minayn*
> *jibū lanā al-a'raj*
> *yajīna'l-mā' wa-yidaḥraj*)

Baybars reacted with fury. He arrested about 300 persons, cut out tongues, punished some with flogging, and ordered others to be carried on camels in disgrace. But things continued to deteriorate for him. Emirs gradually deserted his ranks and joined an-Nāṣir Muḥammad's side. One day in 1310, when Baybars was returning from the Manṣūriyya Madrasa, wearing a ceremonial robe, people gathered to view his ascent to the Citadel. As the royal entourage proceeded, the commoners (*'awāmm*) shouted: "He has neither wit nor grace! (*laysa lahu ḥalāwa wa-lā 'alayhi ṭalāwa*)." One man shouted: "O joy which has not yet ended! (*yā farḥa lā tammat*)", probably meaning that the worst for the sultan was still to come.

Some time later Baybars ordered the arrest of a group of people for cursing him, and had them humiliated in public. Yet this measure only spurred on his opponents. The commoners, among them men on the margins (*ḥarāfīsh*),[10] used to gather time after time below the Citadel, exclaiming: "Rise and surrender to Allah! Vacate the post reserved for a man only! Step down from a throne to which you don't belong!" Attempts by the troops to disperse the crowd proved abortive. Then one night, a rumour about Baybars's abdication spread among the commoners, and they managed to intercept the fleeing sultan. They shouted loudly, some pelting him with stones. An effort to divert their attention by showering money on them failed. The crowd persisted in haranguing Baybars's convoy so that it was necessary to push the commoners back with swords.[11]

Ibn Taghrī Birdī wrote that the alienation (*waḥsha*) of the people from Baybars was a result of what might be called *force majeure*: in the summer of 1309 grain prices were high and from that point on, things just went wrong. This seems to be a simplistic explanation. Perhaps the bad news of yet another food shortage bolstered adverse feelings toward the Egyptian ruler, but it was just the last straw. For Baybars had been detested much earlier. The animosity toward him, as far as we can judge, stemmed from the illegitimacy of his rule in the eyes of the people.

Popular sentiments toward the House of Qalāwūn once again surfaced in 1341, following the death of an-Nāṣir Muḥammad at the end of a second, long reign. Now his two sons and successors, first al-Manṣūr Abū Bakr, then Küçük, were challenged by the viceroy Qawṣūn.[12] Küçük, according to one poetic description, was in Qawṣūn's hands "like a bird caught by an eagle". As a military confrontation between Qawṣūn's army and the troops of the deceased sultan seemed imminent, the people of Cairo assembled in the Rumayla quarter, below the Citadel, and shouted: "O Mamluks of an-Nāṣir! We are with you!" The troops, stationed inside the Citadel, responded to the chants and urged the crowd to turn against Qawṣūn's residence, which it did. People started pillaging, but then were pushed back by the emir's loyal soldiers. A few dozen civilians were killed and others were captured. At that point fights broke out between the Nāṣirī soldiers, who were trying to protect their allies among the commoners, and Qawṣūn's men. The latter had the upper hand, dispersed the crowd, and began a series of summary executions. Nine men were nailed to the Zuwayla Gate.

Qawṣūn's supremacy, however, was short lived. A few months later some leading emirs moved to depose him. Sensing new developments, the people assembled once again below the Citadel "like the spreading locust". They were incited by Aydughmish, the leader of the rebellious officers, to loot (*yā kassāba*) Qawṣūn's property a second time. The crowd broke through the gate of his residence and in a matter of a few hours took away all that was there, including doors and marble plates (Aydughmish was later able to recover much that was taken). Then people rushed to Qawṣūn's *khānqāh*, which stood by the Qarāfa Gate,[13] overpowered the Sufis there, and ransacked the complex, leaving it in shambles, even carrying away Qur'āns. Not only Qawṣūn's residence but the homes of his Mamluks all over Cairo were attacked. The looters sold their spoils cheaply; so much gold appeared in Cairo's markets that its value decreased significantly. The current slogan was "Here is a Qawṣūnī!", and immediately the man would be attacked. Such, for example, was the fate of Ibn al-Muḥsinī, the prefect (*wālī*) of Cairo, who was almost lynched by the mob. Another victim of "Qawṣūnī" association was the chief Ḥanafite qadi, Ḥuṣām ad-Dīn al-Ghawrī. His beard was plucked, his headgear torn, his house looted, and he himself had to find shelter with a Ḥanbalite colleague. The situation prompted Aydughmish to intervene and stop the riots by taking exemplary measures.

The subsequent arrest of Qawṣūn was celebrated with poems (*qaṣīda*) written for the occasion. One of these (its first two lines have been preserved) was by "an ordinary man" (*ba'ḍ 'awāmm Miṣr*). It was entitled "There once was" (*kāna wa-kāna*), and, most likely, mocked the downfall of the hated emir. Also, lollipops (*'alālīq*)[14] in the shape of the deposed Qawṣūn were sold near the Zuwayla Gate. One of them depicted him nailed to a camel, being transferred to Alexandria to be executed there. Ibrāhīm al-Mi'mār, a contemporary Egyptian poet, wrote with obvious irony:

> We saw the figure of nailed Qawṣūn
> In the candies,
> And we marvelled.
> For sweet was the nailing . . . [15]

In January 1342, the emirs, with Aydughmish at their head, decided to replace Küçük by his brother, Shihāb ad-Dīn Aḥmad, the oldest of an-Nāṣir Muḥammad's surviving sons. Shihāb ad-Dīn was then in Kerak, a traditional place of exile of the Qalāwūnid family. When his regnal title (al-Malik an-Nāṣir) was proclaimed in the Friday prayer, the people lifted yellow banners (yellow being the colour of the Mamluk regime), and conveyed to Aydughmish their desire to travel to Kerak and escort the new sultan on his return to Cairo. They also demanded supplies for the journey, which they received. In the same month six other sons of an-Nāṣir Muḥammad returned from exile in Qūṣ, Upper Egypt, and were greeted by the crowd. As the procession of the "princes" passed by the tomb of one Jariktamūr at the Qarāfa Cemetery, the people exclaimed: "This is the tomb of the murderer of our master al-Malik al-Manṣūr!"[16] The tomb was promptly destroyed. Then, below the Citadel, the six princes encountered the former *wālī* of Gīza, who had mistreated them on fleeing Cairo. He was now reminded of his actions, and the crowd, with the approval of one of the princes, stormed the ex-*wālī*'s residence. Troops had to be sent to restore order. Ten people died and a large number were injured.[17]

Legitimacy to rule has been a major issue in Islamic societies, as students of Islamic politics know all too well. It was debated and fought over by political factions and contenders, and occupied the minds of many "people of the pen" in different periods and regions.[18] It must have been of some concern also to the common people. But in what sense? How was it manifested? Here is something we know next to nothing about. In the case of Mamluk Egypt, as we have seen above, the issue of legitimacy surfaced on occasion. In fact, it seems that the right to rule, in the people's view, rested on two premises: a ruler had to be born Muslim; and it was preferable to maintain the dynastic principle.

A known piece of historical information is that in July 1250 'Izz ad-Dīn Aybak, an emir formerly in the service of the Ayyūbids, was crowned as al-Malik al-Mu'izz.[19] This, one can safely argue, was the beginning of the Mamluk regime in Egypt. That the rise of a Mamluk to the Egyptian throne was a watershed in the annals of the Near East is a truism to historians. Contemporaries, however, lacked the benefit of historical hindsight. Does it mean that they considered the rise of the *first* Mamluk sultan a matter of fact? Not necessarily, if we pay attention to what one eyewitness had to tell about this particular event. The people of Cairo, he reported, expressed their dissatisfaction. Whenever the new sultan (Aybak) rode through the city, they (*al-ʿawāmm*) chanted: "We do not want other than a respected sultan, born Muslim (*wulida ʿalā fiṭrat al-islām*)."[20] This, of course, was an explicit rejection of Aybak, who had been born pagan. He consequently tried to placate the people with generous gifts.[21] Whether the people's attitude had a bearing on the decision of the leading emirs, only five days later, to force Aybak to step down in favour of an Ayyūbid child-prince, al-Ashraf Mūsā, we do not know.[22]

Aybak was certainly not the first man of non-Muslim extraction to have become a local ruler in Egypt, let alone in the Abode of Islam. The Cairo of the mid thirteenth century was full of powerful military men who became Muslims only later in their careers. This, however, was small comfort to their contemporaries when the issue at stake was the identity of the *sultan*. Whereas men born as non-Muslims could be accepted as soldiers and generals, as *sultans* they were probably an abomination. Something had to be said about it, and in public.

The nexus of crowds and violence has been much discussed in historical studies[23] and has lately become worthy of investigation also by students of Islamic societies.[24] For the Mamluk period, Lapidus has drawn attention to the frustrations of the common people with the socio-political order, frustrations that "characteristically expressed themselves in mob violence which articulated needs and demands not otherwise served by the city elites". Lapidus has thoughtfully suggested that we should not think of mob violence as necessarily senseless and chaotic; it "fell into patterns which not only reflected the limitations of the social order, but served to integrate the common people into a more complex over-all form of social organization".[25] What these patterns were is far from clear, however, for elsewhere Lapidus concedes that no pattern of popular support of, or opposition to, the Mamluk regime emerges.[26]

The ordinary people in Mamluk towns were, according to Lapidus, capable of rebellions born of resentment, but they had limited effectiveness and were subject to manipulation from above. Their violence was diverted from permanent and revolutionary achievements; their severe grievances could be accommodated in the end.[27] In Cairo,[28] pleas for the removal of abusive officials were uncommon; such officials were rarely dismissed because of popular protest. Petitions to transfer powerful emirs were even less likely to be given attention. Consequently, the more usual popular response to fiscal abuse was direct assault on offending bureaucrats. Sporadic attacks on individuals also took place. Other acts occurred in the context of Mamluk factional strife, as the commoners were enlisted for support by this or that party.[29] In the final analysis (that is, Lapidus's analysis), then, the people in Mamluk Cairo were devoid of political ambitions, and no pattern of support or opposition to the regime emerges. "The mobs had no will of their own . . . The populace behaved as an amorphous mass seeking only the most immediate monetary gains, having no deep attachment to any party."[30]

Popular opportunism was undoubtedly displayed in many acts by the crowd in Mamluk Cairo. The commoners, with remarkably acute intuition, sensed politically weak spots, had no hesitation in plundering the property of defeated emirs, and were eager to attack disgraced officials.[31] Understandably enough, they felt hatred, on occasion extraordinarily intense, toward villains, at least toward those whom they considered to be villains. Two examples will suffice to illustrate the popular "ritual of hate".

The first is the vizier Sanjar ash-Shujāʿī, who was loathed by the Cairenes. After he had been murdered by his rival in 1294, his head was stuck on a javelin and carried all over Cairo. The people paid the javelin bearers so that they could have the head, which they struck with shoes. Jews, as our sources make a point of stressing, also participated in this macabre ritual of revenge; there were claims that they urinated on the victim's head. In a matter of three days, the officials, complying with popular demand, were able to earn a large sum of money.[32]

A second case is that of the hated emir Nashw. When in 1338, or the following year, rumours about his arrest spread, merchants suspended business, and people, in fact whole families, gathered at the Rumayla quarter, below the Citadel, lit candles, raised Qur'āns, waved banners, and cheered. Celebrations lasted for a whole week, music was played, performances (*khayāl*) were staged; people wrote lines of poetry (*azjāl wa-balālīq*) in which they commemorated the event. As in another case, already mentioned, lollipops[33] were made to depict a fantastic (or real?) punishment of the disgraced official and his family: "Nashw" was presented being flogged, his "sister" as led by executioners(?),[34] their "mother", wearing a girdle – the distinguishing sign of a Christian (as was the family) – as beaten by her guards. Sellers of sweets sold many such lollipops and made a good profit. Then a crowd attempted to lynch the imprisoned official. Nashw's brother, who had taken his own life, was carried to be buried in a coffin intended for a woman, for the fear that the crowd would burn his corpse.[35]

There are many more reports in our sources of the hatred toward detested officials by the people of Cairo.[36] Yet this is the place to emphasize that hate was not the sole feeling toward the ruling elite; there were officials who, in contradistinction, gained the people's sympathy. One example will illustrate this point. In 1512, the sultan released the *muḥtasib* ʿAlī az-Zaynī Barakāt b. Mūsā from prison, after a detention lasting eight days. The official then descended from the Citadel in procession, accompanied by a group of dignitaries. The people, learning of the release of their favourite, now decorated the city, lit torches and candles, and perfumed themselves with saffron. At Birkat ar-Raṭlī, where the *muḥtasib* was a resident, people hung cloths to decorate the façades of their homes. Singers, performers, and ordinary women, shrilling, came to greet the procession.[37]

Hate, sympathy, and opportunism combined to form a complex of feelings toward the authorities and specific personages among the ruling elite. However, these feelings were only one dimension of the rather intricate popular politics of Mamluk Cairo. To equate the people's general ineptitude to challenge the system with a lack of political vision is, I contend, incorrect. Our information, scant as it may be, has more to tell us than just amorphousness, lack of loyalty, or greed.

Earlier in this chapter we learnt of some political principles that the commoners adhered to. "Moral economy" is another principle that we should now examine.

That some of the plebeian uprisings in medieval Cairo were from time to time actually grain riots is no surprise. The acquisition of sufficient food to fill one's stomach was a major concern for most people in pre-modern times, and, when hungry, they were ready to rise even against powerful rulers. In medieval Egypt, as in contemporary European communities, rulers were expected to act responsibly in time of shortage. Lapidus's brief discussion of grain riots, although mainly concerned with Syrian towns in the Mamluk period, is perceptive and relevant. Accordingly, riots were not just spontaneous acts, but political demonstrations. They "made every bread shortage a crisis of confidence . . . by pressing the Sultan, in whose hands lay the power to curb abuses, to remove obnoxious officials, curb the speculations of the emirs, and reduce prices . . . Every grain crisis thus became a political game raging around the Sultan without formal organs for articulation of the political struggle."[38]

To comprehend the meaning of Cairene grain riots, it is essential first to review the structure of the grain market in medieval Cairo. As far as ownership is concerned, it contained the main ingredients of what E. P. Thompson has termed paternalism,[39] Egyptian rulers being the major grain owners. Through taxes collected in kind, they amassed and controlled enormous quantities of grain, as well as other agricultural products.[40] Fāṭimid caliphs had control of the product throughout the vast region of Upper Egypt from Cairo southwards (*al wajh al-qiblī*), and of some portion of the grain grown in the rest of Egypt. The Fāṭimid bureau (*dīwān*) of taxation collected 1 million *irdabb*s (about 70,000 tons) of grain annually.[41] In Mamluk times grain was collected as tax mainly in the southern parts of Egypt.[42]

Much of the rulers' grain was stockpiled in the state (i.e., their private) granaries, an important Egyptian institution since Pharaonic times.[43] Grain reserves of the Fāṭimid caliphs and Mamluk sultans normally amounted to over 300,000 *irdabb*s, or about 21,000 tons of grain;[44] during al-Afḍal's vizierate (1094–1121), as much as 1 million *irdabb*s was stored – at least so we are told.[45] Such quantities could probably feed the entire populace of Cairo during a whole year of famine.[46] Emirs and lesser-ranking officers, through the "fief" system (*iqṭā'*), also exacted taxes in kind, and were thus able to store grain of their own.[47] Officials received grain from Mamluk rulers to supplement their cash payment (*jirāyāt*). Thus Baybars I (1260–77) used to distribute a total of 20,000 *irdabb*s of grain each month to various office holders.[48] In 1345 a high-ranking emir received no less than 10,000 *irdabb*s (700 tons) of grain on the occasion of his promotion.[49] A few years later, another emir received a similar amount of barley.[50] In the 1420s gifts of grain amounted to 5,000 *irdabb*s (350 tons) monthly.[51]

Grain was not just a property lying idle, but was a prime commodity in the Cairene market. Surplus in the possession of the elite probably constituted a large share of the market supplies. The rest was provided by what can be reservedly characterized as free trade: that is, peasants, after raising their taxes in kind, consuming part of their grain, and saving part for seeds, sold their surplus – if they had any – to meet their obligations for cash payments. Here merchants and brokers served as mediators between the countryside and urban centres. In 1054 or 1055, according to one report, merchants even concluded agreements of "grain futures"; they paid peasants, who had been under pressure to pay taxes in cash, for the right to the harvest later in the year.[52]

Boats loaded with grain, mainly arriving from Upper Egypt, anchored at the Grain Dock (*sāḥil al-ghalla*), situated in the port of al-Maqs at Būlāq.[53] Prior to reforms in 1315, this dock had been owned by more than 400 Mamluks as a shared "fief" (*iqṭāʿ*) to the value of 4.6 million (*sic*) *dirhams* – the largest single source of income in the Mamluk state. The dock was staffed by sixty officials who were in charge of collecting fees (*maks*) on incoming grain to the amount of 2–2.5 *dirhams* per *irdabb*,[54] about 12.5 per cent of the average price of grain, according to one scholarly calculation.[55] After unloading, grain was transported to an area west of the Canal (*khalīj*), outside Bāb al-Qanṭara known as the Grain Square (*maydān al-qamḥ*, *maydān al-ghalla*).[56] The concentration of supplies within a defined space facilitated not only taxation, but also the estimate of supply and demand and the determination of prices.[57] From the Square grain was distributed to shops[58] by brokers (*simsār*, *dallāl*), some of whom were in the service of grain owners.[59] They charged customers their special fees,[60] which in years of high prices were raised correspondingly.[61]

Direct marketing to consumers, the unchallenged right of the poor to purchase grain before dealers, and the prevention of hoarding and speculation characterized paternalistic marketing in medieval and early modern Europe.[62] In this sense, one can detect some paternalism embedded also in the medieval Cairene grain market, although it was quite fragile, and frequently exposed to breaches. Islamic regimes in Egypt (at least we know this for the Fāṭimid and Mamluk) could not ignore their responsibility as suppliers of sufficient food to their subjects. Aside from their moral obligation to see that people were not hungry, they were cognizant of the fact that a smooth flow of grain and its proper distribution were important prerequisites for maintaining socio-political stability.[63]

On some occasions of shortage and excessively high prices, Egyptian rulers opened their granaries, or ordered other owners to sell their grain to the people at reduced prices. In 1130 the vizier Abū ʿAlī Aḥmad b. Afḍal sold hundreds of thousands of *irdabb*s from the central granaries.[64] In 1137 or 1138 Caliph al-Ḥāfiẓ ordered granaries to be opened and grain sold for "average prices" (*awsaṭ al-athmān*).[65] More information on this policy is available for the Mamluk period. In 1283, in the wake of a price increase, Sultan Qalāwūn was about to order his grain to be sold at lower prices when he was advised by Emir ʿIzz ad-Dīn Aydamūr to impose this measure on the leading officers and thus keep the state's reserves untouched and prevent public anxiety. Indeed the result was a price decrease.[66] The same emir repeated his responsible policy in 1309–10. Now Master of the Royal Household (*ustādār*), he left reserves in his granary for a year and gradually sold the rest. In this he differed from other emirs, who, in the expectation of high profits, refused to sell their grain.[67] Granaries of sultans and emirs were opened for the public at least a dozen times in the fourteenth and fifteenth centuries.[68]

The sale of state-owned grain directly to millers – many of whom were probably employees in sultanic mills[69] – or bakers, obviously to prevent hoarding and speculation, appears to have been an occasional policy.[70] Price control (*tasʿīr*), although a problematic subject in the world of Islam (as in Christendom),[71] was occasionally employed by Egyptian rulers,[72] especially during the extended inflation in the second half of the fifteenth century.[73] It appears, however, that even when a decision to regulate prices was taken, its implementation was by no means easy, because of opposition staged by market forces. Price control did not always bring the desired change, and on occasion had to be abandoned.[74]

Egyptian rulers were concerned with the state of the poor, and saw themselves obligated, especially in times of shortages, to supply grain or bread, either *gratis* or at low prices, to the poor of Cairo. In 1122 2,000 *irdabb*s (about 140 tons) of wheat was distributed as alms (*ṣadaqa*).[75] The Ayyūbid al-ʿĀdil offered grain to the poor in the terrible famine of 1200.[76] Baybars's policy was to grant 10,000 *irdabb*s (4,000 according to another version) each year to the poor (*fuqarāʾ*, *masākīn*)[77] and to dwellers in Sufi lodges (*arbāb az-zawāyā*).[78] In 1264, a year of high prices, the same ruler ordered the rationed sale of 500 *irdabb*s (35 tons) a day directly to the "weaklings" (*ḍuʿafāʾ an-nafs*). Several thousand of these assembled below the Citadel and their names were registered; military officers of various ranks, merchants, and men of means were each assigned a certain number of poor people to feed over a period of three months. The prefect of Cairo, for example, was responsible for 200 persons. The poorest were also provided half a *dirham* each to buy bread baked especially for them. Sufis in lodges were given a total of 100 *irdabb*s (about 7 tons) a day out of the sultan's granaries (*shuwan*).[79] Similar measures were taken in the famines of 1295, 1374, 1416, and 1426.[80] In 1396 Sultan Barqūq ordered that 20 *irdabb*s (1.4 tons) of grain be baked into bread and distributed daily to the poor and prisoners. The number of poor enjoying this "welfare programme" reached 5,000, and those unable to obtain either bread or some other food were financially compensated.[81] The same Barqūq (r. 1382–9, then 1390–9) used to distribute 8,000 *irdabb*s annually to Sufis (*ahl al-khayr wa-arbāb as-ṣalāḥ*).[82] Sometimes in years of shortage, grain had to be imported from abroad; it is unclear, however, whether this measure always involved the initiative of the authorities.[83]

If there was, by and large, paternalism embedded in the medieval Cairene grain market, it was at times inept or even absent altogether. Disruptions of the normal mechanisms of supply were not infrequent. What were their causes? To start with, there was an inherent conflict in the attitude of the Mamluk elite, and even in that of sultans themselves, toward the grain business. On the one hand, as already seen, there was recognition of the importance of an efficient supply system. On the other hand, the grain trade was a resource for accumulating capital. Thus Fāṭimid rulers, at least some time before the mid eleventh century, bought grain each year to the value of 100,000 *dinars* (over 100,000 *irdabbs*, or 7,000 tons)[84] through the Bureau of Commerce (*matjar*), a euphemism for state monopolies.[85] Monopolistic measures recurred mainly in Mamluk days in the practice of *ṭarḥ* or *rimāya*, that is, sales imposed on merchants at excessive prices. In 1386, for example, a Mamluk vizier forced merchants to buy 100,000 (118,000 in another version) *irdabbs* (about 7,000 tons) at a price three(!) times as high as the current price of wheat.[86] Sultan Barsbāy (r. 1422–38), who monopolized some sectors of Egypt's trade and industry, was notorious for this practice. In 1429 he tried to add grain to these. Although he had to backtrack later, he still looked for other means to secure profit from grain. In the same year he banned sales at the Grain Dock and sold his own grain at relatively high prices. It was only after Barsbāy had disposed of his stocks that dealers were allowed to enter the market. However, at that point they found that demand had already subsided and, consequently, they were forced to reduce prices. In 1432, when grain prices were low, the same sultan ordered brokers at the dock to sell their supplies only to the state (i.e., himself), the result this time being an increase in demand. Three years later, various capital owners (*aṣḥāb al-basātīn wa' l-ma'āṣir wa-ghayrihā min ad-dawālīb*) were forced to buy about 700 tons of broad beans and a smaller quantity of wheat from the same ruler. Only those with political influence managed to evade the order. In 1436 Barsbāy once again implemented his repressive policies. This time he purchased over 2,000 tons of grain and stored them in his warehouse. His action was followed by a more general wave of hoarding.[87]

Others among the Mamluk elite acted irresponsibly at times to disrupt the normal marketing of grain in order to increase their profits. One relatively detailed description of the difficulties posed to paternalistic policies is worth examining. At the beginning of 1336 grain prices mounted and, subsequently, emirs stopped selling their stocks with the aim of increasing profits. Bread became scarce. The prefect of Cairo appears to have avoided the main problem (namely, confronting the military elite), and, looking for an easier target, punished millers and bakers. Prices were fixed and penalties for non-compliance were announced. Yet emirs continued to withhold their stocks and thus grain brokers went on charging excessive prices. The sultan, concerned about the situation, and, according to one of our sources, following the model of the biblical Joseph, ordered the importation of grain from Palestine and Syria. He then replaced the market inspectors of both Cairo and Fusṭāṭ and appointed a man known for his steadfastness. The latter first surveyed granaries owned by emirs and then forced the sale, at a fixed price, of surplus to millers. This policy turned out to be quite effective. At one point, an emir who took 400 *irdabbs* (about 28 tons) out of his storage without permission was forced by the *muḥtasib* to make up for that quantity. In another instance, brokers working for two leading emirs were caught speculating; their masters were summoned to the court, beaten, and disgraced. The sultan personally reprimanded one of them in front of his peers, and then, in an eruption of fury, struck the villain with his sword. The act of the sultan, we read, served as a warning for other high-ranking officers, who abandoned all thoughts of speculation. The sultan also ordered a search in the provinces for hoards of grain and the transfer of all grain to Cairo. He publicly approved the plundering of speculators' properties. Grain merchants tampering with weights were seized. Wheat was centrally distributed to millers in quantities equal to the average daily consumption of Cairo's population. Official observers were placed at bakeries to regulate the distribution of dough. The shortage of the early months of 1336 then began to subside as new supplies started to arrive, first from Syria, then from Upper Egypt and the Delta regions.[88]

Grain dealers contributed their share to the sin of speculation[89] by exploiting the dependence on the Nile for irrigation. Since the annual flood of the river decided the fate of hundreds of thousands, a too slow rise of the water between July and September, or its sudden recession during these crucial months, frequently aroused anxiety among the populace. This was the point when merchants and brokers were only too happy to withhold supplies and thus exacerbate the demand for grain and push its prices upward, or even to spread false rumours about a low level of the Nile or about insufficient grain supplies from Upper Egypt, the natural granary of the country.[90] We have numerous brief descriptions of crowds at the docks of the Nile or in front of mills and bakeries, struggling to obtain grain, dough, or bread. On occasion the anxiety could not be contained, and pillaging would occur.[91] Small wonder that medieval Egyptian rulers attempted to conceal information about the condition of the Nile from their subjects.[92]

One should also mention the power of millers, bakers, and shopkeepers to manipulate the market. In 1024, for example, they reacted to the *muḥtasib*'s decision to fix the prices of poor- and fine-quality bread[93] by shutting down their establishments,[94] thus aggravating the existing shortage.[95] The *muḥtasib* was replaced and his successor announced that only bread sold directly from ovens would be regulated, the rest being priced according to the market conditions. Indeed, bread reappeared.[96] In 1412 shopkeepers closed their shops in the wake of monetary reforms. Bread became scarce, and crowds gathered in front of bakeries. This time the sultan reacted with fury. He ordered the crowd to be punished, but he also had the shops burnt down and some shopkeepers disciplined.[97]

How did the people of Cairo view manipulatory operations in the grain market? How did they react to crises of paternalism? They certainly could not afford indifference to affairs that had an immediate bearing on their very lives. They kept a watchful eye on the performance of the authorities, as well as the different market agencies, and reacted to what they perceived as negligence of duty and abuse of office. As early as 1008 the Cairenes protested to the Fāṭimid caliph against the scarcity and poor quality of bread.[98] In 1023, a year when the Nile was low, they assembled below Muqaṭṭam Hill and, carrying Qur'āns, prayed for a better flood. Then they returned to Cairo and crowded in the markets to buy grain, which was difficult to obtain.[99] The following year was possibly one of the hardest years of plague and famine during the Fāṭimid reign. Many died of hunger. As Caliph aẓ-Ẓāhir was riding through Fusṭāṭ, the inhabitants complained bitterly about the situation; the Fāṭimid ruler was even cursed by one man of noble descent. The man was punished, yet the general unrest had to be diffused, especially as prices kept increasing. It was decided that grain was to be sold to millers for a fixed price.[100]

More information on protests is available for the Mamluk period. In 1373 people carrying Qur'āns and banners gathered at the foot of the Citadel and demanded the dismissal of the *muḥtasib*. The sultan complied.[101] In 1394 the commoners complained to the viceroy about high prices. They blamed the *muḥtasib* and in fact conspired to attack him. The Mamluk ruler, attempting to diffuse tension and restore public order, first instructed the prefect to interrogate brokers and millers. Then he ordered grain owners to sell their reserves at "God's price" (*si'r Allāh*), otherwise their grain would not be protected from looters. A number of emirs followed his call, and the prices they now charged were apparently low enough to satisfy the protestors.[102] Yet it took two years and the arrival of new grain supplies for bread prices to tumble. At that point (that is, in 1396), brokers stopped supplying Cairo and instead took grain to Alexandria in search of a more profitable market. Millers and bakers, despite the sultan's objection, slowed down production. The result was general panic. In response to public protest the sultan punished a number of millers and brokers, but his order that the supply of bread should be increased still went unheeded. The market inspector, once again threatened by the crowd and, as the chief "villain", nearly attacked, was dismissed. His follower insisted on an end to forced sales (*ṭarḥ*) at high prices, but he did not last more than a few months in office.[103]

In the shortage of 1415, hungry people from the Delta region, as well as from Syria, came in great numbers to Cairo in search of bread. Yet grain owners withheld supplies. The *muḥtasib* first taxed each grain transaction, but soon had to back down. He was then confronted by a crowd of protestors and was forced to resign. His successor initiated a different policy and announced a price control. This step was probably applauded by the people; yet at the same time it created a new problem, since grain dealers still cut their supplies to a minimum. Peasants in the South also refused to sell their surplus, and joined those opposing the control. There were Cairenes who travelled to the Delta region to purchase grain directly from farmers. The second inspector served only one month before he too resigned. The third *muḥtasib* in line imported grain from various regions in Egypt, then forced grain owners to sell from their reserves directly to millers. Rationing was imposed, and each person was allowed to purchase one *irdabb* (70 kg) only. In 1416 new grain supplies arrived in Cairo. The Egyptian government also purchased wheat in Upper Egypt for 530 *dirham*s per *irdabb* and sold it in Cairo to millers for 600, probably to cover transportation costs, but possibly also to make a profit. Tens of thousands of hungry people gathered at the Grain Dock, even emerging from their homes at midnight to look for bread. Ships loaded with grain had to anchor far from the port of Būlāq to prevent looting. In one incident several women were crushed to death; in another, a small boat sank in the Nile with twenty persons on board. Those lucky enough to obtain grain had to hire protection, which cost them 50 *dirhams* per *irdabb*. Official guards were put in front of bakeries.[104]

In 1435 Sultan Barsbāy, about to impose one of his numerous forced sales, was confronted by a crowd protesting against his policy and accusing him of creating an artificial shortage of bread. The people demanded the sale of grain from sultanic granaries, but, not surprisingly, they were ignored.[105] Protests are also recorded for a later period, in the inflationary years 1452 and 1468.[106] Then, on a single day in 1472, the people confronted the sultan twice and demanded the appointment of a *muḥtasib* to combat petty merchants (*sūqa*), whom they blamed for tampering with the weight of loaves. The sultan appointed an emir to investigate the situation. The next day bread prices were fixed, and the ruler summoned merchants and millers and ordered them to cooperate.[107] In 1480 Sultan Qāyit Bāy, returning from a military campaign, was blocked by a crowd protesting against high grain prices and the temporary absence of a market inspector. The ruler agreed to appoint someone to the vacant post.[108] In 1513, a year of shortage, grain was shipped from Egypt to Syria, where the situation was difficult as well. As Sultan Qānṣawh al-Ghawrī went in procession through Cairo, the people complained and, alluding to the export of grain, exclaimed: "God will make perish him who brings high prices upon Muslims." The sultan, who seems to have been upset by these slogans, cut his ride short.[109]

What clearly emerges in all these descriptions is that the main "villain" in the eyes of the people was the man acting as market inspector. To the cases above one can add the detailed account of 1425. In that year, as bread was in short supply, the target of the people's wrath was Inspector al-ʿAyntābī, better known as Badr ad-Dīn al-ʿAynī, the chronicler. He barely escaped the stones pelted at him and had to find shelter at the Palace. This time the sultan, in affection for al-ʿAynī, his boon companion, disregarded the protestors and even sent troops to disperse them. Twenty-two men of "high status" (*min al-mastūrīn*) among them *ashrāf* (descendants of the Prophet) and merchants, were captured, beaten, and tortured, and then thrown into jail for one night. A few weeks later, however, al-ʿAynī was replaced.[110] Popular protest against other inspectors is mentioned in more than a dozen cases.[111]

One significant feature captures our attention in reading the relevant descriptions. Whereas market inspectors were a frequent target, millers and bakers were generally left in peace. A popular song from the fifteenth century possibly typifies the friendly attitude toward them:

> I find the baker's kindness far from negligible,
> Since I buy from him on credit,
> And he ignores my failure to pay.
> In the past I resembled a lion, devouring raw meat,
> But now I have turned into a nibbling rat.[112]

These lines suggest a somewhat simplistic notion on the part of the people as to who was "good" and "bad" among the market groups. Obviously, bakers too were far from altruists and were sometimes responsible for shortages and high prices. Yet the daily contact with bakers and millers may have been a crucial factor in determining the popular attitude. Whoever was the immediate source of bread for the people enjoyed their affection and thus was granted a great deal of immunity.[113]

E. P. Thompson, in a seminal article which has been a model of analysis for about twenty years now, has contributed the notion of "moral economy", "a consistent traditional view of social norms and obligations, of the proper economic functions of several parties within the community". This view in turn bred a popular consensus which defined the practices in the marketing system that were considered legitimate. An outrage against moral assumptions, quite as much as actual deprivation, was the usual occasion for direct action.[114] Following Thompson's model, another historian reconstructed the principles of the "moral economy" in eighteenth-century France. There, the government should have kept bread prices low by controlling and regulating the sale of bread and by setting the price of grain when necessary; it should have searched out grain supplies, or forced them on to markets at reduced prices; it should also have prevented the movement of grain outside an area unless local needs were satisfied at a reasonable price.[115] Can we also speak about the moral economy of the Cairene crowd?

The material presented above is certainly suggestive in the sense that it reveals a number of expectations about the operation of the market which were shared by the commoners in Cairo. They held the authorities responsible for keeping the prices of grain and bread at a "just" level, although the exact nature of the "just price" was never actually defined.[116] They also expected their rulers to prevent the manipulation of marketing and intervene when real or fabricated shortages occurred. In the case of dearth, the rulers' granaries were thought to provide the solution. There is also some evidence of the people's demand that grain should not be shipped out of Egypt during a local shortage.[117]

The growing prominence of the moral economy among crowds has been linked, in the case of England and France, to structural changes in the political economies of these two countries. In eighteenth-century England the paternalistic tradition of grain supply was eroded and was replaced by what may be described as Adam Smith's new economic model of the self-regulating market.[118] Around the same time in France, paternalism was challenged by an increasing centralization of economic policy-making, the formation of a national market, and growing efficiency in tax collection, which in turn drove peasants into the market and transformed many of them into buyers of food.[119] The new European ideologies and changing systems were in direct conflict with the plebeian consensus on the issue of grain. Seen in this context, grain riots cannot be regarded as an impulsive reaction but have to be viewed as a coherent form of political action, a critique of the rulers.[120]

No structural changes of this sort can be pointed out in the medieval Egyptian economy, not even after the mid fourteenth century,[121] when grain riots and protests emerge as a more frequent phenomenon.[122] Paternalism in medieval Cairo generally remained intact, and we are able to depict it even more clearly after *ca* 1350. Without evidence to the contrary, in the case of Egypt one can speak of temporary, short-term dislocations, as opposed to a secular and total erosion of the system. What, then, explains the grain protests in late medieval Cairo? Although years of protest in Cairo were also years of high grain prices, it is doubtful that the long-term price trend was the only factor in force.[123] More frequent abuse of the system from different directions – that of the government as well as market agents – could have been the major cause for the rise in the frequency of protests.

Be that as it may, one thing is clear. The moral economy of the people of Cairo did not evolve in a vacuum. The hopes of the crowd and the policies of the regime influenced one another. Decisions about price control, the dismissal of inept inspectors, grain distribution from central reserves: all these were a direct response to public anxiety as much as an appropriate context for arousing some definite expectations among the common people. In medieval Cairo the grain market was a stage where plebeian concepts and patrician policies interacted. Grain riots were one notable result of the interaction.

CHAPTER 5

Popular culture and high culture in medieval Cairo

This book has been about the culture of ordinary people in medieval Cairo. One should bear in mind, however, that in the Egyptian city, as in many other places, popular culture was only one cultural block ("subculture" is another term) in a complex system. In the case of Egypt there also existed the cultures of the rulers, of the scholars, of the wealthy merchants and bureaucrats.[1] All these and popular culture did not function in isolation from one another. They were bound to exert an "osmotic" influence on each other and to interact in a variety of ways. It is the interaction in medieval Cairo between popular culture and all the rest – to which, for the sake of brevity, I shall refer as high culture – that this concluding chapter seeks to explore.

From an "ideological" point of view, such interaction would seem questionable, at least at first sight. The information we have, which is about the attitude of the learned toward the culturally "inferior", reveals criticism, perhaps outright rejection, of popular culture – not the concept itself, but its expressions.[2] First and foremost of these were religious beliefs and practices, which in their popular garb were the main target of scholarly disapproval. This disapproval reached an extreme point in the writings of Ibn Taymiyya (1263–1328). This prominent theologian spent almost his entire life in Syria and was rarely in Cairo, sometimes as a prisoner for his theological beliefs. However, between 1310 and 1313, as occasional consultant to Sultan al-Malik an-Nāṣir Muḥammad on Syrian affairs, Ibn Taymiyya issued his *Fatāwā miṣriyya* ("Egyptian Legal Opinions").[3] His first *fatwā*, written in Cairo, was directed against the cult of saints, and earned him the enduring hostility of Ibn ʿAṭāʾ Allāh, at that time the main spokesman for the Shādhiliyya order,[4] and that of Karīm ad-Dīn al-Āmulī, another influential Sufi.[5] Given Ibn Taymiyya's repute, as well as the political and religious unity of the Mamluk state, it stands to reason that his views were known in Cairo no less than in Damascus, and are therefore relevant to our study. In fact, Ibn Taymiyya had disciples in Cairo, some of whom belonged to the ruling elite: Arghūn an-Nāṣirī (d. 1330 or 1331), at one point viceroy, is a prominent example. In the first half of the fifteenth century one scholar wrote that "until the present, the latter [Ibn Taymiyya] has retained admirers and disciples in Syria and Egypt".[6]

Ibn Taymiyya's opinion concerning popular religious practices can best be examined in his *Necessity of the Straight Path against the People of Hell*.[7] The book has a long section condemning customs such as the celebration of the Prophet's birthday (*mawlid*). "Such practices are horrendous to a believer – a believer whose heart is not as yet dead but rather knows the reputable and shuns what is not reputable." The theologian also criticizes those "common people . . . who do not know the essence of Islam", and who are influenced by Christianity. He warns "against that into which we have seen many people fall", namely, the imitation of Christian festivals.[8] Another of Ibn Taymiyya's treatises, *On the Visitation of Graves*, directed against the popular custom of *ziyāra*, contains a detailed refutation of the ceremonies and rituals evolving around the Prophet's tomb, as well as the graves of lesser personages.[9] The worship of tombs, even that of Muḥammad, an exaggerated belief in the spiritual powers of local saints and in their intercession, or any other manifestation of popular belief had to be wiped out, according to Ibn Taymiyya, if faith were to be saved and Allah only to be worshipped. This scholar saw his calling in the eradication of innovations (*bidaʿ*), in redeeming faith from the popular invasion of heretical novelties, and in restoring it to its original simplicity.[10] One should note that Ibn Taymiyya was able on occasion to practise what he preached against popular customs. Thus one day, when he was walking in Cairo, he could not resist stopping briefly to kick over a backgammon board when he spied two men playing the game outside a blacksmith's shop.[11]

From Ibn Taymiyya the way is short to the genre of "anti-*bidaʿ*" tracts: scholarly works written against unsanctioned innovations, hence, containing, almost by definition, criticism of religious practices current among ordinary Muslims. Two examples of such tracts will suffice. One is *al-Madkhal*, by Ibn al-Ḥājj al-ʿAbdarī (d. 1336), Ibn Taymiyya's contemporary and a resident of Cairo. In this book al-ʿAbdarī attacks the visitation of graves, the celebration of dubious festivals, including Christian ones, and the "un-Islamic" behaviour of Muslim women.[12] Al-ʿAbdarī even advises the rulers to ban the sale of various products needed by Christians for their festivals because it is tantamount to sharing in their idolatry (*shirk*).[13] A second tract of the same genre is *Kitāb al-lumaʿ fi'l-ḥawādith wa'l-bidaʿ*, written around 1300 by Idrīs b. Baydākīn at-Turkumānī.[14] In it the author criticized innovations which were widespread among Muslims in Mecca, Egypt, and Syria, such as singing and dancing at mosques during prayer time and the participation of Muslims in Christian holidays. He also condemned the veneration of graves and the cult of the dead, and women's repugnant habit of singing and dancing while performing the Pilgrimage.[15]

The "ideological" picture of the relationship between subcultures is, however, somewhat more complex than has been painted so far. What is important to stress at this juncture is that the learned in medieval Islam were not united in their criticism of popular religious practices. One example of disagreement emerges in a trial in 1326 against Ibn Taymiyya. The council of his judges expressed hostility to any suggestion that "visiting" graves (*ziyāra*) was an unorthodox ritual.[16] In fact, three Egyptian and Syrian scholars wrote tracts against Ibn Taymiyya's view on the subject.[17] When, around the same year, one of his followers spoke in Jerusalem against *ziyāra*s, local officials filed a report to the sultan, with the result that the man, a scholar in his own right, was punished.[18] More than 100 years later, Ibn Ḥajar al-ʿAsqalānī, one of the leading savants of the Mamluk period, expressed a lenient attitude toward the cult of the dead and forbade only extreme veneration and the use of tombs as pointers to the direction to mecca (*qibla*).[19] His contemporary, as-Suyūṭī (d. 1505), approved of the celebration of the Prophet's *mawlid* and characterized it as a "commendable innovation" (*bidʿa ḥasana*). The celebration, in his view, should be carried out, yet restricted to reciting Qur'ānic verses, relating information (*riwāyat al-akhbār*) on the birth of Muḥammad, and serving a special meal (*simāṭ*).[20]

While the learned provided the ideological weaponry, it was mainly rulers who took practical measures to combat and repress those cultural phenomena that could be characterized as popular. Together with scholars, at times under their influence, rulers were concerned with public morals, and understood their task as defending "true" Islam. They were on the alert as regards the state of public order, and thus, from time to time, initiated attacks on what appeared to them to be endangering it. Earlier in this book we had occasion to see how Egyptian rulers attempted occasionally to repress the celebrations of Nawrūz, until the disappearance of this festival from Cairo altogether in the fifteenth century.[21] The *ziyāra* was another popular practice which, as we saw, drew scholarly fire. It also became a target for governmental action.

We have scattered information about its banning. As early as 865 the prefect of Fusṭāṭ forbade women to continue their custom of visiting graves. He also imprisoned women hired as mourners.[22] A ban against women's *ziyāra* was declared once again in 1011.[23] In 1023–4 the gathering of crowds at the Qarāfa Cemetery, most likely for performing *ziyāra*s, was declared to be prohibited.[24] Acts against "visiting" graves continued under the Mamluks. Baybars I (1260–77) even decided at one point to level the Qarāfa. His questionnaire to scholars about that gained an approving *fatwā*. It was only the intervention of his vizier and, subsequently, the sultan's own death which prevented the decision from being put into effect.[25] In the early fourteenth century, Emir ʿAlāʾ ad-Dīn Ṭaybars, the Castellan (*wālī bāb al-qalʿa*), barred women from outings to the Qarāfa on special days (*mawsim*).[26] At the end of the same century, in Ramaḍān of 793 (1391), women were prevented once again from visiting graves at the Qarāfa.[27] A ban on women's custom of performing *ziyāra*s on Fridays was announced in 1421 – this was apparently not unconnected with high mortality rates that year – and again in the following year, around the time of ʿĪd al-Fiṭr,[28] as well as on Fridays in 1432.[29] In 1505, a year in which the plague occurred, the sultan forbade mourning ceremonies which featured tambourines. A female mourner who disregarded the ruler's order was paraded in disgrace on a donkey, tambourines tied to her neck, her face blacked.[30]

Thus far we have largely encountered learned criticism and what could be provisionally termed governmental repression as characterizing the relationship between the Egyptian elite and the culture, especially religion, of the people. This relationship, however, was certainly more complex. For in a dynamic cultural system which consists of subcultures, reality would hardly reflect ideology on a one-to-one basis. In other words, despite the general hostility that the learned and the rulers might develop toward the culture of the commoners, they had to take it into consideration and accommodate it. Sometimes they even succumbed, perhaps unconsciously, or else eagerly, to elements of popular culture. Two cases may help us fathom the cultural process in medieval Cairo in the light of the latter reservations. The first is a case of a meeting point of the cultures of the elite and the people. The second is of a contribution made by popular culture to the larger cultural edifice.

The case of cultural intersection which I intend to discuss is that of the state festival. In opposition to the popular festival of Nawrūz, the state festival was initiated by the regime and was first and foremost intended to serve its needs. Yet a state festival needed a large audience if it was also to convey some (mostly political) message. In terms of location, it therefore had to be staged not within the Citadel, the enclosure of the Mamluk regime, but in the streets of Cairo, in front of thousands of spectators. There the festival would be turned into an encounter between rulers and their subjects, and in a more extended sense, between the culture of the elite and the culture of the people. This encounter helped to create new cultural processes.

What were the state festivals in Mamluk Cairo like? One such annual festival evolved around the "Procession of the Palanquin" (*dawarān al-maḥmil*, or *maḥmal*), a camel carrying a richly decorated, normally empty litter, as part of the Egyptian Pilgrimage caravan to Mecca. It first occurred in the 1260s as a demonstration of Egypt's interest in the Holy Places,[31] and persisted as an annual festival into our own century.[32]

The *maḥmil* procession started on a Monday or a Thursday in or immediately after the middle of the month of Rajab, the seventh month of the Islamic year. The night before the "Day of the *maḥmil*" the camel carrying the decorated litter was stationed near al-Ḥākim Mosque.[33] A festive fire (*nafṭ ḥāfil*) was then lit in the quarter of Rumayla, below the Citadel.[34] The next morning the procession would commence. This is how it appeared to the traveller Ibn Baṭṭūṭa in 1326:

The four Grand Qādis, the Intendant of the Treasury, and the Muḥtasib . . . are mounted, and along with them ride the principal jurists, the syndics of the heads of corporations,[35] and the officers of state. They all proceed together to the gate of the citadel, the residence of al-Malik al-Nāṣir, whereupon the *maḥmil* comes out to meet them, borne on a camel, and preceded by the amīr who has been designated for the journey to the Ḥijāz in that year. With him are his troops and a number of water-carriers mounted on their camels. All classes of the population, both men and women, assemble for this ceremony, then they go in procession with the *maḥmil* round the two cities of al-Qāhira and Miṣr [al-Fusṭāṭ], accompanied by all those whom we have mentioned, and with the camel-drivers singing to their camels in the lead . . . thereupon resolves are inflamed, desires are excited, and impulses are stirred up, and God Most High casts into the heart of whom He will of His servants the determination to set out upon the Pilgrimage, so they start to equip themselves and to make preparations for it.[36]

At the end of the procession, the camel carrying the *maḥmil* was stationed once again near al-Ḥākim Mosque, there to remain until the procession of Shawwāl three months later. The latter featured the march (*musāyara*) of the emir in charge of the Pilgrimage caravan,[37] after which the caravan embarked on its long journey to Mecca to arrive in time for the Ḥajj.[38] Al-Maqrīzī, a fifteenth-century eyewitness, related that, on the day of departure, the Raydāniyya quarter, north of the Succour Gate (Bāb an-Naṣr), was crowded with merchants, entertainers, and many commoners; it was extremely difficult to move between Raydāniyya and the gate known as Bāb al-Futūḥ.[39]

The splendour would have been particularly marked when the Mamluk sultan or members of his family set out themselves for the Pilgrimage. Such was the case in 1457, when the sultan's son, assuming the title of "emir of caravan" (*amīr ḥajj al-maḥmil*), went in a splendid parade watched by his father.[40] In 1514, shortly before the demise of the Mamluk regime, the Pilgrimage caravan included Qānṣawh al-Ghawrī's son, the sultan's wife (*khōnd*), and a senior official in the chancery (*kātib as-sirr*), each with his or her own canopy (*wiṭāq*). Especially impressive was the *khōnd*'s canopy, which was valued at 20,000 *dinar*s and was led by torch bearers. The chronicler Ibn Iyās noted that the participation of the "First Lady" in the procession that particular year was without precedent. There also rode four regiments of cavalry (*ṭulb*) – that of the prince being a combatant regiment (*ṭulb ḥarbī*) – led by a band of drummers and pipers. The "prince's" party also included two teams of camels richly decorated with costly textiles, twenty of the camels carrying objects of Chinese manufacture and other precious vessels, all expensive items "that baffle the eyes". A large crowd gathered in the quarter of Rumayla, whereas the sultan observed the procession from the Citadel. Incidentally, there were occasions when the sultan viewed the *maḥmil* procession, when it reached the quarter of Būlāq, from a golden boat on the Nile.[41] Our source concludes his elaborate report of the procession in 1514 by noting that the people prophetically viewed the event as signifying the end of the sultan's good fortune.[42]

A special pageant during the *maḥmil* celebrations, about which we first learn in the fifteenth century, was the show of Mamluk lancers (*rammāḥa*), dressed in red, riding horses covered with iron masks as in a march to the battlefield, and exercising with lances. This show also featured a "combat" at the foot of the Citadel.[43] It was performed in the presence of Egyptian rulers; at least so we are told with regard to the last stage of the Mamluk period. Furthermore, the *rammāḥa* became a gimmick for impressing foreign visitors, as in 1509, when they marched in front of the Mamluk elite on the occasion of a visit by the Safavid ambassador from Iran.[44] It is noteworthy that in 1444 the lancers' show had to be cancelled because of the death of soldiers from the plague.[45] It was reintroduced only nine years later, but by then the art of the riding lancers had to be learnt anew by a fresh generation of soldiers.[46]

Thus far the *maḥmil* festival from the court's vantage point. Yet the commoners also played a part in the celebrations. First, they added to the decoration of Cairo. Shopkeepers, for instance, were urged to adorn their shops three days in advance.[47] People used to repaint the façades of their homes. According to one report, around 1398, a man known as "the Interpreter" (*turjumān*)[48] exceeded the norm and hung a (live?) donkey with a scourge[49] at the gate of his residence, a spectacle the precise meaning of which eludes us, but which attracted throngs of viewers.[50] Second, ordinary men and women were spectators of the *maḥmil* processions, the audience of the royal spectacle. As such they were naturally disappointed when the performance of the lancers was cancelled in 1444.[51] They used to occupy shops for hours, sometimes the whole night before, even renting seats there as well as on roofs and in private homes,[52] waiting for the procession to pass. Women intermingled with men, with the result that such "immoral behaviour" was banned in 1422, but with little success.[53] Hence in Rajab of 831 (1428), Shaykh ʿAlā' ad-Dīn Muḥammad al-Bukhārī appealed to the sultan to stop the procession of the *maḥmil* altogether, denouncing the "abominations" (*munkarāt, maʿāṣī*) that were part of it. In the ruler's council that convened to deliberate that issue, the famous Ibn Ḥajar al-ʿAsqalānī suggested a compromise: the celebrations would go on, but decorations would be reduced, night lights would be done away with, and thus the commoners would prefer to stay at home.[54]

The ordinary people were also directly involved in an intriguing carnivalesque element which is mentioned in descriptions of the *maḥmil* festivities around the mid fifteenth century. It is the show of the "demons (*ʿafārīt*) of the *maḥmil*". These "demons" were initially "men on the fringes" (*aṭrāf al-qawm*), whose main job was to entertain people. However, at some point they were replaced by soldiers ("the scum (*awbāsh*) of the sultan's Mamluks", according to one description), who put on funny (*muḍḥik*) costumes, but also "extremely terrifying [demon?] masks". They rode horses adorned with bells and *sharāshiḥ*(?) and scolded the commoners.[55] In 1453 a Cairene merchant was stabbed by one of these "demons" and struck from his horse, which provoked the laughter of the crowd. A special couplet was written to commemorate the incident. Another feature of the "demons' show" that incensed the people was the extortion of money by "demons" disguised as "beggars". They would even dare to force their way into residences of emirs in order to obtain their "fees".[56] So much havoc was wreaked that the masquerade was banned in 1467; only to be renewed later.[57] What was the role of the "demons" of Rajab? Was there any symbolism in their appearance beyond sheer merry-making? Regrettably we lack further details.[58]

Another festive occasion in medieval Cairo on which the elite and the people were brought into contact was the celebration of the "Plenitude of the Nile" (*wafā' an-Nīl*). It signalled the rise of the Nile, normally in the Coptic month of Thout, that is, in September, to the level of 16 cubits, which had traditionally been considered necessary for sufficient irrigation of Egyptian land, and thus for breaking the special dam constructed on the river at Cairo. The celebration is first recorded in Fāṭimid sources and recurred annually till the nineteenth century.[59]

As in the case of the *maḥmil*, the plenitude ceremonies were initiated by the Egyptian regime. They consisted of two parts. The first was known as *takhlīq* (or *khalq*) *al-miqyās* (or *al-ʿamūd*); that is, the perfuming with saffron of the Nilometer at Rawḍa Island, in what appears to have been a ritual of good omen or gratitude. The caliph in the Fāṭimid period, and the sultan or his representative in the Ayyūbid and Mamluk periods, led this ritual.[60] At least in the fifteenth century, if not earlier, sultans used to arrive at the Nilometer on a boat equipped with sixty oars and embellished with gold, hence its name "the golden" (*dhahabiyya*). The boats of leading emirs were also decorated.[61] In the ceremony the Mamluk ruler mixed saffron and musk with his own hands in a cup which he handed to the guardian of the Nilometer. The latter would then throw himself, fully clothed, into the water, swim to the *miqyās*, and perfume it with the contents of the cup.[62] In 1451, following a prolonged drought, the joy for the plenitude was so great that the commoners smeared saffron on their own bodies.[63] The ritual of *takhlīq* would be followed by the "breaking of the dam" (*kasr / fatḥ al-khalīj / as-sadd*), the opening of the earthen dam which was annually constructed across the Canal (*khalīj*), near its mouth, to prevent the water from subsiding before the Nile attained the level of plenitude.[64] During that part of the festival Qur'ān reciters and singers performed, sometimes all night. On the following morning, there was a banquet, presided over by the ruler.[65] In 1419, in a display reminiscent of the *maḥmil* festival, Mamluk lancers performed on the bank of the Nile.[66]

Large crowds were drawn to the celebration of the plenitude, and assembled by the Nilometer.[67] In Fāṭimid days, at the public observatory of Dār ibn Maʿshar, situated by the dam, seats were rented to spectators. Some time in the twelfth century the Dār collapsed because of over-crowding, causing many deaths.[68] Another observation point was built for the people in 1124–5, and was intended to replace private, improvised wooden structures that had become hazardous. It was destroyed in a great fire in 1163.[69]

Merry-making, wine drinking, and sexual promiscuity were part of the Nile celebrations, so we are told by the chroniclers.[70] The compound at Zāwiyat al-Ḥamrā', near the Canal, which had been put up by Qadi Ibn al-Jiʿān in the last years of the fifteenth century, was one site of entertainment (*min jumlat muftarajāt al-Qāhira*) to which many people flocked.[71] Celebrations included boat trips.[72] Writing in the early sixteenth century, Leo Africanus reported that "each family gets a boat which it decorates with the finest cloth and the most beautiful rugs and provides itself with a quantity of food, delicacies, and wax torches. The entire population is in boats and amuses itself as best it can." Celebrations of the plenitude lasted seven days and seven nights, "so that what a merchant or an artisan earns all year he spends that week on food, delicacies, torches, perfume, and musicians".[73]

A number of instances are recorded in which the Mamluk authorities attempted to control the popular celebrations, and even to destroy centres of amusement. At least in those years in which the river failed to attain the minimum level of 16 cubits, or its flood was arrested for a time, the people's "abominations" were considered by scholars and rulers to be the reason for the low level of the water.[74]

Turning now from annual festivals to other spectacles in Mamluk Cairo, we find that the royal entry of a sultan or a leading emir or a procession of some dignitary was a quite frequent event. Royal entries, of course, had their forerunners in the Fāṭimid and Ayyūbid periods,[75] but it was the Mamluk regime that turned them into an almost annual event in the life of Cairo. Over 100 such entries have been recorded for the 260 years or so of Mamluk rule.[76]

In the first place one should mention processions occasioned by the accession of a new sultan. In the Ayyūbid and early Mamluk periods such processions went through Cairo, from the gate known as Bāb al-Futūḥ, or else from the Succour Gate (Bāb an-Naṣr), to the Zuwayla Gate. The street connecting these gates, the Khaṭṭ bayna'l-Qaṣrayn (also known as the *qaṣaba*), Cairo's main artery, had to be kept clean for this event. The nominated sultan would don the robe of investiture outside the city wall and then appear to the crowds on horseback, his vizier ahead of him, carrying the letter of investiture (*ʿahd*) which Mamluk sultans used to receive from caliphs. The emirs as well used to march before the sultan, to signal his eminence. The insignia of the sultanate (*shiʿār as-salṭana*) were displayed: a gilded saddle-cover (*ghāshiya*) and a parasol surmounted by the figure of a bird in silver-gilt (*al-qubba waṭ-ṭayr*). The latter, the trappings of the royal horse, the cloth of the sultan's banners, and the livery of his pages were all yellow, the distinctive colour of the Mamluk regime.[77]

There were other processions in Mamluk Cairo, some annual,[78] but most commemorating specific events. Such were the triumphant processions following successful campaigns, in which hundreds of heads of slain soldiers or prisoners in chains could be seen on display in the main streets.[79] One procession which is relatively well documented occurred in 1303, following a successful campaign against the Mongols in Syria. Preparations for welcoming the sultan at the head of his victorious army lasted several weeks. The road leading from the Succour Gate to the Citadel was decorated. People contributed jewellery and expensive cloth for the purpose. All the singers in Cairo and the vicinity were called upon to participate. A total of seventy wooden demi-citadels (*qilaʿ*) were built by the emirs.[80] The prefect, for example, constructed one such citadel by the Succour Gate and staged various kinds of entertainment (*anwāʿ al-jidd wa'l-hazl*) at the site. He also provided several containers of lemon juice for the people to drink. In the procession 1,600 Mongol war prisoners were led in chains, each carrying the head of a fallen fellow soldier; 1,000 more heads were carried on lances. Following the defeated army there entered the sultan, his insignia carried by an emir. The sultan stopped at each of the "citadels" to examine their decorations. Then he halted at the Manṣūrī Hospital and visited the tomb of his father Qalāwūn. Ibn Taghrī Birdī, our source, wryly remarks that in his own day (the fifteenth century) such pageantry would have been highly criticized as extravagant.[81]

Another procession about which we have detailed information took place in 1515, on ʿĪd al-Fiṭr, the holiday which broke the fast of Ramaḍān. It commenced at the Silsila Gate with a banquet organized by the sultan's son during which he also bestowed robes of honour on his personal servants (*ghilmān*). Then the ruler's son, two qadis, and some of the sultan's personal guard entered through the gate. Spectators crowded shops to greet the marching "prince". A delegation of the Jewish community, its members carrying candles, also participated. The quarter where the prince resided, between the Markets of the Papermakers (*warrāqūn*) and the Crossbow Makers (*bunduqāniyyūn*), was decorated, tents and canopies were set up, and candelabra (*aḥmāl*) and lanterns (*tanānīr*) were lit in broad daylight. Singers performed and played tambourines. By the gate of the prince's mansion, a stage(?) (*r.d.k*[?]) had been erected, with trees and bushes made of leather, and fountains spraying water.[82]

In other processions Cairo was also decorated. Torches and candles were lit,[83] and the route was occasionally paved with brocade which, as the marchers passed by, would be seized by spectators.[84] Coins were showered on the proceeding ruler and snatched by the crowd.[85] The sultan occasionally distributed alms,[86] or ordered a banquet to be prepared for the public;[87] musicians and singers provided entertainment.[88]

What role did the people of medieval Cairo play in the many processions and various pageants? First and foremost they were curious spectators to whom the royal show was, at least to a considerable extent, directed and whom it was meant to impress. Indeed, as we have had occasion to see, public eagerness to view processions could on occasion reach to such a pitch that seats in shops and private homes were offered for rent at considerable sums.[89] But the people were not merely passive spectators. They reacted in various ways, according to their mood or the situation. At times they would salute the riding sultan,[90] and women would utter shrill cries (*zaghārīt*).[91] At other times they would consider the procession an appropriate occasion to approach the ruler, express their concerns to him, and ask for redress.[92] Above all, as spectators of a royal procession they were "readers" of a "text" of which they provided their own interpretation. Their "reading" did not usually find its way into our historical sources, but one example of it which we do have is quite revealing. It involves a procession in 1516 of Qānṣawh al-Ghawrī's troops when leaving for Syria to do battle against the Ottomans. The crowd gathering below the Citadel disparaged (*istaqallū*) the size of the cavalry; there were those who compared it, unfavourably, it seems, to earlier military processions, such as in the days of Barsbāy (1422–37).[93] For them, obviously enough, the procession served as a criterion for assessing the power of the regime. Their view, it turned out, had the force of prophecy. The battle in Syria proved to be disastrous for the Mamluk regime.[94]

Thus, royal entries and other processions and pageants in medieval Cairo were, as with similar events in other contexts, plural festivals *par excellence*, in which

"The iconographic and scenographic material . . . offered many readings, certainly as diverse as the different social and cultural groups."[95] These events served as microcosms of both diversity and unity in cultural terms. The elite – the producers of the events – and the people, their consumers, must have had different points of view. Yet they were participants in something which, for a moment, united the city of Cairo.

The phenomena discussed thus far in this chapter, despite their nuances, display one familiar pattern of cultural process: the rulers and the elite in general as dominating the masses, dictating the "rules of the game". The commoners appear as secondary actors, reacting to the initiative of their superiors. This could have characterized most of the cultural exchange in medieval Cairo. Most but not all. For once we have established that the people had a culture that could be defined as "their own", we must assume that it had to be part of a cultural process which was multi-directional. Thus, while there were cultural products which ceased to have high cultural value and were appropriated by the popular, becoming transformed in the process, there also were popular forms which became enhanced in cultural value, went up the cultural escalator, and found themselves on the opposite side. The result was a cultural "dialectic of change"; though the distinction popular/elite remained, the inventories of each of these two subcultures did alter in the process.[96]

An example of the influence of popular culture on the culture of medieval Cairo, and on Egypt in general, is the cult of Sufi saints, a phenomenon which was discussed in Chapter 1. There is the assumption, which as regards Islam was expressed long ago by Goldziher, that this cult had first been practised at, or at least had been clearly associated with, the popular strata of society.[97] If this assumption is correct, then a process of cultural flow from the bottom upward at some point incorporated the cult of saints into the religion of the elite. To give just a few examples: the high-ranking official (*ṣāḥib*) 'Alam ad-Dīn Yaḥyā, known as Abū Kumm "the Copt" (d. 1432), became famous for his frequent *ziyāra*s to both living and deceased saints.[98] Sultan Qāyit Bāy and his entourage of emirs visited the tomb of Sīdī Ibrāhīm ad-Dasūqī in 1479.[99] The same sultan also came one night in 1488 to meet someone whom he believed to be Shaykh ʿAbd al-Qādir ad-Dashṭūṭī (d. 1517),[100] kissed his feet, and asked him to give his blessings to the army marching against the Ottomans; he rewarded the Sufi saint with more than 500 *dinar*s.[101] The veneration of Sufi saints found its way not only into the ruling body, but also into the world of orthodox scholars. In his autobiography, the Egyptian scholar as-Suyūṭī – born in 1445 into a family of qadis, *muḥtasib*s, and wealthy merchants – wrote that as an infant he was blessed by one Shaykh Muḥammad "the possessed" (*al-majdhūb*).[102]

To document the climb of the cult of saints up the cultural ladder phase by phase would be impossible. It is also difficult to explain, and it is a question which certainly requires further study, why Mamluk rulers, and especially devout scholars, were drawn into this cult. Be that as it may, in Mamluk sources we find the final stage of the process in reports about the people, scholars, and dignitaries, all venerating local saints.

The annals of the Mamluk period are replete with figures of Sufi saints who were venerated at all levels of Egyptian society. Some time in the second half of the thirteenth century Abū ʿAbd Allāh ash-Shāṭibī, who dwelt in a *ribāṭ* near Alexandria, became the "*kaʿba* of that outpost" (*thaghr*). Sultans and dignitaries came to see him, and the people were unanimous about ash-Shāṭibī's supremacy (*siyāda*).[103] Muḥammad b. ʿAbd Allāh (d. 1337), known as al-Murshidī (after Minyat Banī Murshid, in the Buḥayra, south of Alexandria, where his *zāwiya* stood), was a saint (*walī*) and *mukāshif*: that is, one who could guess what was on people's minds. He was frequented by the commoners as well as emirs, dignitaries, and religious scholars. Even Sultan an-Nāṣir Muḥammad came to see him a few times and once sent him a large sum of money. People of all classes (*ṭawāʾif an-nās*) came to eat at his residence in what seems to have been a special ritual. "Every one of them would express his desire to eat some flesh or fruit or sweetmeat at his cell, and to everyone he would bring what he had desired, though that was often out of season. Doctors of the law used to come to him to ask for appointment to office, and he gave appointments or dismissed from office." Ibn Baṭṭūta, who himself visited the Shaykh in 1326, met at his *zāwiya* Emir Sayf ad-Dīn Yalmalāk of the sultanic guard (*khāṣṣakiyya*). The famous traveller also recounts a dream he had during his night at the saint's lodge and the interpretation he heard from al-Murshidī.[104] Burhān ad-Dīn Ibrāhīm b. Muḥammad an-Nawfalī, surnamed Ibn Zuqqāʿa (d. 1413), a Sufi *shaykh*, who was also known as an astrologer and botanist,[105] used to arrive every year from his residence in Gaza, at the invitation of Sultan Barqūq, to participate in the *mawlid* of the Prophet, celebrated at the Citadel. On the occasion of his arrival, people used to crowd around the Shaykh and he would heal the sick. Public opinion, however, was divided about him. There were those who admired him as a saint (*walī*) and related miracles about him; others claimed he was a charlatan (*mushaʿbidh*). Barqūq's son, Sultan Faraj, we are told, would not embark on a military expedition without asking Ibn Zuqqāʿa's opinion.[106] To give yet another example, the *mawlid* at Ṭanṭā of the leading saint Aḥmad al-Badawī, which, as we saw at the beginning of this book,[107] was an important popular gathering, was also attended by dignitaries. Thus we find that in 1462 Shukr Bāy, wife of Sultan Khushqadām, and her entourage participated in the festival.[108] Sultan Qāyit Bāy visited al-Badawī's tomb in 1483 and ordered it to be enlarged.[109] In 1498 his successor, an-Nāṣir Abū Saʿadāt, intended to take part in the *mawlid*, but, for reasons which elude us, was prevented from doing so by his emirs.[110] In the same year, however, he came to the nocturnal celebration (*layla*) of Sīdī Ismāʿīl al-Inbābī.[111] One could put together a much longer list of *shaykh*s who were venerated by all classes of the Cairene population.[112]

Thus, drawing on the cult of saints, a subject on which we have some information, we come to the argument that, in the final analysis, a refined approach to the history of culture should transcend the "-chotomous" view, the tendency to emphasize the dichotomy between "high" and "low".[113] Despite the existence of cultural division (if one is to avoid the notion of hierarchy) – and it has been the main task of this book to emphasize the popular element in that division – there has been in most cultures, at a given point in time, a common cultural domain consisting of shared practices and meanings, the very links between high and low cultures. The Cairene case was no exception: in medieval Cairo the cult of saints created a cultural common ground for the people and the elite.

APPENDIX

Sufi *shaykh*s in Mamluk Cairo

Note: The following list should be considered as preliminary and probably does not exhaust all the *shaykh*s who lived and were active in Cairo and its vicinity during the Mamluk period.

Abbreviations

Aḥ. Aḥmad
Ibr. Ibrāhīm
Maḥ. Maḥmūd
Muḥ. Muḥammad

No.	Name	Dates	Sources
1	Yaḥayā b. Sulaymān Abū Zakariyyā' as-Sabaṭī	d. 1257	*Dhayl*, Vol. I, pp. 83–4; Ibn Ẓāfir, *Risāla*, pp. 86–7 (French trans., p. 183).
2	Abū'l-'Abbās Aḥ. b. Muḥ. al-Fāsī	d. 1259	*Tuḥfa*, p. 183.
3	Abū 'Abd Allāh Muḥ. b. 'Alī al-Mawṣilī (= Ibn Ṭabbākh)	d. 1271	*'Iqd*, pp. 96–7.
4	Musallam b. 'Antar al-Barqī al-Badawī	d. 1274	Ibid., p. 136; *Dhayl*, Vol. III, p. 103; Suyūṭī, *Ḥusn*, Vol. I, p. 521.
5	Aḥ. as-Salāmī al-Maghribī	d. 1276	Ibn Furāt, Vol. VII, p. 60.
6	Muḥ. b. Aḥ. b. Manẓūr b. 'Abd Allāh	d. 1277	*Dhayl*, Vol. III, pp. 280–1.
7	Abū Muḥ. Yūsuf b. 'Abd Allāh at-Takrūrī	d. *ca* 1250–1300	*Khiṭaṭ*, Vol. II, p. 326.
8	Amīn ad-Dīn Mubārak b. 'Abd Allāh al-Hindī	d. 1282	*Tuḥfa*, pp. 97–8.
9	Ḥasan at-Tustarī	d. *ca* 1301	*Ṭabaqāt kubrā*, p. 54.
10	'Abd al-'Azīz ad-Dīrīnī	d. 1298	Ibid., p. 161.
11	Ibn 'Aṭā' Allāh	d. 1309	Chapter 1 n. 52 below.
12	Muḥ. b. Maḥ. al-Mawṣilī	d. 1314	*Nujūm*, Vol. IX, p. 227.

No.	Name	Dates	Sources
13	Jalāl ad-Dīn Ibr. b. Muḥ. al-Qalānisī	d. *ca* 1300	*Sulūk*, Vol. II, p. 238.
14	Abū'l-Fatḥ Naṣr b. Salmān al-Musabbiḥī	d. 1319 or 1320	*Nihāya*, Leiden MS OR 2-O, fos. 111a–12a.
15	Najm ad-Dīn al-Ḥusayn b. Muḥ. b. ʿAbūd	d. 1322	*Sulūk*, Vol. II, p. 238.
16	Ayyūb as-Suʿūdī	d. 1324	*Khiṭaṭ*, Vol. II, p. 434.
17	ʿAbd al-ʿĀl	d. 1332	*Nujūm*, Vol. IX, p. 295; *Sulūk*, Vol. II, p. 355; Suyūṭī, *Ḥusn*, Vol. I, p. 525.
18	Yāqūt b. ʿAbd Allāh al-Ḥabashī	d. 1332	Suyūṭī, *Ḥusn*, Vol. I, p. 525.
19	Muḥ. b. ʿAbd Allāh al-Murshidī	d. 1337	*Nujūm*, Vol. IX, p. 313; *Bidāya*, Vol. XIV, p. 179.
20	Shihāb ad-Dīn Aḥ. b. Muḥ. al-Azdī	d. 1338 or 1339	*Tuḥfa*, p. 177.
21	Muḥ. b. Ḥasan b. Muslim as-Sulamī	d. 1362	*Badāʾiʿ*, Vol. I, pt 1, p. 590.
22	Abū Zakariyyāʾ Yaḥyā b. ʿAlī as-Ṣanāfīrī	d. 1371	Ibid., Vol. I, pt 2, pp. 93, 104; *Nujūm*, Vol. XI, pp. 118–19.
23	ʿAbd Allāh ad-Darwīsh	d. 1372	*Nujūm*, Vol. XI, p. 122; *Tuḥfa*, p. 299.
24	Bahāʾ ad-Dīn Muḥ. b. al-Kāzarūnī	d. 1373	*Nujūm*, Vol. XI, p. 125.
25	ʿAbd Allāh Abī Bakr	d. 1375	*Badāʾiʿ*, Vol. I, pt 2, p. 162.
26	ʿAlī al-ʿUqaylī	d. 1376	*Sulūk*, Vol. III, p. 302.
27	ʿAbd Allāh b. ʿAbd Allāh al-Jabartī	d. 1378	*Inbāʾ*, Vol. I, p. 184.
28	Ṣāliḥ b. Najm	d. 1379	*Sulūk*, Vol. III, p. 349.
29	Aḥ. b. Badr al-ʿAjamī	d. 1378 or 1379	Ibid., p. 349.
30	Ḥasan b. ʿAbd Allāh as-Sabbān	d. 1379	*Inbāʾ*, Vol. I, p. 203.
31	Shams ad-Dīn Muḥ. al-Qināwī	d. 1382	*Badāʾiʿ*, Vol. I, pt 2, p. 297.
32	Sīdī ʿAlī al-Berberī	*fl.* 1382	Ibid., p. 303.
33	Sīdī ʿIsmāʿīl b. Yūsuf al-Inbābī	d. 1388	*Nujūm*, Vol. XI, p. 315; *Badāʾiʿ*, Vol. I, pt 2, p. 391.
34	Ḥasan al-Khabbāz	d. 1389	*Nujūm*, Vol. XI, p. 385.
35	ʿAlī al-Mugharbil	d. 1390	*Nujūm*, Vol. XII, p. 122.
36	ʿAlī ar-Rūbī	d. 1391	Ibid., p. 124; *Sulūk*, Vol. III, p. 467.
37	Abū ʿAbd Allāh Muḥ. ar-Rakrākī	d. 1392	*Khiṭaṭ*, Vol. II, p. 433; *Sulūk*, Vol. III, p. 779.
38	Ṭalḥa al-Maghribī	d. 1392	*Nujūm*, Vol. XII, p. 130; Ibn Furāt, Vol. IX, p. 320.
39	Rashīd al-Takrūrī al-Aswad	d. 1394	*Nujūm*, Vol. XII, p. 139.
40	ash-Shaykha al-Baghdādiyya	d. 1394	Ibid., p. 142.
41	Abū Bakr al-Bijāʾī al-Maghribī	d. 1395	Ibid., pp. 143–4.
42	Nāṣir ad-Dīn Muḥ. (= Ibn Bint Maylaq)	d. 1395	Ibid., p. 146.

No.	Name	Dates	Sources
43	Muḥ. as-Samalūṭī	d. 1396	Ibid., p. 150.
44	Shams ad-Dīn Muḥ. al-Maqsī	d. 1396	Ibid., p. 150.
45	Zayn ad-Dīn Abū'l-Faraj 'Abd ar-Raḥmān (= Ibn ash-Shaykha)	d. 1397	Ibid., p. 157.
46	(Muḥ. b. 'Abd Allāh) az-Zawharī	d. 1398	*Nujūm*, Vol. XIII, p. 10; *Ḍaw'*, Vol. VIII, pp. 120–1.
47	Khalaf b. Ḥasan b. Ḥusayn aṭ-Ṭūkhī	d. 1398	*Nujūm*, Vol. XIII, p. 6.
48	Khalīl b. 'Uthmān b. 'Abd ar-Raḥmān (= Ibn al-Mushayyab)	d. 1398	Ibid., p. 6.
49	Salīm as-Sawwāq al-Qarāfī	d. 1399	Ibid., p. 18.
50	Shihāb ad-Dīn Aḥ. b. Muḥ. (= Ibn an-Nāṣiḥ)	d. 1402	Ibid., p. 28; *Manhal*, Vol. II, p. 87; *Ḍaw'*, Vol. II, p. 205 (No. 543).
51	Ibr. b. 'Abd Allāh ar-Rifā'	d. 1402	*Ḥusn*, Vol. I, p. 528; *Ḍaw'*, Vol. I, p. 72.
52	Badr ad-Dīn Ḥasan b. 'Alī b. al-'Āmidī	d. 1403	*Nujūm*, Vol. XIII, p. 30.
53	Muḥ. b. 'Abd Allāh aṣ-Ṣāmit	d. 1403	*Ḥusn*, Vol. I, p. 528.
54	Muḥ. b. Ḥasan b. Muslim al-Sulamī	d. 1404	Ibid., p. 528.
55	Sīdī 'Iwaḍ(?)	d. 1404	*Badā'i'*, Vol. I, pt 2, p. 691.
56	Muḥ. b. 'Alī b. Ja'far al-'Ajlūnī	d. 1409 or 1410 or 1417 or 1418	*Ḥusn*, Vol. I, p. 529; *Ḍaw'*, Vol. VIII, pp. 178–9.
57	Muḥ. ad-Daylam	d. 1416	*Nujūm*, Vol. XIV, p. 137.
58	Aḥ. az-Zāhid	d. 1416	*Khiṭaṭ*, Vol. II, pp. 327–8.
59	Yūsuf b. 'Abd Allāh al-Būṣīrī	d. 1417	*Nuzha*, Vol. II, p. 407.
60	Abū Bakr b. 'Umar aṭ-Ṭarīnī	d. 1424	*Nujūm*, Vol. XV, pp. 124–5.
61	Khalīfa al-Maghribī	d. 1425	Ibid., p. 134.
62	Aḥ. b. Ibr. (= Ibn 'Arab)	d. 1426	Ibid., pp. 139–40; Petry, *Civilian Elite*, p. 71.
63	Sa'īd al-Maghribī	d. 1428	*Sulūk*, Vol. IV, p. 786; *Inbā'*, Vol. III, p. 411; *Nujūm*, Vol. XV, pp. 149–50.
64	Sīdī 'Umar b. 'Alī b. Ḥijjī al-Bisṭāmī	d. 1434	*Badā'i'*, Vol. II, pp. 157–8; *Ḍaw'*, Vol. VI, p. 106.
65	Salīm b. 'Abd ar-Raḥmān al-Janānī	d. 1436 or 1437	*Inbā'* (Hyderabad), Vol. VIII, p. 437; *Ḍaw'*, Vol. III, p. 271.
66	'Abd al-Malik b. Muḥ. az-Zankalāwī	d. 1437	*Badā'i'*, Vol. II, p. 179; 'Abd al-Bāsiṭ, *Ḥawādith*, fo. 3a.
67	Shams ad-Dīn Muḥ. b. Ḥasan al-Ḥanafī ash-Shādhilī	d. 1443	*Badā'i'*, Vol. II, p. 238; 'Abd al-Bāsiṭ, *Ḥawādith*, fo. 44a; *Ṭabaqāt kubrā*, Vol. II, pp. 71–2, 78.

No.	Name	Dates	Sources
68	Muḥ. b. ʿUmar al-Ghamrī	d. *ca* 1446	*Ṭabaqāt kubrā*, Vol. II, p. 71; *Ḍaw'*, Vol. VIII, pp. 238–40.
69	Muḥ. b. ʿAbd ar-Raḥmān b. ʿĪsā ash-Shādhilī	d. 1449	ʿAbd al-Bāsiṭ, *Ḥawādith*, fo. 68a.
70	Muḥ. Abū'l-Fayḍ b. Sulṭān	d. 1449	*Badā'iʿ*, Vol. II, p. 273.
71	Muḥ. Abū ʿAbd Allāh al-Hiwī (= as-Safārī)	d. 1451	*Ḥawādith*, p. 108; *Tibr*, p. 375.
72	Aḥ. at-Turābī	d. 1452	*Nujūm*, Vol. XVI, p. 11; *Ḍaw'*, Vol. II, p. 261.
73	Muḥ. b. al-Munajjim	d. 1452	ʿAbd al-Bāsiṭ, *Ḥawādith*, fo. 88a.
74	Muḥ. al-Maghribī	d. 1455	*Nujūm*, Vol. XVI, pp. 177–8; *Ḍaw'*, Vol. X, p. 125.
75	ʿUmar b. Ibr. al-Bābānī	d. 1458	*Nujūm*, Vol. XVI, p. 191; *Ḍaw'*, Vol. X, pp. 150–2.
76	Maydān b. Aḥ. b. Muḥ.	d. 1458	*Ḍaw'*, Vol. VI, p. 64 (No. 219).
77	Ibn az-Zayyāt	d. 1458	*Nujūm*, Vol. XVI, p. 195; *Ḍaw'*, Vol. I, p. 184.
78	Aḥ. b. Khidr as-Saṭūḥī (= Shaykh Kharūf)	d. 1461	*Nujūm*, Vol. XVI, p. 314; *Ḍaw'*, Vol. I, p. 292.
79	Abū ʿAbd Allāh Muḥ. al-Fūwī	d. 1461	*Nujūm*, Vol. XVI, p. 315; *Ḍaw'*, Vol. VI, p. 300.
80	ʿUmar al-Bābānī	d. 1463	*Nujūm*, Vol. XVI, pp. 328–9; *Ḍaw'*, Vol. VI, p. 84 (No. 219).
81	Ibr. al-Ghannām	d. 1465	*Nujūm*, Vol. XVI, p. 344; ʿAbd al-Bāsiṭ, *Ḥawādith*, fo. 170a.
82	Muḥ. b. Ṣāliḥ al-Azharī	d. 1471	*Inbā' al-haṣr*, p. 334; *Ḍaw'*, Vol. VII, p. 687.
83	Sīdī Ibr. b. ʿAlī b. ʿUmar al-Matbūlī	d. 1473	*Badā'iʿ*, Vol. III, p. 88; ʿAbd al-Bāsiṭ, *Ḥawādith*, fo. 245a.
84	Sīdī Muḥ. al-Isṭanbūlī (= al-Iqbāʿī)	d. 1474	*Badā'iʿ*, Vol. III, p. 95.
85	ʿAlī b. Shihāb ash-Shāmī	d. 1486	*Ṭabaqāt kubrā*, Vol. II, p. 91.
86	Sīdī ʿAbd al-ʿAẓīm b. Nāṣir b. Khalaf as-Saddār	d. 1487	*Badā'iʿ*, Vol. III, p. 239; ʿAbd al-Bāsiṭ, *Ḥawādith*, fo. 362b.
87	ʿAlī al-Laḥḥām	*fl.* 1489	ʿAbd al-Bāsiṭ, *Ḥawādith*, fo. 388b.
88	ʿAlī an-Nabtītī aḍ-Ḍarīr	d. 1512	*Ṭabaqāt kubrā*, p. 100.
89	Muḥ. b. Zuraʿa al-Aḥmadī al-Badarshīnī	d. 1514 or 1515	*Badā'iʿ*, Vol. IV, p. 386.
90	Sīdī Muḥ. b. ʿInān	d. 1516	*Badā'iʿ*, Vol. V, p. 7.
91	Tāj ad-Dīn adh-Dhākir	d. 1516	Ibid., p. 57.
92	ʿAbd al-Qādir ad-Dashṭūṭī	d. 1518	*Ḍaw'*, Vol. IV, pp. 300–1.
93	ʿAbd ar-Raḥmān al-Bahnasāwī	d. 1519	*Badā'iʿ*, Vol. V, p. 300.

Notes

Introduction

1 *The Travels of Ibn Baṭṭūṭa A.D. 1325–54*, trans. H. A. R. Gibb (3 vols., Cambridge, 1958–71), Vol. I, p. 41.
2 Janet L. Abu Lughod, *Cairo: 1001 Years of the City Victorious* (Princeton, 1971), p. 38 n. 7.
3 Gaston Wiet, *Cairo: City of Art and Commerce* (Norman, 1964), p. 76.
4 Nelly Hanna, *An Urban History of Būlāq in the Mamluk and Ottoman Periods* (Cairo, 1983), p. 19.
5 For an estimate of 250,000 in the Fāṭimid period (970–1171) see Thierry Bianquis, "Une crise frumentaire dans l'Egypte fatimide", *JESHO* 23 (1980), 96. For the same figure prior to 1348 see André Raymond, "La Population du Caire et de l'Egypte à l'époque ottomane et sous Muḥammad ʿAlī", in *Mémorial Ömer Lûfti Barkan* (Paris, 1980), pp. 171–2. For about 450,000 prior to 1348 see Michael W. Dols, *The Black Death in the Middle East* (Princeton, 1977), p. 202. For half a million see Abu Lughod, *Cairo*, p. 37.
6 For 150,000 see André Raymond, "La Population du Caire de Maqrīzī à la Description de l'Egypte", *BEO* 28 (1975), 205. For 150,000–200,000 see Raymond, "La Population du Caire et de l'Egypte". For 300,000 see Dols, *Black Death*, p. 223.
7 For 100,000 see Raymond, "La Population du Caire de Maqrīzī", 206 (quoting Russell). For over 200,000 at the beginning of the fourteenth century see Bronislaw Geremek, *The Margins of Society in Late Medieval Paris* (Cambridge, 1987), p. 7.
8 Wiet, *Cairo*, pp. 36, 39.
9 Abu Lughod, *Cairo*, p. 33, citing al-Maqrīzī.
10 Susan Jane Staffa, *Conquest and Fusion: The Social Evolution of Cairo A.D. 642–1850* (Leiden, 1977), pp. 128–98. For a similar, though not identical, presentation see Ira Marvin Lapidus, *Muslim Cities in the Later Middle Ages* (Cambridge, Mass., 1967). The latter, although dealing mainly with Syrian towns, implies that the picture also suits Cairo.
11 Staffa, *Conquest*, p. 176.
12 See especially the many works by David Ayalon, as listed in the volumes of *Index Islamicus*.
13 Karl Stowasser, "Manners and Customs at the Mamluk Court", *Muqarnas* 2 (1984), 13–20.
14 David Ayalon, "Notes on the *Furūsiyya* Exercises and Games in the Mamluk

Sultanate", *Scripta Hierosolymitana* 9 (1961), esp. 53–7; Ahmad Abd ar-Raziq, "Deux jeux sportifs en Egypte au temps des Mamlūks", *AI* 12 (1974), 95–130.

15 For Turkish translations under Mamluk patronage see A. Bodrogligeti, "Notes on the Turkish Literature at the Mameluke Court", *Acta Orientalia* (Budapest) 14 (1962), 273–82; Barbara Flemming, "Šerīf, Sulṭān Ġavrī und die 'Perser'", *Islam* 45 (1969), 81–93; Ulrich Haarmann, "Arabic in Speech, Turkish in Lineage: Mamluks and their Sons in the Intellectual Life of Fourteenth-Century Egypt and Syria', *JSS* 33 (1988), 90. Ḥusayn b. Muḥammad al-Ḥusaynī, who spent ten months, in 1504–5, at Qānṣawh al-Ghawrī's court, recorded the literary sessions that took place there in his *Nafā'is al-majālis as-sulṭāniyya*. Another book on these sessions is *al-Kawkab ad-durrī fī masā'il al-Ghawrī*, of which only the first volume has survived. See Mohammad Awad, "Sultan al-Ghawri, his Place in Literature and Learning (Three Books Written under his Patronage)", *Actes du XXe congrès international des orientalistes, Bruxelles 5–10 Septembre 1938* (Louvain, 1940), 321–2. See also Barbara Flemming, "Aus den Nachtgesprächen Sultan Ġaurīs", in H. Franke *et al.* (eds.), *Folia Rara Wolfgang Voigt* (Wiesbaden, 1976), pp. 22–8. For Sultan Qāyit Bāy's own writings in Arabic and "barbaric Turkish" see Haarmann, "Arabic in Speech", 85 and n. 14.

16 A *furūsiyya* guide, *Nihāyat as-su'l wa'l-umniyya fī ta'allum a'māl al-furūsiyya*, which could be roughly translated as *All One Need Know about Horsemanship*, was dedicated by its author, Muḥammad b. 'Īsā al-Aqsarā'ī (d. Damascus 1348), to the Mamluk viceroy in Damascus. See G. Rex Smith, *Medieval Muslim Horsemanship: A Fourteenth-Century Arabic Cavalry Manual* (London, 1979); David James, "Mamluke Painting at the Time of the 'Lusignan Crusade', 1365–70", *Humaniora Islamica* 2 (1974), 74. A copy of the *Nihāya* was owned in 1386 by one Ṭaybughā al-Azjī, most likely a Mamluk officer. Of the eleven surviving manuscripts of the *Nihāya*, ten were copied within one hundred years of the author's death. See Geoffrey Tantum, "Muslim Warfare: A Study of a Medieval Muslim Treatise on the Art of War", in Robert Elgood (ed.), *Islamic Arms and Armour* (London, 1979), p. 188. For *furūsiyya* guides see also Hassanein Rabie, "The Training of the Mamluk Fāris", in V. J. Parry and N. E. Yapp (eds.), *War, Technology and Society in the Middle East* (London, 1975), pp. 153–63.

17 Thus al-Aqsarā'ī's afore-mentioned *Nihāya* and similar manuals soon became a special category of books for artistic adoration. One illustrated copy of the *Nihāya*, produced in 1366, and now at the Chester Beatty Library, had been dedicated to a Mamluk emir. It was later *ex-libris* of Sultan Jaqmaq (1438–53) and read to his son. See James, "Mamluke Painting", 75; Esin Atil, *Renaissance of Islam: Art of the Mamluks* (Washington, D.C., 1981), pp. 252, 262; Duncan Haldane, *Mamluk Painting* (Warminster, 1978), p. 48. An illustrated manuscript of a book on farriery (*bayṭara*) by Ibn Akhī Khuzām was produced in 1470, probably in Egypt, for a high court personage, possibly Sultan Qāyit Bāy (1468–96). See Haldane, *Mamluk Painting*, p. 90; Atil, *Renaissance*, pp. 252 and 254 n. 27. The only illuminated manuscript of al-Ḥarīrī's *Maqāmāt* whose patron is known was copied in 1337, most likely in Egypt, for the Mamluk emir Nāṣir ad-Dīn Muḥammad, son of Ṭaranṭāy. See Haldane, *Mamluk Painting*, p. 83; Oleg Grabar, *The Illustrations of the Maqāmāt* (Chicago, 1984), p. 15. For a short note on this patron (whose year of death is 1330 – was the manuscript completed posthumously?) see *Sulūk*, Vol. II, p. 338. An illustrated Turkish translation of the Persian epic *Shāhnāma* was prepared between 1500 and 1511 at the request of Qānṣawh al-Ghawrī. See Nurhan Atasoy, "Un manuscrit

Mamlūk illustré du Šāhnāma", *REI* 37 (1969), 151–8. The so-called Baptistère de Saint Louis, which was made in the first quarter of the fourteenth century for a Mamluk emir, is engraved with court scenes, battles, and hunting expeditions. Two medallions show a crowned figure seated on a throne, flanked by attendants on each side, bearing the emblem of government. See D. S. Rice, "The Blazons of the 'Baptistère de Saint Louis'", *BSOAS* 13 (1949–51), 367–80; Eva Baer, *Metalwork in Medieval Islamic Art* (Albany, 1983), pp. 230–1. For Mamluk patronage of metalwork see, e.g., James W. Allan, *Metalwork in the Islamic World: The Aron Collection* (London, 1986), esp. pp. 48–61.

18 Carl F. Petry, *The Civilian Elite of Cairo in the Later Middle Ages* (Princeton, 1981).

19 See especially S. D. Goitein, *A Mediterranean Society*, Vol. IV: *Daily Life* (Berkeley, 1983). For an argument about the validity of the Geniza (which is primarily concerned with the Jewish community) for conclusions about the Egyptian society in general, see Goitein, *A Mediterranean Society*, Vol. I: *Economic Foundations* (Berkeley, 1967), pp. 70–4. For middle-class housing in the Mamluk period see Laila A. Ibrahim, "Middle-Class Living Units in Mamluk Cairo: Architecture and Terminology", *Art and Archeology Research Papers* 14 (1978), 24–30. For a Cairene middle-class dwelling, the construction of which is dated to 1522, see Mona Zakariya, "Le *Rabʿ* de Ṭabbāna", *AI* 16 (1980), 275–97.

20 Lapidus, *Muslim Cities*, pp. 81–2; Goitein, *Economic Foundations*, pp. 99–116.

21 The private lives of the medieval Cairene bourgeoisie are revealed occasionally in Geniza letters.

22 This is clearly demonstrated in Goitein, *Economic Foundations*, and Lapidus, *Muslim Cities*.

23 For taxation and the people's resentment see Lapidus, *Muslim Cities*, pp. 144–53. For monetary instability and high grain prices see Boaz Shoshan, "From Silver to Copper: Monetary Changes in Fifteenth-Century Egypt", *Studia Islamica* 56 (1983), 97–116; Boaz Shoshan, "Money Supply and Grain Prices in Fifteenth-Century Egypt", *Economic History Review* 36 (1983), 47–67.

24 This is a subject that deserves to be studied.

25 Compare J. Huizinga's statement that "No other epoch has laid so much stress as the expiring Middle Ages on the thought of death", *The Waning of the Middle Ages* (Garden City, 1954), p. 138. Huizinga's discussion of the "Vision of Death" seems to lack concrete connection with the contextual circumstances.

26 Dols, *Black Death*, pp. 223–7; Boaz Shoshan, "Notes sur les épidémies de peste en Egypte", *Annales de démographie historique* (1981), 387–404.

27 For the problems involved in estimating plague mortality in medieval Islamic societies see Dols, *Black Death*, pp. 193–223.

28 *Sulūk*, Vol. II, pp. 780–3; Dols, *Black Death*, pp. 240–1.

29 *Inbā'*, Vol. III, p. 438. For white as the normal colour of shrouds see A. S. Tritton, "Djanāza", *EI*^{2}. For a different interpretation of the contemporary metaphor see Dols, *Black Death*, pp. 240–1.

30 *Inbā'*, Vol. III, p. 438 (for 1430); *Badā'iʿ*, Vol. II, p. 359 (for 1460).

31 *Sulūk*, Vol. II, pp. 780–3; Dols, *Black Death*, pp. 240–1.

32 *Badā'iʿ*, Vol. III, p. 36.

33 *Badā'iʿ*, Vol. I, pt 1, pp. 532–3. My translation is slightly different from that in Dols, *Black Death*, p. 240, which is based on the Būlāq edition of *Badā'iʿ*. Dols ascribes

these lines to Ibrāhīm al-Mi'mār, who, incidentally, died of the plague later in that year. In fact, the author is anonymous.

34 *Sulūk*, Vol. II, p. 783; Dols, *Black Death*, p. 246.

35 *Badā'i'*, Vol. III, p. 125.

36 Dols, *Black Death*, pp. 245–6, after *Nujūm*, English trans. (= *History of Egypt*), Vol. XVIII, p. 72.

37 *Badā'i'*, Vol. II, p. 136; *Nujūm*, Vol. XIV, p. 338.

38 *Nujūm*, English trans. (= *History of Egypt*), Vol. XVIII, pp. 149–50, cited in Dols, *Black Death*, pp. 243–5. See also *Sulūk*, Vol. IV, pp. 1038–40.

39 *Sulūk*, Vol. I, pp. 386–8. For this revolt see Jean-Claude Garcin, *Un centre musulman de la Haute-Egypte médiévale: Qūṣ* (Cairo, 1975), pp. 184–6.

40 *Badā'i'*, Vol. II, p. 311.

41 Huizinga, *Waning of the Middle Ages*, p. 11.

42 *Nujūm*, Vol. XI, pp. 184–6.

43 Robert Muchembled, *Popular Culture and Elite Culture in France, 1400–1750* (Baton Rouge, 1985), p. 31.

44 *Muṣṭafā 'Alī's Description of Cairo of 1599*, ed., trans., and annot. Andreas Tietze (Vienna, 1975), p. 49.

45 David Hall, Introduction to Steven L. Kaplan (ed.), *Understanding Popular Culture: Europe from the Middle Ages to the Nineteenth Century* (Berlin, 1984), p. 14.

46 Aron Gurevich, *Medieval Popular Culture: Problems of Belief and Perception* (Cambridge, 1988), pp. xv–xvi.

47 According to Edward Shorter popular culture belongs to virtually all strata of the population beneath the level of large landowners, wholesale merchants, or the educated upper-middle class in general. See Edward Shorter, "Towards a History of *La Vie Intime*: The Evidence of Cultural Criticism in Nineteenth-Century Bavaria", in Michael R. Marrus (ed.), *The Emergence of Leisure* (New York, 1974), p. 40.

48 Gurevich, *Popular Culture*, pp. xv–xvi.

49 See, e.g., Pierre Boglioni, "La Culture populaire au moyen âge: thèmes et problèmes", in *La Culture populaire au moyen âge* (Montreal, 1979), pp. 13–14.

50 The difficulties of defining popular culture are still expressed in works written in the 1980s. See remarks by Kaplan, Hall, and Löttes in Kaplan (ed.), *Understanding Popular Culture*, pp. 1, 5, 7–8, 10, 147–8. See also Peter Burke, "Popular Culture between History and Ethnology", *Ethnologia Europaea* 14 (1984), 5–13.

51 Georges Duby states that "dividing lines between the cultural strata are blurred and shifting and they seldom coincide exactly with those defining the economic conditions". See his *The Chivalrous Society* (London, 1977), p. 14. Cf. David Hall's opinion: "Culture has a social basis, but the relationship of culture to society is more fluid", and also: "Culture lived more freely than any one-to-one relationship [with social structure] can recognize." See Kaplan (ed.), *Understanding Popular Culture*, pp. 5, 11.

52 Carlo Ginzburg, *The Cheese and the Worms: The Cosmos of a Sixteenth-Century Miller* (Baltimore, 1980).

53 Roger Chartier, "Culture as Appropriation: Popular Cultural Uses in Early Modern France", in Kaplan (ed.), *Understanding Popular Culture*, pp. 233–6. In the same vein is Chartier's argument that "the classification of professional groups [which] corresponds with a classification of cultural products and practices can no longer be

accepted uncritically". See ibid., p. 233, and also Roger Chartier, *The Cultural Uses of Print in Early Modern France* (Princeton, 1987), p. 3.

54 Jacques Le Goff, "The Learned and Popular Dimensions of Journeys in the Otherworld in the Middle Ages", in Kaplan (ed.), *Understanding Popular Culture*, pp. 19–22.

55 H. C. Eric Midelfort, "Sin, Melancholy, Obsession: Insanity and Culture in 16th Century Germany", in Kaplan, p. 114.

56 Le Goff, "Learned and Popular", in Kaplan, p. 19.

1 Sufism and the people

1 For Companions of the Prophet see Ignaz Goldziher, "Aṣḥāb", *EI*[1].

2 *Sulūk*, Vol. II, pp. 649–50.

3 This claim, it appears, drew inspiration from Muḥammad's alleged heavenly journey. For the latter see J. Horovitz, "Miʿrādj", *EI*[1].

4 *Inbāʾ*, Vol. III, p. 99. Physicians diagnosed the man as insane, and thus he escaped execution. For the Manṣūrī Hospital see, e.g., Dols, *Black Death*, p. 176.

5 For al-Ḥākim Mosque see most recently J. M. Bloom, "The Mosque of al-Ḥākim in Cairo", *Muqarnas* 1 (1983), 15–36.

6 *Sulūk*, Vol. IV, p. 511.

7 *Badāʾiʿ*, Vol. IV, p. 161.

8 Margaret Spufford, *Small Books and Pleasant Histories: Popular Fiction and its Readership in Seventeenth-Century England* (Athens, Ga., 1982), p. 194.

9 For the differences between "official" and "popular" religions, see, e.g., R. W. Scribner, "Ritual and Popular Religion in Catholic Germany at the Time of the Reformation", *Journal of Ecclesiastical History* 35 (1984), 47–8.

10 Keith Thomas, *Religion and the Decline of Magic* (New York, 1971), esp. pp. 154, 159–66.

11 Jean Delumeau, *Catholicism between Luther and Voltaire: A New View of the Counter-Reformation* (London, 1977), p. 161. For a survey of scholarly literature on this subject see John van Engen, "The Christian Middle Ages as an Historiographical Problem", *AHR* 91 (1986), 519–52.

12 Margaret Aston, "Popular Religious Movements in the Middle Ages", in Geoffrey Barraclough (ed.), *The Christian World: A Social and Cultural History* (New York, 1981), p. 157.

13 See e.g., Jacques Toussaret, *Le Sentiment religieux en Flandre à la fin du moyen âge* (Paris, 1963).

14 To some examples given at the beginning of this chapter one can add, for instance, reports on eating and wine drinking during the month of Ramaḍān. See, e.g., *Khiṭaṭ*, Vol. II, p. 24 (year 1191); *Ḥawādith*, pp. 301–2 (year 1457).

15 For such a definition of popular religion see Natalie Z. Davis, "From 'Popular Religion' to Religious Cultures", in Steven Ozment (ed.), *Reformation Europe: A Guide to Research* (St Louis, 1982), pp. 321–2.

16 For this term see n. 26 below.

17 *Nujūm*, Vol. XI, pp. 118–19; *Badāʾiʿ*, Vol. I, pt 2, pp. 93, 104 (10,000 and 50,000 respectively).

18 *Ṭabaqāt ṣughrā*, pp. 65–6.

19 For this term, see n. 26 below.

20 *Khiṭaṭ*, Vol. II, p. 415, cited also in Annemarie Schimmel, "Some Glimpses of the Religious Life in Egypt during the Later Mamlūk Period", *Islamic Studies* 4 (1965), 376. For Saʿīd as-Suʿadāʾ see *Khiṭaṭ*, Vol. II, pp. 415–16; J. Spencer Trimingham, *The Sufi Orders in Islam* (Oxford, 1971), p. 18.

21 A number of eminent Sufis were Egyptians, at least by adoption: Dhū an-Nūn (d. 860), ʿUmar b. al-Farīd (d. 1234), and al-Buṣīrī (d. 1296). See Trimingham, *Sufi Orders*, pp. 44–5. Dancing Sufis of an unspecified order (*ṭarīqa*) are already mentioned in the reign of the Fāṭimid al-Āmir (1101–29). See *Ittiʿāẓ*, Vol. III, p. 131. Salāḥ ad-Dīn welcomed Sufis to Egypt, and he and his followers founded and endowed many hospices, of which al-Maqrīzī gives a long list. See Trimingham, *Sufi Orders*, pp. 17–19.

22 Muhammad Umar Memon, *Ibn Taimiya's Struggle against Popular Religion* (Mouton, 1976), p. 61. Information on orders in the Mamluk period is meagre, however. On the Qalandāriyya see Tahsin Yaziçi, "Ḳalandāriyya", *EI*[2]; Trimingham, *Sufi Orders*, pp. 267–8. According to *Khiṭaṭ*, Vol. II, p. 433, a *zāwiya* was built for this order in the last years of the thirteenth century. On the Shādhiliyya and the Aḥmadiyya see Michael Winter, *Society and Religion in Early Ottoman Egypt: Studies in the Writings of ʿAbd al-Wahhāb al-Shaʿrānī* (New Brunswick, 1982), pp. 88–101. On the Wafāʾiyya see Trimingham, *Sufi Orders*, p. 49.

23 Trimingham, *Sufi Orders*, pp. 39 (contrast p. 21 n. 4), 45–6, 76; Winter, *Society and Religion*, pp. 102–12; Ernst Bannerth, "La Rifāʿiyya en Egypte", *Mélanges de l'Institut dominicain d'études orientales du Caire* 10 (1970), 4–6.

24 For material support see, e.g., Leonor Fernandes, "Three Sufi Foundations in a 15th Century Waqfiyya", *AI* 17 (1981), 141–56; Fernandes, "The Foundation of Baybars al-Jashankir: Its Waqf, History, and Architecture", *Muqarnas* 4 (1987), 21–42; Fernandes, *The Evolution of a Sufi Institution in Mamluk Egypt: The Khanqah* (Berlin, 1988), pp. 96–7. For the penetration of Sufism into circles of Egyptian scholars already in the second half of the thirteenth century see Denis Gril, "Une source inédite pour l'histoire du *taṣawwuf* en Egypte au XII/XIIIe siècle", in *Livre du centenaire 1880–1980* (Cairo, 1980), p. 445. Biographical literature on Egyptian *ʿulamāʾ* in the fourteenth and fifteenth centuries abounds with information (which has hardly been studied) on men who combined both orthodox scholarship and Sufism. Winter writes, apparently as regards the fifteenth and early sixteenth centuries, that the number of scholars who left their religious posts at the peak of their careers in order to devote the rest of their lives to Sufism, under the guidance of *shaykh*s often inferior to themselves in learning, was legion. "In many cases the difference between a Sufi and an *ʿālim* was not a matter of conviction and religious attitude but simply of occupation. The '*ʿulamāʾ* class was permeated with Sufism to such an extent that the distinction between the two categories is sometimes difficult to define." See *Society and Religion*, pp. 30–1.

25 Lapidus, *Muslim Cities*, pp. 105–6, writing of the "closely knit [Sufi] bodies" as "important foci of communal aggregation", concludes, however, that "the nature of their ties with the population at large remains obscure". What follows below is an attempt to go beyond this statement and to provide some concrete information.

26 For a most recent discussion of Sufi institutions in Mamluk Egypt see Donald P. Little, "The Nature of *Khānqāh*s, *Ribāṭ*s, and *Zāwiya*s under the Mamlūks", in Wael B. Hallaq and Donald P. Little (eds.), *Islamic Studies Presented to Charles J. Adams* (Leiden, 1991), pp. 91–105. By the latter part of the fourteenth century there

were nine *zāwiya*s in Fusṭāṭ and more than twenty in Cairo. See *Intiṣār*, Vol. IV, pt 1, pp. 103–4; *Khiṭaṭ*, Vol. II, pp. 430–6. For *zāwiya*s in the fourteenth and fifteenth centuries, see, e.g., *'Iqd*, pp. 96–7; *Nujūm*, Vol. XVI, pp. 191, 214. Recent excavations in the courtyard of 'Amr b. al-'Āṣ Mosque in Fusṭāṭ brought to light the foundations of residences which were most likely the *zāwiya*s mentioned by chroniclers. See Layla 'Ali Ibrāhīm, "The Zāwiya of Šaiḫ Zain ad-Dīn Yūsuf in Cairo", *Mitteilungen des Deutschen Archäologischen Institut: Abteilung Kairo* 34 (1978), 97 and n. 81. One of these was possibly the "convent" of Muḥammad as-Safārī (d. 1451). For further information on him see *Ḥawādith*, pp. 106–7 and p. 21 above. There were *zāwiya*s also in al-Azhar Mosque and, according to al-Maqrīzī, seven hundred and fifty persons inhabited them in the year 1415. See Ibrāhīm, "Zāwiya", 97 and n. 81. For the organization of one *zāwiya*, established in the years following the Ottoman conquest of Egypt, see Leonor Fernandes, "Two Variations on the Same Theme: the *zāwiya* of Ḥasan al-Rūmī, the *takiyya* of Ibrāhīm al-Ğulšanī", *AI* 21 (1985), 95–111.

27 Fernandes, *Khanqah*, p. 33.

28 *Inbā'*, Vol. I, pp. 49–50.

29 For some speculations see Winter, *Society and Religion*, pp. 131–2.

30 Ibid., pp. 131–2.

31 *Ṭabaqāt kubrā*, Vol. II, p. 137; Winter, *Society and Religion*, p. 126 and n. 2.

32 *Khiṭaṭ*, Vol. II, p. 434; Ibn Furāt, Vol. VIII, pp. 72–3. For further information on him see also *Manhal*, Vol. I, pp. 177–8; *Nujūm*, Vol. VII, pp. 374–5.

33 *Nujūm*, Vol. VIII, p. 280.

34 *Nujūm*, Vol. X, p. 242.

35 *Nujūm*, Vol. XI, p. 385; Ibn Furāt, Vol. IX, pp. 173–4; *Ḍaw'*, Vol. II, p. 50.

36 *Khiṭaṭ*, Vol. II, pp. 434–5; *Ṭabaqāt kubrā*, Vol. II, p. 2. The term *talḥīn* (composing a melody) should probably be read as *talqīn* [*adh-dhikr*].

37 *Khiṭaṭ*, Vol. II, pp. 327–8; *Inbā'*, Vol. III, p. 105; *Ḍaw'*, Vol. II, pp. 111–13. Ash-Sha'rānī (*Ṭabaqāt kubrā*, Vol. II, pp. 66–7) claimed to have seen an autograph of the sermons in sixty quires. See also Winter, *Society and Religion*, p. 94.

38 *Sulūk*, Vol. IV, pp. 815–16; *Ḍaw'*, Vol. II, p. 50; *Tuḥfa*, p. 209. He was first a Shāfi'ite student, then became acquainted with a Sufi named Muḥammad b. az-Zayyāt (d. 1402), an associate of the above-mentioned Yaḥayā aṣ-Ṣanāfīrī, who was apparently successful in directing him into Sufism. The above-mentioned Ḥusayn al-Khabbāz initiated him to the Shādhilite order by dressing him in the special Sufi garment (*khirqa*). He also had close contacts with members of the Qādiriyya order. Later in his life he migrated from Cairo to Damascus, where he founded a *zāwiya* as well. For his writings see *GAL*, Vol. II, pp. 147–8; *GAL Suppl.*, Vol. II, pp. 149–50.

39 Ibn 'Arabshāh, *at-Ta'līf aṭ-ṭāhir fī shiyam al-Malik aẓ-Ẓāhir*, London, British Library MS BM Or. 3026, fo. 123b. For further information on him see also *Badā'i'*, Vol. II, p. 238.

40 *Ḥawādith*, p. 33; *Nujūm*, Vol. XVI, p. 164. Ibn Taghrī Birdī notes: "We have profited from his blessing and the blessings of his ancestors" (*wa-nafa'nā bi-barakatihi wa-barakāt salafihi*).

41 He arrived in Cairo in the 1440s and became wealthy from alms he received. See *Nujūm*, Vol. XVI, p. 347; *Badā'i'*, Vol. II, p. 437. There is a detailed biography in *Ḍaw'*, Vol. I, pp. 363–6.

42 *Ṭabaqāt ṣughrā*, p. 77.

43 This *ribāṭ* was built for women in 1285 or 1286 and was situated near the *khānqāh* founded by Baybars. See *Khiṭaṭ*, Vol. II, pp. 427–8.
44 She died in 1394. See *Sulūk*, Vol. III, p. 823.
45 For references see n. 37 above.
46 ʿAbd al-Bāsiṭ, *Ḥawādith*, fo. 393b.
47 D. L. d'Avray, *The Preaching of the Friars: Sermons Diffused from Paris before 1300* (Oxford, 1985), pp. 258–9, quoting Mark Pattison. See also John C. Somerville, *Popular Religion in Restoration England* (Gainesville, 1977), p. 2; Gurevich, *Popular Culture*, pp. 1–6.
48 Cf. d'Avray's qualification that "sermons take us to water but do not let us drink", since we never know how much the audiences of popular preachers assimilated, or how far preachers were really bound by the preconceptions of their hearers. *Preaching*, p. 259. For the use of medieval sermons for studying popular religion see, e.g., Alexander Murray, "Religion among the Poor in Thirteenth-Century France: The Testimony of Humbert de Romans", *Traditio* 30 (1974), 285–324.
49 See n. 1 above.
50 *Sulūk*, Vol. II, p. 408.
51 *Inbā'*, Vol. II, pp. 87–8: "wa-badat minhu alfāẓ munkara wa-fīhā jar'a ʿaẓīma ʿala kitāb Allāh". Ibn Ḥajar al-ʿAsqalānī gives a few examples of the Shaykh's peculiar readings of the Qur'ān. For further information on him see *Ḍaw'*, Vol. X, p. 426.
52 His full name was Tāj ad-Dīn Abū'l-Faḍl Aḥmad b. Muḥammad. For his biography see G. Makdisi, "Ibn ʿAṭā' Allāh", *EI²*; *Ibn ʿAtā' illāh's Sufi Aphorisms (Kitāb al-Ḥikam)*, trans. with intr. and notes by Victor Danner (Leiden, 1973), pp. 1–12; Abū'l-Wafā' at-Taftazānī, *Ibn ʿAṭā' Allāh al-Iskandarī wa-taṣawwufuhu*, 2nd edn (Cairo, 1969).
53 For this institution see, e.g., Petry, *Civilian Elite*, pp. 331–2.
54 Ibn ʿAṭā' Allāh's most important works are the following:

I. *Miftāḥ al-falāḥ wa-miṣbāḥ al-arwāḥ* (*The Key of Success and the Lamp of Spirits*), a concise and comprehensive exposition of the Sufi ritual of invocation (*dhikr*). There are several Arabic editions, e.g., on the margins of ash-Shaʿrānī, *Laṭā'if al-minan* (Cairo, 1331/1913). It is quite popular in present-day Sufi circles. For further information see *Aphorisms*, p. 12; Taftazānī, *Ibn ʿAtā' Allāh*, pp. 108–11. Most of the Arabic text has been translated into German by Florian Sobieroj, "Der Schlüssel des Heils, Ibn ʿAṭā' Allāhs Sufi-Schrift über das Gottgedenken", MA thesis, Freiburg i. Br., 1985.

II. *Kitāb al-ḥikam* (*Book of Aphorisms*), which centres around the notion of *ma'rifa* (gnosis) and relies on the metaphysical postulate, a classical Sufi doctrine, that the Divine Unity alone is the absolute or the infinite or the real; everything else is relative or finite or unreal. There are several Arabic editions. For a critical edition with a French translation and commentary see Paul Nwyia, *Ibn ʿAṭā' Allāh (m. 709/1309) et la naissance de la confrérie Šaḏilite* (Beirut, 1972). For an English translation and a commentary see *Aphorisms*.

III. *Al-Qaṣd al-mujarrad fī ma'rifat al-ism al-mufrad* (*The Pure Goal concerning Knowledge of the Unique Name*), sets out the doctrine of the Supreme Name (Allāh), both in itself and in relation to the other divine names of God. It has been characterized by its French translator as "un traité purement metaphysique et spirituel". For further information on this work see *Aphorisms*, p. 13. There is an

Arabic edition (Cairo 1348/1930), and a French trans., *Ibn 'Aṭā' Allāh, traité sur le nom Allah*, trans. and annot. Maurice Gloton (Paris, 1981).

IV. *Kitāb an-tanwīr fī isqāṭ at-tadbīr* (*The Book of Illumination concerning the Elimination of Self-Direction*), a simple and clear exposition of the Shādhilite approach to virtues such as patience and sincerity, and feelings such as hope, love, fear, etc. They are all seen as contained in a single virtue, "the elimination of self-direction". See *Aphorisms*, p. 13.

V. *Laṭā'if al-minan* (*Niceties of Blessings*), a biographical work on the two great masters of the Shādhiliyya order, Abū'l-Ḥasan ash-Shādhilī and Abū'l-'Abbās al-Mursī. See *Aphorisms*, p. 6 n. 1; p. 8 n. 1; p. 13; Taftazānī, *Ibn 'Aṭā' Allāh*, pp. 104–5.

55 Taftazānī, *Ibn 'Aṭā' Allāh*, p. 89.
56 *Aphorisms*, pp. 28–9.
57 Ibid., p. xiii.
58 Examples abound. See, e.g., *Aphorisms*, Nos. 77, 80.
59 Paris, Bibliothèque Nationale MS arabe 1299. For other titles of this work see Taftazānī, *Ibn 'Aṭā' Allāh*, pp. 106–7.
60 Taftazānī, *Ibn 'Aṭā' Allāh*, pp. 105–7.
61 I disagree with Danner (*Aphorisms*, pp. 13–14), who characterizes it as being of minor importance, though still quite popular, a composite work of extracts from other works.
62 *Tāj al-'arūs*, p. 69.
63 Ibid., pp. 24, 30, 62.
64 Ibid., p. 24.
65 Ibid., p. 77.
66 E.g., p. 22.
67 E.g., pp. 18, 43, 46–7, 49, 53, 55, 58, 59, 63, 64.
68 Ibid., pp. 2–4. See also pp. 7, 45–6, 62, 65.
69 Ibid., p. 61. See also pp. 39–40, 66.
70 Ibid., pp. 13, 57, 80.
71 E.g., pp. 11, 28, 29, 31, 32, 33, 36, 49, 57, 60, 77, 78, 81.
72 Ibid., p. 36.
73 Ibid., p. 59.
74 Ibid., p. 78.
75 Ibid., p. 31.
76 Ibid., p. 46.
77 Ibid., p. 49.
78 Ibid., pp. 62–3.
79 Ibid., p. 63.
80 Ibid., pp. 84–5.
81 Ibid., p. 55.
82 Ibid., p. 21.
83 Ibid., p. 25.
84 Ibid., p. 25.
85 Ibid., p. 21.
86 Ibid., p. 22.
87 He is mentioned as a source in, e.g., pp. 3, 25, 26, 52, 56. On p. 3 he is described as one of the "seven substitutes" (*abdāl*).

88 Taftazānī, *Ibn 'Aṭā' Allāh*, p. 52.
89 Ibid., p. 57.
90 Ibid., p. 30.
91 Ibid., p. 9.
92 See L. Gardet, "Dhikr", *EI*².
93 See n. 54, No. I above.
94 *Tāj al-'arūs*, p. 20.
95 Ibid., p. 21. See also p. 42.
96 Ibid., p. 53.
97 Ibid., p. 62.
98 E.g., pp. 5, 20.
99 Ibid., p. 22.
100 See p. 12 and n. 33 above.
101 See p. 11 and n. 20 above. According to an hagiographical account, the man was Karīm ad-Dīn al-Āmulī. See Memon, *Ibn Taimiya*, pp. 54–5.
102 The matter was referred to the Shāfi'ite qadi, who called for a council. A great part of the accusations against Ibn Taymiyya were found groundless, but the matter assumed a grave aspect when Ibn 'Aṭā' Allāh called in question the validity of Ibn Taymiyya's views on the role of the Prophet as an intercessor. Subsequently, Ibn Taymiyya was offered the choice between residence in Alexandria or Damascus under certain conditions, and prison. He opted for Damascus. See ibid., pp. 54–5; *Sulūk*, Vol. II, p. 40 (the name there is Ibn 'Aṭā'). See also *Nujūm*, Vol. VIII, p. 280; *Bidāya*, Vol. XIV, p. 45; Makdisi, "Ibn 'Aṭā' Allāh", *EI*². For Ibn Taymiyya's polemics against the Sufis see, e.g., Memon, *Ibn Taimiya*, pp. 51, 62–6. For his anti-Sufi works see pp. 377–8.
103 *Durar*, Vol. I, pp. 291–2, No. 700, notes that Ibn 'Aṭā' Allāh had followers among the commoners (*'āmma*).
104 H. Fuchs, "Mawlid", *EI*¹; H. Fuchs and F. de Jong, "Mawlid", *EI*². For the celebration of Muḥammad's *mawlid* in Egypt at the beginning of our century see J. W. McPherson, *The Moulids of Egypt* (Cairo, 1941), pp. 263–73.
105 *Dhayl*, Vol. III, pp. 280–1.
106 *Badā'i'*, Vol. II, p. 437.
107 *Sulūk*, Vol. III, p. 576; Ibn Furāt, Vol. IX, pp. 27, 42–3; *Inbā'*, Vol. I, pp. 350–1; *Durar*, Vol. I, p. 410, No. 973. *Nuzha*, Vol. I, p. 169, has 1,000 jugs.
108 *Nujūm*, Vol. XI, p. 315.
109 Many of the Egyptian *mawlids*, however, were initiated in the sixteenth century. See Winter, *Society and Religion*, p. 178.
110 For al-Badawī's biography see K. Vollers and E. Littmann, "Aḥmad al-Badawī", *EI*².
111 *Tibr*, p. 176; *Ṭabaqāt kubrā*, Vol. I, p. 148. This is what Lane had to say on this particular *mawlid* in the early nineteenth century: "The tomb of the saint attracts almost as many visitors, at the period of the great annual festival, from the metropolis, and from various parts of Lower Egypt, as Mekkah does pilgrims from the whole of the Muslim world." Quoted in Vollers and Littmann, "Aḥmad al-Badawī". Lane noted that many Egyptians who made the Pilgrimage first went to Ṭanṭā, and therefore al-Badawī was called "Door of the Prophet" (*bāb an-nabī*).
112 *Badā'i'*, Vol. II, p. 258; *Tibr*, pp. 176–7; Ignaz Goldziher, *Muslim Studies*, Vol. II (London, 1971), p. 310. The year mentioned by Goldziher is AH 852. K. Vollers, "Aḥmed al-Badawī", *EI*¹, misinterpreted the passage in *Badā'i'* (Būlāq, 1311–12/

(1893–5)), Vol. II, p. 30 l. 5. The word *baṭala* should not be understood as "sunk into neglect", but "was suppressed", as the passage in the Wiesbaden edition clearly shows.

113 *Ṭabaqāt kubrā*, Vol. II, p. 107; Winter, *Society and Religion*, pp. 57, 98.
114 Some information on him in *Inbā'*, Vol. I, p. 357.
115 According to McPherson, *Moulids*, p. 228, this *mawlid* was probably established soon after Inbābī's death (1388), and has been one of the oldest in Egypt. It absorbed an ancient festival of Isis, the *laylat an-nuqṭa*, when multitudes once watched for the falling of a precious tear of Isis into the Nile. The *mawlid* took place at the spot where the tear was believed to have fallen. For celebrations in our own century see pp. 228–9.
116 *Badā'i'*, Vol. II, p. 37.
117 *Badā'i'*, Vol. I, pt 2, p. 391. Celebrations are mentioned in the following years: 1475 ('Abd al-Bāsiṭ, *Ḥawādith*, fo. 261a); 1491 (ibid., fo. 403a); 1507 (*Badā'i'*, Vol. IV, p. 114); 1508 (ibid., p. 132); 1509 (ibid., p. 152); 1510 (ibid., p. 182); 1511 (ibid., p. 214); 1514 (ibid., p. 375). See also Annemarie Schimmel, "Sufismus und Heiligenverehrung im Spätmittelalterlichen Ägypten", in E. Gräf (ed.), *Festschrift Werner Caskel* (Leiden, 1968), pp. 277–8; Schimmel, "Religious Life", 372, with some inaccuracies.
118 *Badā'i'*, Vol. IV, p. 114; Schimmel, "Religious Life", 372–3. Her suggestion about the identity of Suwaydān is questionable.
119 Winter, *Society and Religion*, pp. 212–13 nn. 119, 120.
120 Hamilton A. R. Gibb, *Studies on the Civilization of Islam* (Boston, 1962), p. 215.
121 Memon, *Ibn Taimiya*, p. 58.
122 Ibid., pp. 58–9.
123 Marshall G. S. Hodgson, *The Venture of Islam* (Chicago, 1974), Vol. II, pp. 458–9. For the nexus of self-styled saints and miracles and its importance for popular Christianity in medieval times see Gurevich, *Popular Culture*, pp. 69–74.
124 Hodgson, *Venture*, Vol. II, p. 207.
125 *'Iqd*, p. 136.
126 Ibid., pp. 96–7.
127 Arabic *al-fuqarā' as-saṭḥiyya*. For Aḥmad al-Badawī dwelling on a roof of a house in Ṭanṭā see *Badā'i'*, Vol. I, pt 1, p. 336. For Saṭūḥī as one of al-Badawī's surnames see *Nujūm*, Vol. VII, p. 252. Cf. Aḥmad Ṣafī Ḥusayn, *al-Adab aṣ-ṣūfī fī Miṣr fi'l-qarn as-sābi' al-hijrī* (Cairo, 1964), p. 39. A Sufi *shaykh* named Aḥmad as-Saṭūḥī, also known as ash-Shaykh Kharūf (d. 1461), had a *zāwiya* on the road to Būlāq. See *Ḍaw'*, Vol. I, p. 292.
128 *Beiträge zur Geschichte der Mamlukensultane in dem Jahren 690–741 der Hiǧra nach arabischen Handschriften*, ed. K. V. Zetterstéen (Leiden, 1919), p. 129.
129 Emile Dermenghem, *Vies des saints musulmans* (Paris, 1981), p. 236, explains *majdhūb* as "un attiré, jouet passif de l'attraction divine, dont l'esprit est au ciel, absorbé dans le monde des Réalités, tandis que son corps est encore en retard sur la terre. Il représente à sa façon l'aspect passif de la vie mystique, la primauté de la grâce, de la *jadzba* qui vaut tout le travail des hommes et des génies."
130 *Sulūk*, Vol. III, p. 467; *Inbā'*, Vol. I, p. 231.
131 *Ṭabaqāt kubrā*, Vol. II, p. 76.
132 *Ḥawādith*, pp. 62–4; *Nujūm*, Vol. XV, pp. 406–7; *Tibr*, pp. 302–3.
133 *Ṭabaqāt kubrā*, Vol. II, p. 146.
134 Tahsin Yaziçi, "Ḳalandāriyya", *EI*[2].

135 Memon, *Ibn Taimiya*, pp. 64–6.

136 For the tendency of the majority of saints' miracles in medieval Christendom to address human needs see Donald Weinstein and Rudolph M. Bell, *Saints & Society: The Two Worlds of Western Christendom, 1000–1700* (Chicago, 1982), pp. 143–4.

137 Leonor Fernandes, "Some Aspects of the *zāwiya* in Egypt at the Eve of the Ottoman Conquest", *AI* 19 (1983), 15. Fernandes associates this *topos*, chronologically, with the late Mamluk period.

138 *Badā'i'*, Vol. I, pt 2, pp. 6, 14.

139 *Ṭabaqāt kubrā*, Vol. II, p. 68. For more information on him see also *Ḍaw'*, Vol. I, pp. 85–6; Winter, *Society and Religion*, pp. 95–6.

140 *Ṭabaqāt kubrā*, Vol. II, pp. 88, 90. For further information on him see also Jean-Claude Garcin, "Histoire et hagiographie de l'Egypte musulmane à la fin de l'époque mamelouke et au début de l'époque ottomane", in *Hommages à la mémoire de Serge Souneron 1927–1976*, Vol. II: *Egypte post-pharaonique* (Cairo, 1979), pp. 293–6, rep. in Garcin, *Espaces, pouvoirs et idéologies de l'Egypte médiévale* (London, 1987); Winter, *Society and Religion*, pp. 43–4.

141 *Ṭabaqāt kubrā*, Vol. II, pp. 94–5.

142 On this mosque see J.-C. Garcin, "Index des Ṭabaqāt de Sha'rānī", *AI* 6 (1966), 32 n. 3; Garcin, "L'Insertion sociale de Sha'rānī dans le milieu cairote", *Colloque international sur l'histoire du Caire* (Cairo, 1969), p. 163.

143 *Ṭabaqāt kubrā*, Vol. II, pp. 116–17; *Ṭabaqāt ṣughrā*, p. 61.

144 Doris Behrens-Abouseif, "An Unlisted Monument of the Fifteenth Century: The Dome of Zāwiyat al-Damirdāš", *AI* 18 (1982), 106.

145 Franz Rosenthal, *The Herb: Hashish versus Medieval Muslim Society* (Leiden, 1971), p. 100.

146 Weinstein and Bell, *Saints & Society*, p. 13. The following is another passage worthy of quotation:

> As in the case of medieval Christian saints . . . it is the *perception* we are documenting, the *reputation* we are gauging, more than the actual fact of the saint's acts of humility or charity. This is the case whether a saint was a real historical personage with a verifiable holy life, or a person for whom a reputation for sanctity was somehow well constructed . . . As Delooz summed it up so well, "the reputation of sanctity is the collective mental representation of someone as a saint, whether based on a knowledge of facts that have *really* happened, or whether based on facts that have been at least in part *constructed* if not entirely imagined. But in truth, all saints, more or less, appear to be constructed in the sense that being necessarily saints in consequence of a reputation created by others and a role that others expect of them, they are remodelled to correspond to collective mental representations.

See ibid., p. 9.

147 Sa'īd 'Abd al-Fattāḥ 'Ashūr, *al-Mujtama' al-miṣrī fī 'aṣr salāṭīn al-mamālīk* (Cairo, 1962), p. 31.

148 *Sulūk*, Vol. III, p. 71.

149 *Inbā'*, Vol. II, p. 70: "wa-shafā'atuhu maqbūla 'inda as-sulṭān wa-man dūnahu".

150 For high grain prices around that time see *Ḥawādith*, pp. 100, 105.

151 Ibid., pp. 106–8; *Nujūm*, Vol. XVI, p. 5. In the event, the Shaykh died shortly afterwards. See the interesting commentary in *Nujūm*.

152 For further information on him see also p. 17 above.

153 *Ṭabaqāt kubrā*, Vol. II, pp. 106–7.

154 Fernandes, "Aspects of the *zāwiya*", 9, 11. In Lapidus, *Muslim Cities*, the role of mediator is placed exclusively on the *'ulamā'*. They feature as the sole communal

leadership in Mamluk cities. For a summary of this role see, e.g., pp. 141–2. Sufi *shaykhs* are seldom discussed, and despite some recognition of Sufism's communal role, Sufis are portrayed as a marginal element. See pp. 105–6. Lapidus's presentation of the *'ulamā'* should be contrasted with the following: "In Cairo, under the watchful eye of the sultan, the upper ranks of the juridical-scholarly establishment stood somewhat aloof from the problems of the masses. Although they were acknowledged by the common people as the leaders of the Muslim community, the impact of their litigation, especially on the lower orders, is difficult to assess. Moreover, the Sharī'a courts could do little to mitigate the excesses from on high that ordinary people endured as a fact of life." Petry, *Civilian Elite*, p. 321.

155 Shujā'ī, p. 16.

156 *Ḍaw'*, Vol. I, p. 201; *Nujūm*, Vol. XV, p. 139. For further information on him see also *Manhal*, Vol. I, No. 111; Petry, *Civilian Elite*, p. 71.

157 *Nujūm*, Vol. XVI, pp. 328–9; *Ḍaw'*, Vol. VI, p. 64, No. 219.

158 See sources in n. 156 above.

159 *Sulūk*, Vol. II, p. 50. For further information on him see also Ṣafī al-Dīn Ibn Abī'l-Manṣūr Ibn Ẓāfir, *La Risāla: biographies des maîtres spirituels connus par un cheikh égyptien du VIIe–XIIIe siècle*, ed. and trans. Denis Gril (Cairo, 1986), pp. 217–20.

160 Thus, in 1011, Egyptian women were banned from performing the cult. See *Khiṭaṭ*, Vol. II, p. 287. In 1326 Ibn Baṭṭūṭa recorded in Alexandria the people's habit of visiting graves after concluding their prayers. See *Riḥla* (Beirut, 1379/1960), p. 28. Al-Maqrīzī, writing in the first half of the fifteenth century, leaves no doubt that *ziyāra* in the Mamluk period was an important part of popular religion. In his description of a fabricated grave of one Abū Turāb, he tells how "ignorant men and women now turn in times of need, when only Allāh should be prayed to, and request from graves what they should have done only from God. Of the graves they expect release of debts, the supply of daily bread. Sterile women pray at graves for offspring, here they make their offerings of oil and other gifts in the belief that through these they would be delivered of their difficulties and improve their conditions." See *Khiṭaṭ*, Vol. II, pp. 49–50.

161 The famous Fāṭimid vizier Badr al-Jamālī is credited with cultivating the public cult of 'Alīd saints. The building of shrines was part of his policy to build up popular devotion to the 'Alīds and to the Fāṭimid dynasty itself. Later, the Ayyūbids, in a triumphant assertion of their own Sunni rule, built Shāfi'ī's mausoleum in the midst of 'Alīd tombs. See Caroline Williams, "The Cult of 'Alīd Saints in the Fāṭimid Monuments of Cairo, Part II: The Mausolea", *Muqarnas* 3 (1985), 57. For a recent criticism of this argument see Christopher S. Taylor, "The Cult of Saints in Late Medieval Egypt", *Newsletter of the American Research Center in Egypt* 139 (1987), 13–16. It seems to me that Taylor fails to make the necessary distinction between an organized form of the cult, for which the Fāṭimids were responsible, and a private, spontaneous form, which could have preceded Fāṭimid policies.

162 For a brief treatment of the ritualistic practices during *ziyāra*s in modern Cairo see F. de Jong, "Cairene *Ziyāra*-Days: A Contribution to the Study of Saint Veneration in Islam", *Welt des Islams* NS 17 (1976–7), 27. Christopher S. Taylor has studied the cult of saints in medieval Egypt in a recent doctoral dissertation which I have been unable to consult.

163 *Badā'i'*, Vol. I, pt 1, p. 390.

164 *Khiṭaṭ*, Vol. II, pp. 434–5, who comments that the claim was "from the Devil".

165 *Badā'i'*, Vol. I, pt 1, p. 528.

2 Al-Bakrī's biography of Muḥammad

1 *Mīzān al-i'tidāl fī naqd* (or *tarājim*) *ar-rijāl* (Cairo, 1325/1907–8), Vol. I, p. 53. In the 1382/1963 edition of this text the passage is in Vol. I, p. 112, No. 440. References in F. Rosenthal, "al-Bakrī, Abū'l-Ḥasan", *EI*[2].

2 See M. Canard, "Dhū'l-Himma", *EI*[2]; M. Canard, "Baṭṭāl", *EI*[2]; Udo Steinbach, *Dāt al-Himma, Kulturgeschichtliche Untersuchungen zu einem arabischen Volksroman* (Wiesbaden, 1972).

3 See R. Hartmann, "'Antar, Romance of", *EI*[1]; B. Heller, "'Antar, Sīrat", *EI*[2]; H. T. Norris, *The Adventures of Antar* (Warminster, 1980).

4 Ahlwardt, No. 9171, lists parts II–VIII of the "History (*ta'rīkh*) of Aḥmad ad-Danif the Brave, the Shrewd and the Noble" (*min dhawī az-za'āra wash-shaṭāra wash-sharaf*). No. 9172 is the "Story (*qiṣṣa*) of Aḥmad ad-Danif". Ahlwardt has noted that a much shorter and substantially different version is found in the *Thousand and One Nights*. For Aḥmad ad-Danif in the *Nights* see Muḥammad Rajab an-Najjār, *Hikāyāt ash-shuṭṭār wa'l-'ayyārīn fi't-turāth al-'arabī* (Kuwait, 1981), pp. 259–78. The story of ad-Danif does not appear, however, in Muhsin Mahdi's recent edition of the *Nights*. The Egyptian chronicler Ibn Taghrī Birdī mentions one Aḥmad Danif as a popular archetype of robbers in the early centuries of Islam. According to Ibn Taghrī Birdī, he was in the category of other medieval heroes such as the Baghdadi Ḥamdī or Ibn Ḥamdī,who had been executed in 943 or 944. See *Nujūm*, Vol. III, p. 281. Strangely enough, in other sources we read that in 1486 the Mamluk sultan Qāyit Bāy ordered the execution of the gangster (*min kibar al-minsar*) Aḥmad ad-Danif, "with whom too many stories of the art of robbery are connected". See *Badā'i'*, Vol. III, p. 234; 'Abd al-Bāsiṭ, *Ḥawādith*, fo. 358b. It seems that the way to explain this rather late reference to Danif is that the fifteenth-century figure was named after his earlier namesake. Najjār, *Shuṭṭār*, pp. 65, 66–7, seems to imply the same. Aḥmad ad-Danif served as a popular thief model in Ottoman Egypt. See ibid., p. 69. Around the turn of our century, a *mawlid* ("birthday") of Aḥmad ad-Danif used to be celebrated at the Qarāfa Cemetery in Cairo. See L. Massignon, "La Cité des morts au Caire", in his *Opera Minora* (Beirut, 1963), Vol. III, pp. 253–4. For Egyptian youths called Aḥmad ad-Danif in the 1940s see Najjār, *Shuṭṭār*, p. 71. For *danif* meaning "gravely ill", probably for some disease that the hero had contracted in his youth, see ibid., p. 102 n. 99.

5 *Bidāya*, Vol. IX, p. 334. H. T. Norris, "The Rediscovery of the Ancient Sagas of the Banū Hilāl", *BSOAS* 51 (1988), 470 n. 15, refers to another of al-Bakrī's works, *Futūḥ al-Yaman* (see below), as mentioned by Ibn Kathīr. I suspect that Fārūq Khūrshīd, on whom Norris relies, confused Ibn Kathīr's *Bidāya* and his *Tafsīr*.

6 *Lisān al-mīzān* (Hyderabad, 1929/1911), Vol. I, p. 202, reference in Rosenthal, "al-Bakrī".

7 *Ṣubḥ*, Vol. I, p. 454, reference in Franz Rosenthal, *A History of Muslim Historiography*, 2nd edn (Leiden, 1968), p. 191 n. 1.

8 For further information on him see *GAL* Suppl., Vol. II, p. 72; *Manhal*, Vol. I, pp. 147–53; *Ḍaw'*, Vol. I, pp. 138–45. He died in Aleppo, not in Cairo (as stated in *GAL*).

9 *Nūr an-nibrās 'alā sīrat Ibn Sayyid an-Nās*, Paris, Bibliothèque Nationale MS arabe 1968, fo. 2b: *wa-iyyāka wa-siyar al-Bakrī Aḥmad b. 'Abd Allāh Muḥammad b. al-Ḥasan fa-innahu kadhdhāb dajjāl wāḍi'l-qiṣaṣ*. Reference in Rosenthal,

Historiography, p. 191 n. 1. *Nūr an-nibrās* is a commentary on *'Uyūn al-āthār*, a *sīra* written by Ibn Sayyid an-Nās.

10 See the reference to as-Ṣafadī in n. 160 below. The editor of al-Majilisī's *Biḥār al-anwār*, 2nd edn (Tehran, 1956–72), Vol. XV, p. 26 n. 1, states that Ibn Taymiyya characterized al-Bakrī as an Ash'arite, and that Samhūdī, in his history of Medina, composed around 1483, mentioned the "lies" (*al-buṭlān wa'l-kidhb*) in al-Bakrī's *sīra*. I have been unable to verify these references, as they lack precise details.

11 Ibn Ḥajar al-Haytamī, *al-Fatāwā al-ḥadithiyya* (Cairo, 1353/1934), p. 116, reference in Rosenthal, "al-Bakrī". For further information on him see C. van Arendonk and J. Schacht, "Ibn Ḥadjar al-Haytamī", *EI*2.

12 I. *Ḍiyā' al-anwār*, undoubtedly the biography of Muḥammad (see below). It appears identical, despite the difference in titles, with the work mentioned by al-'Asqalānī as *adh-Dharwa(?) fī's-sīra an-nabawiyya*. Cf. *GAL* Suppl., Vol. I, p. 616, No. 2 (the Berlin manuscripts are 9525–6, not as listed). Nos. 2 and 3 in *GAL* Suppl., Vol. I, p. 616, are identical.

II. *Ra's al-ghūl*, undoubtedly the work known as *Futūḥ al-Yaman al-ma'rūf bi-ra's al-ghūl*. The Berlin manuscripts are listed in Ahlwardt, Nos. 9012–13. There are also Paris manuscripts (Bibliothèque Nationale MS arabe 1816, fos. 50–89; MS arabe 3837–9, which vary substantially). For printed editions see *GAL* Suppl., Vol. I, p. 616, No. 6; Rudi Paret, *Die legendäre Maghāzi – Literatur, arabische Dichtungen über die muslimischen Kriegszüge zu Mohammeds Zeit* (Tübingen, 1930), p. 131; Yūsuf A. Sarkīs, *Mu'jam al-maṭbū'āt al-'arabiyya wa'l-mu'arraba* (Cairo, 1928), col. 578. For a summary see Rosenthal, *Historiography*, pp. 191–3. Rosenthal implies distaste for this and similar works; see his sarcastic remarks on pp. 190, 192–3.

III. *Sharr ad-dahr*, unidentified.

IV. *Kitāb Kalandaja*(?), unidentified.

V. *Ḥiṣn ad-dawlab*, unidentified.

VI. *Kitāb al-ḥuṣūn as-sab'a wa-ṣāḥibihā Haḍḍām b. al-Hajjaf wa-ḥurūb al-imām 'Alī ma'ahu*, probably identical with *Qiṣṣat sayr al-imām 'Alī b. Abī Ṭālib wa-muḥārabatihi al-malik al-Haḍḍām b. al-Hajjaf wa-qatlihi al-ḥuṣūn as-sab'a*. For a Berlin manuscript see Ahlwardt, No. 9006. For several printed editions see *GAL* Suppl., Vol. I, p. 616, No. 7 (probably identical with No. 14). For a summary see Paret, *Maghāzi*, pp. 99–106. Sarkīs, *Mu'jam*, cols. 2009, 2016, lists the author as anonymous.

13 I. *Qiṣṣat az-Zibriqān b. Badr malik wādī Jayḥūn wa-wufūdihi 'alā an-nabī*. Cf. *GAL* Suppl., Vol. I, p. 616, No. 8. For other editions and a summary see Paret, *Maghāzi*, pp. 142–5. Sarkīs, *Mu'jam*, col. 1020, lists the author as anonymous.

II. *Futūḥ Ifrīqyā*. Cf. *GAL* Suppl., Vol. I, p. 616, No. 9. For a work entitled *Futūḥ Ifrīqyā*, recounting the adventures of a Maghribī hero named 'Abd Allāh b. Ja'far and the conquest of Tunis by Arab armies, see Bridget Connelly, *Arab Folk Epic and Identity* (Berkeley, 1986), pp. 4–5.

III. *Qiṣṣat as-sayyida Khadīja bint Khuwaylid wa-zawājihā bin-nabī*. Cf. *GAL* Suppl., Vol. I, p. 616, No. 10. This fragment could be the last part of the biography of Muḥammad (see p. 31 above).

IV. *Ghazwat al-aḥzāb* . . . Cf. *GAL* Suppl., Vol. I, p. 616, No. 11; Paret,

Maghāzi, pp. 33–6; Sarkīs, *Mu'jam*, col. 578; 'Ā'ida Ibrāhīm Nuṣayr, *al-Kutub al-'arabiyya llātī nushirat fī Miṣr 1900–1925* (Cairo, 1983), p. 122, No. 2/2476. The library of the London School of Oriental and African Studies possesses *Waq'at al-khandaq wa-ghazwat al-aḥzāb*, 2nd edn (Cairo, 1951), which I have been unable to consult.

V. *Islām aṭ-Ṭufayl b. 'Āmir ad-Dawsī*. Cf. *GAL*, Vol. I, p. 362, No. 15; Nuṣayr, *Kutub*, p. 309, No. 9/361 (erroneous title). For a summary see Paret, *Maghāzi*, pp. 54–8.

VI. *Kitāb* (or *Qiṣṣat*) *al-mi'rāj*. Cf. *GAL* Suppl., Vol. I, p. 616, No. 4. There is a Paris manuscript of this fragment, Bibliothèque Nationale MS arabe 1931, fos. 71a–91a.

VII. *Ghazwat Badr*. For a Berlin manuscript see Ahlwardt, No. 9627/1. For other versions and a summary see Paret, *Maghāzi*, pp. 1–11.

VIII. *Ghazwat Uḥud*. For a Berlin manuscript see Ahlwardt, Nos. 8982, 9627/2. For a summary see Paret, *Maghāzi*, pp. 16–26.

IX. *Futūḥ Makka*. For a Berlin manuscript see Ahlwardt, No. 9627/3. For a Tübingen manuscript see Max Weisweiler, *Verzeichnis der arabischen Handschriften der Universitätsbibliothek Tübingen* (Leipzig, 1930), No. 139/8. Both Weisweiler and Paret (*Maghāzi*, p. 38) followed Brockelmann's (*GAL* Suppl., Vol. I, p. 616, No. 5) erroneous identification of the *Futūḥ* with *ad-Durra al-mukallala* (see below), another work attributed to al-Bakrī. For a summary see Paret, *Maghāzi*, pp. 38–44.

X. *Ad-Durra al-mukallala fī futūḥ Makka al-mubajjala*. For manuscripts see *GAL* Suppl., Vol. I, p. 616, No. 5 (with the exception of the Tübingen manuscript); Paris, Bibliothèque Nationale MS arabe 4839 (*ad-Durra al-mukalkala* (*sic*). For printed editions see Sarkīs, *Mu'jam*, col. 581. Elsewhere Brockelmann attributed this work to Muḥammad b. 'Abd ar-Raḥmān Abū'l-Makārim al-Bakrī (1492–1545). See C. Brockelmann, "al-Bakrī, Muḥammad b. 'Abd al-Raḥmān . . . ", *EI*².

XI. *Ghazwat Banī Qurayẓa*. For a Berlin manuscript see Ahlwardt, No. 9627/4. For a summary see Paret, *Maghāzi*, pp. 128–30.

XII. *Ghazwat Tābūk*. For a Berlin manuscript see Ahlwardt, No. 9627/5. For other versions and a summary see Paret, *Maghāzi*, pp. 49–54.

XIII. *Ḥadīth Talḥa wa-Ghamra wa-abūhā* [*sic*] *al-'Abbās* . . . For a Berlin manuscript see Ahlwardt, No. 9054/2. For a summary see Paret, *Maghāzi*, pp. 136–7.

XIV. *Ghazwat Banī Naẓīr*. For a Berlin manuscript see Ahlwardt, No. 8989/2. For a summary see Paret, *Maghāzi*, pp. 126–7.

XV. *Sīrat al-imām 'Alī b. Abī Ṭālib ilā'l-ḥiṣn al-azraq*. For a Berlin manuscript see Ahlwardt, No. 9021. For a summary see Paret, *Maghāzi*, pp. 109–11.

XVI. *Sīrat al-imām 'Alī b. Abī Ṭālib wa-Khālid b. al-Walīd* . . . For a Berlin manuscript see Ahlwardt, No. 9005/2. For a summary see Paret, *Maghāzi*, p. 66.

XVII. *Ghazwat Bi'r Ma'ūna*. For a Berlin manuscript see Ahlwardt, No. 9020/2. For a summary see Paret, *Maghāzi*, pp. 26–7.

XVIII. *Sīrat . . . 'Alī b. Abī Ṭālib ilā'l-Muqaffa'*. For a Berlin manuscript see Ahlwardt, No. 9020/1. For a summary see Paret, *Maghāzi*, pp. 125–6.

XIX. *Ghazwat al-imām 'Alī 'alā 'Abd Habbār b. 'Abd Zinjīr*. For a Berlin manuscript see Ahlwardt, No. 9019. For other manuscripts and a summary see Paret, *Maghāzi*, pp. 11–14.

XX. *Khabar al-Mayyāsa b. Jābir ad-daḥḥāk ma'a'l-Miqdād*. For a Berlin manuscript see Ahlwardt, No. 8993/1. For other manuscripts and a summary see Paret, *Maghāzi*, pp. 118–22.

XXI. *Qiṣṣat islām sayyidina 'Abd ar-Raḥmān b. Abī Bakr* . . . For a Berlin manuscript see Ahlwardt, No. 8995. For a summary see Paret, *Maghāzi*, pp. 58–9.

XXII. *Ghazwat al-'Ajjāj*. For a Berlin manuscript see Ahlwardt, No. 9005/1. For a summary see Paret, *Maghāzi*, pp. 64–6.

XXIII. *Qiṣṣat Bi'r Dhāt al-'Alam* (or *Sīrat ghazāt Abī Sa'd al-Khadarī*) *wa-Ḥudhayfa al-Yamanī*. For a Berlin manuscript see Ahlwardt, No. 9007. For other manuscripts and a summary see Paret, *Maghāzi*, pp. 66–7.

XXIV. *Ghazwat al-'ankabūt*. For a Berlin manuscript see Ahlwardt, No. 9015. For other manuscripts and a summary see Paret, *Maghāzi*, pp. 67–71.

XXV. *Qiṣṣat qatl Waḥsh al-Hindī wa-islām ahl madīnat at-tuffāḥ*. For a Berlin manuscript see Ahlwardt, No. 9016. For other manuscripts and a summary see Paret, *Maghāzi*, pp. 137–9.

XXVI. *Qiṣṣat Ḥammād al-Fazārī*. For a Berlin manuscript see Ahlwardt, No. 9018. For a summary see Paret, *Maghāzi*, pp. 108–9.

XXVII. *Ghazwat Ghashshām* . . . For a Berlin manuscript see Ahlwardt, No. 9105/8. For other manuscripts and a summary see Paret, *Maghāzi*, pp. 96–7.

XXVIII. *Ghazwat al-Arqat*. For a Berlin manuscript see Ahlwardt, Nos. 9138–9. For a summary see Paret, *Maghāzi*, pp. 71–83.

XXIX. *Mawlid al-imām wa'l-layth al-hammām 'Alī b. Abī Ṭālib* . . . Al-Bakrī is mentioned as a source. For a Berlin manuscript see Ahlwardt, No. 9001.

XXX. *Maqtal Banī Umayya*. Al-Bakrī is a source. For a Berlin manuscript see Ahlwardt, No. 9046.

It may be worthy of notice that two works listed by Brockelmann as attributed to Abū'l-Ḥasan al-Bakrī (*GAL* Suppl., Vol. I, p. 616, Nos. 12–13) are most likely not his (No. 12, *Faḍā'il* [*laylat*] *an-niṣf min Sha'bān*, is by the sixteenth-century Abū'l-Makārim al-Bakrī, for whom see No. X above and Sarkīs, *Mu'jam*, cols. 580–1. The common name al-Bakrī is probably the reason for this error). For the attribution to al-Bakrī of what seems to be a late medieval or early modern work, the *Futūḥ al-Bahnasā*, see E. Wagner (*Arabische Handschriften, Teil I* (Wiesbaden, 1976), pp. 421–2), in the series *Verzeichnis der orientalischen Handschriften in Deutschland*. For *Kitāb futūḥ al-Bahnasā wa-mā waqa'a li'ṣ-ṣaḥāba ma'a'l-Baṭlūs*, a work composed by Abū 'Abd Allāh Muḥammad al-Maqqarī (or al-Maqqurī), see H. T. Norris, "The *Futūḥ al-Bahnasā* and its Relation to Pseudo-Majāzi . . . ", *Quaderni di Studi Arabi* 4 (1986), 75. Norris suggests that it was composed no earlier than the Ayyūbid or Mamluk periods. See further ibid., 80–1, 85.

14 For the *mab'ath* in the Prophet's career see, e.g., *Bidāya*, Vol. II, pp. 306–56; Vol. III, pp. 2–235.

15 Vatican MS Borg 125, erroneously listed as 126 in *GAL* Suppl., Vol. I, p. 616, No. 1. It is dated 694 (1295) (cf. Levi Della Vida, *Elenco dei manoscritti arabi islamici della Biblioteca Vaticana* (Vatican City, 1935), p. 258). According to 'Abd Allāh Afendī,

Kitāb riyāḍ al-ʿulamā' (Qumm, 1401/1980), Vol. I, pp. 42–3, there exists a manuscript of this work dating to AH 696. See also al-Majlisī, *Biḥār*, Vol. XV, p. 26 n. 1. I thank Professor E. Kohlberg of the Hebrew University for locating for me the statement in the *Riyāḍ*.

I have also used the following versions:

I. Berlin MS Spr. 744 (Ahlwardt, No. 9525), dated 1021 (1621).
II. Berlin MS Pet. 628 (Ahlwardt, No. 9526/1), dated 1182 (1768).
III. Berlin MS Spr. 130 (Ahlwardt, No. 9526/3), entitled *Sīrat an-nabī*, dated *ca* 1750.
IV. Berlin MS We. 128 (Ahlwardt, No. 9624), entitled *Sīrat an-nabī*, incomplete, dated 910 (1504).
V. Berlin MSS We. 163 and 314 (Ahlwardt, Nos. 9625–6), entitled *Nasab ar-rasūl*, dated *ca* 1150 (1737).
VI. London, British Library MS Or. 4281, possibly dating to the fifteenth or sixteenth centuries (see Ch. Rieu, *Supplement to the Catalogue of the Arabic Manuscripts in the British Museum* (London, 1894), No. 514).
VII. India Office Library MS No. 1034, fos. 225–337, n.d.
VIII. Hamburg MS Orient. 138/139, entitled *Intiqāl anwār mawlid al-muṣṭafā al-mukhtār* . . . dated 1061 (1650–1). Cf. C. Brockelmann, *Katalog der orientalischen Handschriften . . . zu Hamburg*, Vol. I (Hamburg, 1908), p. 51.
IX. A complete version which has been incorporated into al-Majlisī, *Biḥār*, Vol. XV, pp. 26–7, 34–104, 299–329, 371–84; Vol. XVI, pp. 20–76.
X. Printed edn (Cairo, 1330/1912), published by Dār al-kutub al-ʿarabiyya al-kubrā.
XI. Printed edn (Cairo, 1959), published by Maṭbaʿat al-Bābī al-Ḥalabī. It is, with some "grammatical corrections", a reproduction of No. X. It was reprinted by al-Maktaba ash-Shaʿbiyya (Beirut, n.d.). A more recently printed edition (Najaf, 1385/1965) is entitled *al-Anwār fī mawlid an-nabī Muḥammad*. I have been unable to compare it thoroughly with Nos. IX–XI above. My general impression is that it is based on yet another version.

16 The headings which follow are my own and are provided as a matter of convenience.
17 Vatican MS Borg 125 (henceforth Vat.), fos. 1a–1b; Cairo edition of 1959 (henceforth C), pp. 4–8. For the convenience of the reader I also refer, wherever possible, to the corresponding pages in the latter version.
18 For discussion and sources see U. Rubin, "Pre-existence and Light, Aspects of the Concept of Nūr Muḥammad", *Israel Oriental Studies* 5 (1975), esp. 67–71.
19 Vat., fo. 1a; *ṭīb mubārak* in C, p. 5.
20 C has Salsabīl, possibly a copyist's corruption or editor's error.
21 For this theme as current among ninth-century mystics see L. Massignon, "Nūr Muḥammadī", *EI*[1].
22 For *mīthāq* as a pact with prophets see also *Bidāya*, Vol. II, p. 322.
23 For an echo of the motif of light see ibid., p. 321 (quoting Abū Nuʿaym al-Iṣfāhānī): God distinguished the prophets from the rest of mankind by fixing light to their foreheads.
24 In Vat., fos. 3b–12a, there is a lacuna up to the passage dealing with the birth of Hāshim. For the missing part see C, pp. 7–8.
25 There is an echo of this in IH, Vol. I, pp. 135–6. The standard report about Hāshim's

business trips and the famous *īlāf* pact is mentioned very briefly. Compare, e.g., IH, Vol. I, pp. 56, 136; Ṭabarī, Vol. I, p. 1089; *Bidāya*, Vol. II, p. 253.

26 There is a close approximation between Vat., fo. 4a, and C, p. 9. The former has two more lines.

27 For these terms see, e.g., W. Montgomery Watt, *Muhammad at Mecca* (Oxford, 1953), pp. 8–10.

28 See G. Levi Della Vida, "Niẓār b. Maʿadd", *EI*[1].

29 Ṭabarī, Vol. I, p. 1082; *Bidāya*, Vol. II, p. 253.

30 For the number forty (and multiplications of it) and its symbolic usage as literary *topoi* in medieval Islam see Lawrence I. Conrad, "Abraha and Muḥammad: Some Observations Apropos of Chronology and Literary *Topoi* in the Early Arabic Historical Tradition", *BSOAS* 50 (1987), esp. 230–2.

31 The text in C, p. 10, is more elaborate than in Vat. It does not mention the flag, however.

32 The dialogue in Vat., fos. 4b–5a (somewhat defective), bears a close approximation to C.

33 There are some differences between Vat., fo. 5b, and C, p. 13.

34 See, for example, her story to al-Muṭṭalib about her earlier marriage in Vat., fo. 10a; C, p. 19.

35 Vat., fo. 5b, and C, p. 13, are at some variance.

36 The dialogue in Vat., fo. 6b, is more elaborate than in C, p. 15.

37 There seems to be a lacuna in Vat. between fos. 7a and 7b. The missing text should have dealt with preparations for that ceremony.

38 Vat., fo. 8a, and C, pp. 16–17, are at some variance.

39 "Armalūn b. Qayṭūr" in C.

40 "Seventy" in C.

41 There seems to be a lacuna in Vat. See C, p. 18, for more details about the wedding.

42 Vat., fo. 10b; C, p. 20.

43 Vat., fos. 12b–17b; C, pp. 24–33.

44 This is a standard piece of information. See, e.g., Ṭabarī, Vol. I, p. 1082; *Nihāya*, Vol. XVI, p. 40.

45 See also *Nihāya*, Vol. XVI, p. 40; Muḥammad b. Yūsuf as-Ṣāliḥī, *Subul al-hudā war-rashād fī sīrat khayr al-ʿibād* (= *as-Sīra ash-shāmiyya*) (Cairo, 1392/1972–1402/1982), Vol. I, p. 309. There is a laconic sentence in *Bidāya*, Vol. II, p. 253.

46 See the different version in *Nihāya*, Vol. XVI, pp. 40–2.

47 There is a difference between Vat., fos. 14b–17a, and C, pp. 28–32.

48 For the number 400 denoting "a large indeterminate number" see n. 30 above; A. F. L. Beeston, "The Genesis of the *Maqāmāt* Genre", *Journal of Arabic Literature* 2 (1971), 2.

49 Compare the dialogue between ʿAbd al-Muṭṭalib and Salma in IH, Vol. I, pp. 137–8.

50 Al-Bakrī has no details on this event. Compare ibid., pp. 137–8; *Nihāya*, Vol. XVI, pp. 42–3.

51 C, pp. 32–3, is more elaborate on this than Vat., fo. 17b. *Badāya*, Vol. II, p. 253, has more concrete information about ʿAbd al-Muṭṭalib's digging of Zamzam and painting the Kaʿba in gold. For the story of Zamzam see also IH, pp. 143–7; *Nihāya*, Vol. XVI, pp. 43–8.

52 Vat., fos. 17b–21a; C, pp. 33–40.

53 For its characterization as "legendary" see M. J. Kister, "Some Reports concerning Mecca from Jāhiliyya to Islam", *JESHO* 15 (1972), 71 n. 3.
54 For this version of his name see also ibid., 68.
55 In C Abraha is vizier to the "Abyssinian king" (*malik al-Ḥabash*).
56 In C there is a different version, according to which a group of Meccan merchants feasted in the church, roasted meat, and forgot to extinguish the fire. For standard versions of the event see Kister, "Mecca", 63, 67–8.
57 Vat. and C are at considerable variance as regards details.
58 Maḥmūd in C, p. 36. Cf. IH, Vol. I, p. 52.
59 This detail is also in Kister, "Mecca", 68.
60 See IH, Vol. I, p. 46. For the men of Khathʿam as responsible for the destruction of the church see Kister, "Mecca", 63–4. Reports by Ibn Ḥabīb and Ibn Saʿd tally with al-Bakrī's. See Kister, "Mecca", 69–70. For information on this tribe see G. Levi Della Vida, "Khathʿam", *EI*[2].
61 The same in IH, Vol. I, pp. 46–7. Cf. Kister, "Mecca", 67, 71.
62 "Eighty" in C, pp. 35, 36, probably a copyist's or editor's error (*thamānīn* and *mi'atayn* are close).
63 For a different version of the reasons for this meeting see IH, Vol. I, p. 48.
64 See IH, Vol. I, p. 49. For ʿAbd al-Muṭṭalib sitting to the side of Abraha see also *Bidāya*, Vol. II, p. 172; Rubin, "Light", 95.
65 See IH, Vol. I, pp. 49–50.
66 For this motif see also IH, Vol. I, p. 52; *Bidāya*, Vol. II, p. 173. Compare the (learned/farcical) question in the latter whether an elephant can actually go down on its knees (see also p. 35 above).
67 There are more details in C, pp. 38–9.
68 Compare IH, Vol. I, p. 54; *Bidāya*, Vol. II, p. 173, on the authority of Ibn Saʿd.
69 Vat., fos. 21a–7b; C, pp. 42–3.
70 Vat., fos. 21a, 22a; C, pp. 43, 53–4. For *ghurra bayḍā'* see also IH, Vol. I, p. 157. W. Montgomery Watt, "The Materials Used by Ibn Ishāq", in Bernard Lewis and P. M. Holt (eds.), *Historians of the Middle East* (London, 1962), p. 29, remarks that this is "an invented anecdote".
71 For similar statements regarding Ṣāliḥ, the pre-Islamic prophet in Arab tradition, see Ṭabarī, Vol. I, p. 247. For the same regarding Abraham see ibid., pp. 255, 257.
72 In C, p. 41, the reason is a dispute with Quraysh on the digging of Zamzam. Cf. IH, Vol. I, p. 151; *Bidāya*, Vol. II, p. 248. For a vow to God in return for his help in digging Zamzam see Ṭabarī, Vol. I, p. 291. Contrast Vol. I, p. 1074 for another version.
73 The monologue in Vat., fos. 22b–3a, is missing in C.
74 Vat. has the interesting piece of information that ʿAbd al-Muṭṭalib paid the soothsayer a bribe (*rashwa*), "according to the custom".
75 Cf. the version of the whole episode in IH, Vol. I, pp. 151–5; Ṭabarī, Vol. I, pp. 1074–8; *Bidāya*, Vol. II, pp. 248–9 (quoting Ibn Ishāq); *Nihāya*, Vol. XVI, pp. 51–2 (quoting Ibn Saʿd). All versions neglect the emotions involved and so well described by al-Bakrī. IH and Ṭabarī, for example, give an extended, tedious description of the technique of drawing arrows. Ṭabarī, Vol. I, p. 291, reports that the sacrifice was prevented by ʿAbd Allāh's maternal uncle, who suggested that ransom be paid instead.
76 Vat., fos. 25a–b, is more elaborate than C, pp. 48–9; Vat., fos. 26a–7a, is at variance

with C, pp. 51–2. Cf. IH, Vol. I, p. 154. The end of the sacrifice story in the *Anwār* recalls, of course, the biblical *Aqeda* story. For the latter and its version in Islamic tradition see *The Tales of the Prophets of al-Kisā'ī*, trans. W. M. Thackston, Jr (Boston, 1978), pp. 160–2.

77 See the following section.

78 Vat., fos. 28a–33b; C, pp. 57–61.

79 The same also in IH, Vol. I, pp. 155–6, where it is less clear, since the motif of the light is not explicated.

80 Cf. ibid., pp. 155–6; Ṭabarī, Vol. I, pp. 379–86, 1078; Muḥammad b. 'Abd al-Bāqī az-Zurqānī, *Sharḥ 'alā'l-mawāhib al-laduniyya*, Vol. I (Cairo, 1325/1907), p. 110, quoting *ahl as-siyar*. The scene of Joseph's trial is briefly alluded to in the *Qur'ān*, XII/23.

81 These stories do not appear in C. Compare similar versions in IH, Vol. I, pp. 155–6; *Bidāya*, Vol. II, pp. 249–50, 262–3 (the woman is the sister of Waraqa b. Nawfal); IS, Vol. I, pp. 94–5. For further material see Rubin, "Light", 84–5.

82 Vat. and C are at variance as regards the phrasing. Contrast the laconic report of the marriage in Ṭabarī, Vol. I, p. 1078: 'Abd al-Muṭṭalib simply brings 'Abd Allāh to Wahb and the marriage is arranged.

83 For "scholarly" versions on the circumstances of his death see, e.g., *Bidāya*, Vol. II, p. 263. C, p. 82, lacks the second version.

84 Vat., fos. 35a–7b; C, pp. 82–9. The story of the birth of Muḥammad in C is preceded (pp. 62–82) by a long story of Saṭīḥ, the *kāhin* of Yamāma (for his "biography" see, e.g., *Bidāya*, Vol. II, pp. 270–1), and Zarqā', Queen of Yemen, their reaction to the imminent birth, and their attempt to eliminate Āmina.

85 For the same (*yamsaḥu 'alā fu'ādī*) see also Zurqānī, *Sharḥ*, Vol. I, p. 111, quoting Abū Nu'aym al-Iṣfahānī, on the authority of Ibn 'Abbās.

86 Cf. ibid., p. 111.

87 Cf. *Nihāya*, Vol. XVI, pp. 69–71.

88 The same in ibid., pp. 69–71; Zurqānī, *Sharḥ*, Vol. I, p. 112, on the authority of at-Ṭabarānī. See also *Bidāya*, Vol. II, pp. 264–5.

89 The same in Zurqānī, *Sharḥ*, Vol. I, pp. 112–13, on the authority of Ibn 'Abbās and Wahb.

90 C, p. 84, has a different version. See also *Nihāya*, Vol. XVI, p. 70.

91 There is an elaborate discussion of these qualities in Zurqānī, *Sharḥ*, Vol. I, pp. 113–14.

92 Cf. ibid., p. 115. Zurqānī comments on this report: "It contains peculiarities [?]" (*wa-fīhi nakāra*).

93 For this motif see also *Nihāya*, Vol. XVI, p. 65, on the authority of Ka'b al-Aḥbār, and pp. 71–2, on the authority of al-Qurṭubī.

94 E.g., *Bidāya*, Vol. II, pp. 267–72.

95 Vat., fos. 37b–42a, and C, pp. 89–96, are at variance.

96 Compare the standard report in IH, Vol. I, pp. 162–3; *Bidāya*, Vol. II, pp. 273–4 (Ḥalīma nearly rejects Muḥammad).

97 There is apparently a lacuna in Vat. between fos. 40b and 41b, and only the end of this story has been preserved. For the complete episode see C, pp. 94–5.

98 Compare, for example, the laconic description in IS, Vol. I, p. 113, of Ḥalīma's encounter with the *Jews*.

99 Vat., fos. 43b–4b, and C, pp. 98–103, are at variance. The latter is more elaborate.

100 For the same see *Bidāya*, Vol. II, p. 276; Ṣāliḥī, *Subul*, Vol. I, p. 474 (both quote Muslim's *Ṣaḥīḥ*).

101 For an allusion to this see IH, Vol. I, p. 167. There is a similar version in Ṣāliḥī, *Subul*, Vol. I, pp. 475–6. For a laconic sentence see *Nihāya*, Vol. XVI, p. 85.

102 Vat., fos. 44b–6a, seems to suffer from a lacuna.

103 C, pp. 106–62 (pp. 113–28 are missing in the copy in my possession and I have used instead the Cairo edition of 1330/1912, pp. 93–106); al-Majlisī, *Biḥār*, Vol. XVI, pp. 20–76; London, British Library MS BM Or. 4281, fos. 92b–130a; Berlin MS Pet. 628 (Ahlwardt, No. 9526), fos. 116a–130a. Al-Majlisī, *Biḥār*, Vol. XV, p. 282, contains also the episode of Muḥammad's sore eye (*ramd* or *ramda*) and the miracle involved. Cf. Ibn al-Jawzī, *al-Wafā' bi-aḥwāl al-muṣṭafā* (Cairo, 1386/1966), Vol. I, p. 101. Muḥammad's role as an arbitrator in the dispute over rebuilding the Ka'ba appears in al-Majlisī, *Biḥār*, Vol. XV, pp. 383–4; C, pp. 104–5; London, British Library MS BM Or. 4281, fos. 92b–93a. It could be a short echo of "Ḥadīth bunyān al-Ka'ba" in IH, Vol. I, pp. 192–9; *Bidāya*, Vol. II, pp. 298–305.

104 Thematically, the different versions are almost identical. There is also a general similarity in phrasing. For example, in Vat. and C we find the phrase *thumma raja'nā ilā'l-ḥadīth* (fo. 24a and p. 46, respectively), at exactly the same point, which suggests a careful copying from a common text. A comparison between Nos. IX and XI in n. 15 above reveals a close approximation to the extent that even the poetical verses vary only slightly, at least until about the middle of the work. The differences increase, however, in its second half. No. VIII in n. 15 above seems to form an independent version, since it provides a *sīra* in the manner of Ibn Hishām's (i.e., the chapter on Muḥammad's mission (*mab'ath*) included). The same can be observed as regards No. IV, although it ends with *mabda' al-waḥyi*. My impression is that the Berlin and London manuscripts use a more colloquial style than the version which served as a basis for the Cairo printed edition (or was this edition "corrected" stylistically?). Compare, e.g., *fa-lammā sāra ibn sab'a sinīn* (No. II, fo. 93a; No. VI, fo. 86a) with *fa-lammā balagha* (No. XI, p. 96). Compare also *tkhallīhi yakhruj* (No. II, fo. 93a; No. VI, fo. 86a) with *tatrukinahu* (No. XI, p. 97). There are, it should be noted, differences in the lines of poetry interwoven throughout the *Anwār*. Compare, e.g., the following passages in Vat. and C: fo. 11a and p. 22, respectively; fos. 11b–12a and pp. 23–4; fo. 23b and p. 45; fo. 25a and p. 46. There are two lines in C which recur several times (e.g., p. 20) and are missing in Vat. In other manuscripts there are additions which seem late when compared with Vat. See, e.g., Berlin MS Pet. 628 (Ahlwardt, No. 9526), fos. 5b–9a, where an extended passage ends as follows: "thumma narji' alān ilā mā qālahu Abū'l-Ḥasan al-Bakrī". A comparison among the available manuscripts and the edited versions of al-Bakrī's *sīra* leads me to one major observation concerning the treatment of this particular work by its copyists. I think it stands half-way between a scholarly text and a popular romance. That is to say, while critical, modern editions of works in historical, religious, and other scholarly fields have established that these works had been copied with general accuracy, with resultant minimal textual variations, versions of popular *siyar* demonstrate total laxity on the part of the storytellers or copyists. The case of al-Bakrī's text, however, is a category in itself: no two versions are identical, yet the differences are not so pronounced as to create totally different stories, as is often the case with the *siyar*.

105 IH, Vol. I, pp. 180–2, 188; IS, Vol. I, pp. 121–30; Ṭabarī, Vol. I, pp. 1124–5; *Bidāya*,

Vol. II, pp. 283–6, 293–4; *Nihāya*, Vol. XVI, pp. 90–2, 95–7; Ṣāliḥī, *Subul*, Vol. II, pp. 188–91, 214–17.

106 Muḥammad the child sitting under a tree, the cover (*ghimāma*) over his head, and the banquet prepared by the monk are motifs which appear in the standard versions of the story of Baḥīrā. See, e.g., IH, Vol. I, pp. 181, 188; IS, Vol. I, p. 130; Ṭabarī, Vol. I, pp. 1124–5; *Bidāya*, Vol. II, pp. 283, 285; *Nihāya*, Vol. XVI, pp. 90–1, 96; Ṣāliḥī, *Subul*, Vol. II, pp. 189, 215.

107 Compare Khadīja's vision in the *Anwār* (e.g., al-Majlisī, *Biḥār*, Vol. XVI, pp. 48–9), with a faint echo in IS, Vol. I, pp. 130–1.

108 E.g., al-Majlisī, *Biḥār*, Vol. XVI, pp. 53–76.

109 Compare ibid., pp. 55–6, with the brief sentence in IS, Vol. I, p. 131.

110 The marriage of Muḥammad to Khadīja receives a very brief treatment in IH, Vol. I, p. 190; IS, Vol. I, pp. 131–3; Ṭabarī, Vol. I, p. 1129; *Bidāya*, Vol. II, p. 294; *Nihāya*, Vol. XVI, pp. 97–8; Ṣāliḥī, *Subul*, Vol. II, pp. 222–4. All standard versions are mainly concerned with the question who was Khadīja's mentor in the engagement procedure: her father or a relative?

111 C, pp. 163–76, has an appendix entitled *Ḥadīth inshiqāq al-qamar*, attributed to al-Bakrī. For a different version of this story in the romance *Sīrat 'Antar* see Urbain Vermeulen, "L'Apparition du prophète dans la Sīrat 'Antar'", *Quaderni di Studi Arabi* 7 (1989), 153–61.

112 Vat., fo. 5a and C, p. 12, are at variance.

113 Vat., fo. 8b; C, p. 17.

114 This term is missing in C.

115 See n. 30 above.

116 Vat., fo. 7a. This is missing in C.

117 Vat., fo. 9b; C, p. 17.

118 Vat., fo. 10b; C, p. 20.

119 Vat., fo. 12b; C, p. 25 (more elaborate). The prediction of the destruction of the Jews by 'Abd al-Muṭṭalib is repeated in Vat., fo. 13b; C, p. 27. The motif of Jewish prior knowledge of the birth of Muḥammad (or Aḥmad) appears in various "scholarly" versions. See, e.g., *Bidāya*, Vol. II, pp. 267–8.

120 Vat., fo. 13b; C, p. 27.

121 Daḥiya in C.

122 Vat., fo. 15a.

123 Ibid., fo. 22a. In C, p. 43, they send spies. Cf. Abū'l-Ḥasan 'Alī al-Mas'ūdī(?), *Ithbāt al-waṣiyya li'l-imām 'Alī b. Abī Ṭālib* (Najaf, 1374/1955), p. 105. It is noteworthy that in C, p. 53, the Jews are also blamed for an attempt to poison 'Abd al-Muṭṭalib's family after the sacrifice episode. In Vat., fos. 27b–28a, these are *kahāna* of Quraysh.

124 Vat., fos. 30a–31a; C, pp. 56–7.

125 Vat., fos. 27b–8a; C, p. 53.

126 Vat., fos. 32b–3a; C, p. 60.

127 Vat., fo. 7a; missing in C. Cf., however, C, p. 17, where there is a vague reference to this dream.

128 Vat., fos. 21a–b; C, p. 42. Cf. Rubin, "Light", 64 and n. 22. This dream should be compared with that recounted in *Bidāya*, Vol. II, pp. 317–18: 'Abd al-Muṭṭalib dreams of a tree reaching Heaven and its branches stretching to East and West. A light comes out of the tree, brighter than the light of the sun, and gets brighter each hour. All nations (*al-'arab wa'l-'ajam*) prostrate themselves before the tree. One group of Qurayshites

cling to the branches and another group try to cut the tree down. At their rear there is the most handsome lad who "breaks their backs and plucks their eyes". The *kāhin* predicts to ʿAbd al-Muṭṭalib that one of his descendants will be "king of East and West" and the founder of a new religion (*wa-yadīnu lahu an-nās*). Ironically, ʿAbd al-Muṭṭalib is ignorant of the identity of this descendant, and has Abū Ṭālib in mind.

129 Vat., fo. 29b. In C, p. 55, the equation apes = Jews is explicit.

130 It is noteworthy that in *Bidāya*, Vol. II, pp. 332–47, there is a chapter entitled "hawātif al-jānn" ("The Invisible Calls of the Demon"), which is based on quotations from a collection (entitled *hawātif al-jinn wa-ʿajīb mā yuḥkā ʿan al-kuhhān*), compiled by Abū Bakr Muḥammad b. Jaʿfar al-Kharāʾiṭī (d. 939. See "al-Kharāʾiṭī", *EI*[2]). One of the stories in it is about a *kāhin* who tells ʿUmar, at the time of his caliphate, of a dream he had about the rise of the Prophet. ʿUmar himself tells of a *hātif* he had heard, prior to his conversion to Islam, concerning the Message. A *hātif* announces to the *ḥunafāʾ* Zayd b. ʿAmr b. Nufayl and Waraqa b. Nawfal the imminent birth of Muḥammad.

131 Vat., fo. 5a; C, p. 10. Contrast IS, Vol. I, pp. 78–9: Hāshim marries Salma because of the good impression she makes on him.

132 Vat., fo. 10b; C, p. 20.

133 Vat., fo. 12b; C, p. 24.

134 Vat., fo. 20a; C, pp. 54–5.

135 Vat., fo. 34b; C, p. 82.

136 Vat., fo. 37b; C, p. 89.

137 Vat., fo. 38a; C, p. 90.

138 See A. J. Wensinck and L. Gardet, "Iblīs", *EI*[2].

139 Vat., fos. 6b–7a; C, p. 14. In C there is the additional interesting observation, which seems to be a later insertion: "At that time the Devil (*shayṭān*) used to come in the open, captivate people's minds, and order them to and prevent them from certain deeds; they were deceived by him and regarded him as a human being."

140 Vat., fo. 9a; C, pp. 16–17.

141 For the Devil appearing in the assembly of Quraysh on the eve of Muḥammad's migration to Medina and his manoeuvring the assembly to pass a death verdict on the Prophet see Ṭabarī, Vol. I, pp. 1229–31.

142 Vat., fo. 3a; C, p. 6. Cf. Rubin, "Light", 93, quoting al-Masʿūdī's (?), *Ithbāt*, and Kharghūshī.

143 Vat., fol. 12b (*shayṭān*); C, p. 24 (Iblīs).

144 Vat., fo. 6b.

145 *Bidāya*, Vol. II, pp. 252–305: "Kitāb sīrat rasūl Allāh."

146 Cf. ibid., p. 289. See further J. W. Fück, "Fidjār", *EI*[2].

147 Cf. *Bidāya*, Vol. II, pp. 290–3. See further Ch. Pellat, "Ḥilf al-Fuḍūl", *EI*[2].

148 Cf. *Bidāya*, Vol. II, pp. 298–305.

149 E.g., ibid., pp. 279–80.

150 There are numerous examples. See, for instance, the version of *sharḥ aṣ-ṣadr* in ibid., pp. 274–9. For a critical approach see ibid., pp. 284–5.

151 Ibid., pp. 259–62: "Bāb mawlid rasūl Allāh". See also *Nihāya*, Vol. XVI, pp. 67–8.

152 *Bidāya*, Vol. II, p. 265.

153 Ibid., p. 173.

154 Ibid., p. 267.

155 Ibid., pp. 267–70.

156 For the full name see, e.g., the source cited in n. 1 above; Berlin MS We. 517

(Ahlwardt, No. 9138), fos. 2a, 18a; Tübingen MS Ma VI 142, fo. 32a. The name Aḥmad b. Muḥammad al-Bakrī appears in Berlin MS We. 702 (Ahlwardt, No. 8989/2). For the name Abū'l-Ḥasan ʿAlī al-Bakrī see Berlin MS We. 702 (Ahlwardt, No. 9054/2). For Abū'l-Ḥasan b. Aḥmad al-Bakrī see Berlin MS We. 128 (Ahlwardt, No. 9624), fo. 79a.

157 Al-Majlisī confused "our" al-Bakrī with one ʿAlā' ad-Dīn Abū'l-Ḥasan ʿAlī al-Bakrī aṣ-Ṣiddīqī (d. 1545 or 1546), a teacher of the Shiite scholar ash-Shahīd ath-Thānī (d. 1559). See al-Majlisī, *Biḥār*, Vol. I, p. 22; Vol. XV, p. 26. See the editor's arguments (Vol. XV, p. 26 n. 1) against this erroneous identification. See also Āqā Buzurg aṭ-Ṭehrānī, *adh-Dharīʿa ilā taṣānīf ash-Shīʿa* (Beirut, 1978–83), Vol. II, pp. 409–11. For ʿAlā' ad-Dīn Abū'l-Ḥasan ʿAlī al-Bakrī see Ibn ʿImād, *Shadharāt adh-dhahab* (Beirut, 1979), Vol. VIII, pp. 292–3.

158 Wüstenfeld saw the Hamburg manuscript of the *Anwār* (n. 15, No. VIII above). See Ferdinand Wüstenfeld (ed.), *Das Leben Muhammeds nach Muhammed Ibn Ishak* (Göttingen, 1858–9), Vol. II, pp. li–lii. Elsewhere Wüstenfeld identified the author of the *Anwār* as Abū'l-Makārim Shams ad-Dīn Muḥammad b. 'Abd ar-Raḥmān (see on him n. 13, No. X above). See further for this confusion F. Wüstenfeld, *Die Geschichtschreiber der Araber und ihre Werke* (Göttingen, 1882), No. 520: "Er soll auch eine Chronik geschrieben haben."

159 *Sharḥ majānī al-adab fī ḥadā'iq al-ʿarab* (Beirut, 1886–8), Vol. I, p. 312, reference in Ziriklī, *al-Aʿlām*, 2nd edn (Cairo, 1954–7), Vol. I, pp. 148–9. The latter goes even further to mention al-Bakrī's year of death as 250 (865), without documentation. In the *Sharḥ*, a book entitled *Kitāb al-ḥukm* is attributed to al-Bakrī. For dating al-Bakrī to the ninth century see more recently G. Levi Della Vida, "Manoscriti Arabi di origine Spagnola nella Biblioteca Vaticana", *Collectanea Vaticana in honorem Anselmi M. Card. Abbareda*, Studi e Testi 220 (Vatican City, 1962), pp. 167–8. See also Rosenthal, *Historiography*, p. 191 n. 1.

160 Ahlwardt suggested as a *terminus post quem* the year 694 (1295), since in one of the works attributed to al-Bakrī there are quotations from two authors who died in that year. See Ahlwardt, No. 9624. These quotations, however, in the light of more recent information (see below), cannot be regarded as part of the original text. Paret suggested as a *terminus ante quem* the year 784 (1382), citing a Turkish manuscript in the Dresden Library, written in that year, and quoting from one of al-Bakrī's works (the *Anwār*). See Paret, *Maghāzi*, p. 156. For this manuscript see H. O. Fleischer, *Catalogus Codicum . . . Dresdensis* (Leipzig, 1831), Nos. 31, 35, 47, 106, 147, 175 (all are fragments of *Siyer-i nabi* by Muṣṭafā b. Yūsuf aḍ-Ḍarīr; see below). The year of aḍ-Ḍarīr's death is actually 1388, not 1382. See Ernst J. Grube, "The Siyar-i Nabi of the Spencer Collection in the New York Public Library", *Atti del secondo congresso internationale di arte turca* (Venice, 1963), esp. 155 n. 1. Still an earlier *terminus* known to Paret is 764 (1363), the year of the death of the famous compiler of biographies, Khalīl b. Aybak aṣ-Ṣafadī, who criticized al-Bakrī's "unsurpassed lies". The quotation from aṣ-Ṣafadī first appeared in *Majānī al-adab* (Beirut, 1885), Vol. II, p. 234 n. See Paret, *Maghāzi*, p. 156. In the most recent treatment of al-Bakrī Rosenthal pushed the *terminus ante quem* back to 694 (1295), the date of the Vatican manuscript of the *Anwār*. Rosenthal warned, however, that this dating is "highly speculative". See "al-Bakrī".

161 See n. 159 above.

162 Raif Georges Khoury, *Les Légendes prophétiques dans l'Islam depuis le Ier jusqu'au*

IIIe siècle de l'Hegire (Wiesbaden, 1978), pp. 341–4. Khoury makes no comment about al-Bakrī.

163 Cf. Levi Della Vida, "Manoscriti".

164 For the identity of the copyist see Khoury, *Légendes*, p. 37.

165 Rosenthal, "al-Bakrī".

166 For these see, e.g., A. A. Duri, "The Iraq School of History to the Ninth Century – A Sketch", in Bernard Lewis and P. M. Holt (eds.), *Historians of the Middle East* (London, 1962), pp. 47–8.

167 For Ibn Sharya and the question of his historicity see A. A. Duri, *The Rise of Historical Writing among the Arabs* (Princeton, 1983), p. 16 n. a. For al-Kisā'ī see T. Nagel, "Al-Kisā'ī, Ṣāḥib Ḳiṣaṣ al-Anbiyā'", *EI*[2]; Ján Pauliny, "Kisā'ī und sein Werk Kitāb 'Aǧā'ib al-Malakūt: Untersuchungen zur arabischen religiösen Volksliteratur", *Graecolatina et Orientalia* 6 (1974), 160–75; Aviva Schussman, *Stories of the Prophets in Muslim Tradition* (in Hebrew) (Jerusalem, 1981).

168 For these see n. 13 above.

169 Paret, *Maghāzi*, pp. 155–6. For Paret's list of *maghāzī* works which are attributed to al-Bakrī see pp. 1–14, 16–27, 33–6, 38–44, 49–59, 64–83, 96–7, 99–106, 108–11, 118–22, 125–7, 128–30, 131, 136–9, 142–5. N. 13 above lists further *maghāzī* fragments which carry the same attribution.

170 Rosenthal, "al-Bakrī".

171 See Nos. XIX, XXIV in n. 13 above.

172 Berlin MS We. 132 (Ahlwardt, No. 9628), fo. 93b. For further information on him see *EI*[2], s.v.

173 See No. XXIII in n. 13 above.

174 Reference as n. 172 above. For further information on him see, e.g., G. Levi Della Vida, "Salmān al-Fārisī", *EI*[1].

175 See Ahlwardt, No. 9005.

176 Ibid., No. 9015.

177 See H. A. R. Gibb, "Abū Mikhnaf", *EI*[2]; Ursula Sezgin, *Abū Miḫnaf, ein Beitrag zur Historiographie der umaiyadischen Zeit* (Leiden, 1971).

178 Ahlwardt, No. 9046; al-Bakrī – Muḥammad b. Qatād – Zayd b. 'Alī. I have been unable to identify al-Bakrī's sources in this *isnād*. The title, however, is not found in Sezgin, *Abū Miḫnaf.*

179 Vat., fos. 1a, 3a.

180 Israel Wolfensohn, *Ka'b al-Aḥbār und seine Stellung im Hadīth und in der islamischen Legendenliteratur* (Gelnhausen, 1933), pp. 62–81. See also Haim Schwarzbaum, *Biblical and Extra-Biblical Legends in Islamic Folk-Literature* (Walldorf-Hessen, 1982), pp. 56, 148–9.

181 Wolfensohn, *Ka'b*, p. 65.

182 Ibid., p. 86.

183 Raif Georges Khoury, *Wahb B. Munabbih*, pt I: *Der Heidelberger Papyrus PSR Heid. Arab. 23* (Wiesbaden, 1972), pp. 12, 222–41. See also Schwarzbaum, *Legends*, pp. 58–62, 151–2.

184 Duri, *Historical Writing*, p. 133. Duri notes that Wahb's *Maghāzī* was not referred to in *sīra* books. Is al-Bakrī's *Anwār* an exception in this regard?

185 Kisā'ī, *Qiṣaṣ al-anbiyā'*, ed. Isaac Eisenberg (Leiden, 1922), passim; *The Tales of the Prophet of al-Kisā'ī*, trans. Thackston, Jr, p. 337 n. 1. For Ibn 'Abbās's importance as regards the legends known as *isrā'īliyyāt* and the attribution to him of anonymous

ḥadīth reports see Gordon Darnell Newby, *The Making of the Last Prophet: A Reconstruction of the Earliest Biography of Muḥammad* (Columbia, S.C., 1989), p. 10. See also Schwarzbaum, *Legends*, pp. 57–8, 150. Other authorities mentioned in al-Bakrī's *isnād* (Vat., fo. 1a) are Abū Muḥammad ʿAbbās (?) b. ʿAbd Allāh (d. 880 or 881. See Ibn Ḥajar al-ʿAsqalānī, *Tahdhīb at-tahdhīb* (Hyderabad, 1325–7/1907–9), Vol. V, pp. 119–20); Faḍl b. Jaʿfar (b.) ʿAbd Allāh (d. 871 or 872. See *Tahdhīb*, Vol. VIII, p. 269); Abū Muḥammad al-Balkhī (= as-Sīrī (?) b. ʿUthmān), whom I am unable to identify.

186 Abū Isḥāq Aḥmad ath-Thaʿlabī, *ʿArāʾis al-majālis* (Cairo, 1950), pp. 22–3: God sends Gabriel to bring him *qabḍa min turābihā*; then commands Gabriel to bring him *qabḍa bayḍāʾ*, "which is the heart of the Earth". The angel takes it from the Prophet's future grave and dips it in Tansīm. It starts to glitter like a white pearl (*durra bayḍāʾ*). Then it is dipped in all the streams of Paradise. Cf. p. 24 above. P. 398: ʿAbd al-Muṭṭalib sitting next to Abraha (see n. 64 above). P. 402: the phrase uttered by Abraha as he learns of the destruction of the church, *ahdimuhā ḥajaran ḥajaran* (cf. p. 27 above) is identical to al-Bakrī's phrasing. Ibn Kathīr, *Qiṣaṣ al-anbiyāʾ* (Cairo, 1968), Vol. I, p. 39: Adam is created from a *qabḍa min jamīʿiʾl-arḍ*. P. 40: Angel of Death taking sand of *turba bayḍāʾ*. Pp. 50–1: God has a covenant (*ʿahd wa-mīthāq*) with Adam's descendants.

187 E.g., Berlin MS We. 708 (Ahlwardt, No. 9016) dated 1197 (1783); Berlin MS Pet. 259 (Ahlwardt, No. 9105/8) dated 1260 (1844); Berlin MS We. 702 (Ahlwardt, Nos. 9019, 9020, 9021) dated 1742. Also Berlin MS Pet. 128 (Ahlwardt, No. 9526), fo. 5b, has an insertion in the text, dealing with the creation of Muḥammad, which is not originally al-Bakrī's (fo. 9a: "thumma narjiʿ alān ilā mā qālahu Abūʾl-Ḥasan al-Bakrī") and which appears in a brief form in Thaʿlabī, *ʿArāʾis*, p. 22.

188 Watt, "Materials", pp. 25–6.

189 P. Crone, *Meccan Trade and the Rise of Islam* (Princeton, 1987), pp. 214–30.

190 E.g., Berlin MS We. 702 (Ahlwardt, No. 8993/2), fo. 130b. Paret, *Maghāzi*, pp. 155–6, lists other Berlin manuscripts.

191 Duri, "Iraq School", p. 47.

192 See No. IX in n. 15 above.

193 Al-Majlisī, *Biḥār*, Vol. I, p. 41.

194 For an assumption about al-Bakrī's Shiism, based on the (apparently erroneous) postulate that he wrote *Wafāt Fāṭima*, and that his rejection by the Sunnis stemmed from his Shiism, see aṭ-Ṭehrānī, *Dharīʿa*, Vol. II, pp. 410–11.

195 Tarif Khalidi, *Islamic Historiography: The Histories of Masudi* (Albany, 1975), pp. 58–9.

196 See n. 12, No. VI and n. 13, Nos. XV, XVI, XVIII, XIX, XXIX above. See also Fuat Sezgin, *Geschichte des arabisches Schrifttums*, Vol. I (Leiden, 1967), p. 278 n. 1. For 'Alī as depicted in (al-Bakrī's) *maghāzī* literature see Paret, *Maghāzi*, pp. 190–200.

197 Vat., fo. 24a; C, pp. 46–7. In C, however, the "elders of Quraysh and Banū ʿAbd Manāf" are credited with the initial move against ʿAbd al-Muṭṭalib, and only afterwards does Abū Ṭālib hold on to ʿAbd Allāh and offer himself as a sacrifice instead. Abū Ṭālib's speech is longer in Vat.

198 M. J. Kister, "The *Sīrah* Literature", in A. F. L. Beeston *et al.* (eds.), *Arabic Literature to the End of the Umayyad Period* (Cambridge, 1983), p. 362.

199 This is found only in Vat.

200 Vat., fo. 33b. In addition, there is material which appears only in C: Abū Ṭālib confronts Abū Jahl (pp. 69–71); Abū Ṭālib expresses sorrow upon ʿAbd Allāh's death (p. 82); the prophecy of Saṭīḥ the *kāhin* as regards ʿAlī (pp. 69–73).

201 Charles Pellat, "Masʿūdī et l'imāmisme", in *Le Shi'isme imâmite* (Paris, 1970), pp. 69–90, raises some doubts about the attribution of the *Ithbāt* to al-Masʿūdī. He concludes, however, that there are no firm reasons to reject the authenticity of the work. His opinion is shared by Corbin (ibid., p. 90). My own inclination, based on the comparison of al-Masʿūdī's *Murūj* with the passages in the *Ithbāt* dealing with the motif of *nūr Muḥammadī*, is to reject al-Masʿūdī's authorship of the *Ithbāt*.

202 Already Ibn Ḥajar al-ʿAsqalānī (d. 1449) had concluded, on the basis of al-Masʿūdī's own writings, that he was a Shiite as well as a Muʿtazilite. See Pellat, "Masʿūdī", p. 71; Ahmad M. H. Shboul, *al-Masudi & his World: A Muslim Humanist and his Interest in Non-Muslims* (London, 1979), p. 39. Medieval and modern Shiite writers considered him a Shiite *rāwī*. See Pellat, "Masʿūdī", pp. 71–2; Shboul, *Masudi*, pp. 39, 40. Al-Masʿūdī's Shiism has also been argued for by modern scholars. See André Miquel, *La Géographie humaine du monde musulman jusqu'au milieu du 11e siècle*, Vol. I (Paris, 1967), pp. 205–8. Miquel even claims (unconvincingly, according to Shboul, pp. 39–40) that al-Masʿūdī was a traveller who propagated the Shiite, perhaps Ismāʿīlī, creed. For more discussion of al-Masʿūdī's possible Shiʿism see Khalidi, *Islamic Historiography*, pp. 136–45; Pellat, "Masʿūdī", pp. 69–77; Shboul, *Masudi*, p. 40.

203 Following is a list of similarities (I have used the 4th impression (Najaf, 1374/1955). P. 90: some similarity in the story of the creation of the special substance (*qabḍa bayḍā'*); pp. 91–9: a very elaborate version of the transfer of the light to Hāshim; p. 99: Hāshim's dream about Salma; p. 99: Hāshim rejects offers of marriage; p. 103: ʿAbd al-Muṭṭalib whispers in the ear of the elephant, which goes down on its knees; p. 109: the story of ʿAbd Allāh's marriage; pp. 110, 111: certain phrases concerning the birth of the Prophet are identical; pp. 112–13: similarities in ʿAbd al-Muṭṭalib's report of his experiences at the time of Muḥammad's birth.

204 One can point out the parts of the *Anwār* which were incorporated into Ḍarīr's *Siyer* by studying the contents of the Turkish edition of the text and the list of illustrations in Carol G. Fisher, "The Pictorial Cycle of the 'Siyer-I Nebi': A Late Sixteenth Century Manuscript of the Life of Muḥammad', unpublished doctoral dissertation, Michigan State University (1981), p. 268, No. 71 ("The Story of the Love of the Soothsayer Zerka for Abdullah" – compare p. 28 above), and illustrations on pp. 159, 261, 263, 332 (Nos. 9, 10, 11, 12), 333 (Nos. 17, 18), 334 (Nos. 38, 39, 47, 51, 52, 53), and 335 (Nos. 58, 63).

205 V. Minorsky, *The Chester Beatty Library: A Catalogue of the Turkish Manuscripts and Miniatures* (Dublin, 1958), pp. 30–1; Carol G. Fisher, "A Reconstruction of the Pictorial Cycle of the Siyar-i Nabi of Murad III", *Ars Orientalis* 14 (1984), 75–94; Zeren Tanindi, *Siyer-i Nebi: An Illustrated Cycle of the Life of Muhammad and its Place in Islamic Art*, pt 2, English trans. Maggie Quigly-Pinar (Istanbul, 1984), pp. 10–11. There is a modern Turkish translation of Ḍarīr's work by M. Frank Gurtunel (Istanbul, 1977), which I have been unable to consult.

206 Barqūq's original patronage of this work was commemorated in the frontispiece of the Ottoman manuscript. It depicts Ḍarīr kissing the hand of the Mamluk ruler. See Esin Atil, "Mamluk Painting in the Late Fifteenth Century", *Muqarnas* 2 (1984), 169 and 171 n. 15. Cf. E. Atil (ed.), *Turkish Art* (Washington, D.C., 1980), pp. 198, 206–7,

figs. 100–1. For the artistic value of one surviving part see Ernst J. Grube, "The Siyar-i Nabi of the Spencer Collection in the New York Public Library", *Atti del secondo congresso internazionale di arte turca* (Venice, 1963), 149–76; Fisher, "Reconstruction"; idem, "Pictorial Cycle"; Emil Esin, *Turkish Miniature Painting* (Rutland, 1960), pp. 14–21. Eighty miniatures of the part preserved at the Topkapi Sarayi are reproduced in Zeren Tanindi, *Siyer-î Nebi: Islam Tasvir sanatinda Hz. Muhammed in Hayat* (Istanbul, 1984).

207 Anwar G. Chejne, *Islam and the West: The Moriscos, a Cultural and Social History* (Albany, 1983), pp. 98 and 198 n. 13. I am indebted to Dr H. T. Norris of the University of London for this reference. Chejne suggests (p. 113) that the *Anwār* was popular because the theme of preordination at creation suited Morisco spiritual needs at a time when their Prophet was denied and vilified. For a summary of the *Anwār*, based on a manuscript at the Biblioteca Nacional de Madrid (BMM 4995), see pp. 98–101. Chejne dates al-Bakrī to 1493–1545, gives his name as Aḥmad b. Muḥammad, and identifies him as an Egyptian scholar.

208 Chejne, *Islam and the West*, pp. 98, 162, has two slightly different titles of the work.

209 Most of the surviving manuscripts date to these centuries. See n. 15 above.

210 C, p. 4.

3 The festival of Nawrūz: a world turned upside down

1 *Khiṭaṭ*, Vol. I, p. 269: "wa-lam yabqa alān li'n-nās min al-farāgh mā yaqtaḍī dhālika wa-lā min ar-rifh wa'l-baṭar mā yūjib lahum 'amaluhu".

2 Mary Boyce, "Iranian Festivals", in Ehsan Yarshater (ed.), *The Cambridge History of Iran*, Vol. III, pt 2: *The Seleucid, Parthian and Sasanian Periods* (Cambridge, 1983), pp. 794, 797–8; Ehsan Yarshater, "Nawrūz", in Mircea Eliade (ed.), *The Encyclopedia of Religion* (16 vols., New York, 1987), vol. X.

3 See U. Huart and H. Massé, "Djamshīd", *EI*².

4 *Khiṭaṭ*, Vol. I, p. 268; *Ṣubḥ*, Vol. II, p. 418; *Nihāya*, Vol. I, p. 185; Yarshater, "Nawrūz", referring to the *Shāhnāma*.

5 The source is allegedly Wahb (b. Munabbih). See *Khiṭaṭ*, Vol. I, p. 262.

6 The source is allegedly 'Abd Allāh (b. 'Abbās); the mediator of this information is the Damascene chronicler Ibn 'Asākir. See ibid., pp. 267–8.

7 Shaul Shaked, "Aspekte vom Noruz, dem iranischen Neujahrsfest", in Jan Assmann and Theo Sundermeier (eds.), *Studien zum Verstehen fremder Religionen*, Vol. I: *Das Fest und das Heilige* (Gütersloh, 1991), p. 90 n. 5. I am indebted to Professor Joseph Sadan of Tel-Aviv University for drawing my attention to this article.

8 *Khiṭaṭ*, Vol. I, pp. 268, 494. See also al-Bīrūnī, *The Chronology of Ancient Nations*, trans. C. Edward Sachau (London, 1879), p. 199. For an expanded and somewhat different version of the Solomon legend see Ṭabarī, Vol. I, pp. 586–97. The story about Solomon is an exegesis on Qur'ān XXXVIII/34, and, according to scholarly opinion, derives from Talmudic material. See D. Sidersky, *Les Origines des légendes musulmanes dans le Coran et dans les vies des prophètes* (Paris, 1933), p. 120.

9 *Khiṭaṭ*, Vol. I, p. 268.

10 This tribe, we are informed, is the one mentioned in Qur'ān II/244: "Knowest thou not of those who went forth from their homes in their thousands, fearing death? Allah said to them: be you as the dead. Thereafter He bestowed life upon them."

11 Boyce, "Iranian Festivals", pp. 798–800; Yarshater, "Nawrūz"; Muhammad Manazir

Ahsan, *Social Life under the Abbasids 170–289 AH 786–902 AD* (London, 1979), p. 286. Ahsan rejects all these explanations as improbable, but leaves the issue at this. For further information in Islamic sources on the customs see especially al-Bīrūnī, *Chronology*, pp. 200–4.

12 Al-Bīrūnī, *Chronology*, pp. 202–3; *Ṣubḥ*, Vol. II, p. 419.

13 Michael Morony, *Iraq after the Muslim Conquest* (Princeton, 1984), pp. 201–2; Shaked, "Noruz".

14 Shābushtī, *ad-Diyārāt* (Baghdad, 1966), p. 39 and n. 37; Adam Mez, *The Renaissance of Islam* (London, 1937), p. 424.

15 *Der Diwān des 'Abdallāh ibn al-Mu'tazz*, ed. B. Lewin, Vol. IV (Istanbul, 1945), pp. 61–2. Cf. Muḥammed b. Yaḥyā aṣ-Ṣūlī, *Ash'ār awlād al-khulafā'*, ed. J. Hyworth-Dunne (Cairo, 1936), p. 249. I owe these two references and the English translation to Professor Shmuel Moreh of the Hebrew University.

16 Ṭabarī, Vol. III, p. 2163, ref. in R. Levy, "Nawrūz", *EI*[1].

17 Ignaz Goldziher, *Muslim Studies*, Vol. I (London, 1967), p. 192 n. 5.

18 For September in the agricultural cycle in Roman Egypt see Naphtali Lewis, *Life in Egypt under Roman Rule* (Oxford, 1983), p. 115.

19 *Sulūk*, Vol. IV, p. 875; *Nuzha*, Vol. III, p. 241. For Nawrūz coinciding with the height of the Nile in Mamluk times see, e.g., *Sulūk*, Vol. IV, pp. 618, 728, 881, 903, 927, 1164.

20 In the celebration in 1122 presents were exchanged between the leading officials in the Fāṭimid court. See Ibn Muyassar, *Akhbār Miṣr (Choix de passages de la chronique d'Egypte d'Ibn Muyassar)*, ed. Ayman Fuad Sayyid (Cairo, 1981), p. 92.

21 *Badā'i'*, Vol. I, pt 2, pp. 364–5.

22 See *EI*[2], s.v.

23 Ibn Ma'mūn al-Baṭā'iḥī, *Passages de la chronique d'Egypte*, ed. Ayman F. Sayyid (Cairo, 1983), p. 65; *Khiṭaṭ*, Vol. I, pp. 68, 69, French trans. R. G. Coquin, "Les Fêtes coptes vues par les Musulmans", *Nouvelle revue du Caire* 2 (1978), 72.

24 *Badā'i'*, Vol. I, pt 2, p. 364. For wine drinking see also *Madkhal*, Vol. II, p. 51; *Khiṭaṭ*, Vol. I, p. 269.

25 *Madkhal*, Vol. II, pp. 48, 49. Barbara Langner, *Untersuchungen zur historischen Volkskunde Ägyptens nach mamlukischen Quellen* (Berlin, 1983), pp. 61–2, suggests, on the basis of comparative data, that slapping with leather originated in fertility rituals. For flogging as a pagan rite see Emmanuel Le Roy Ladurie, *Carnival in Romans* (New York, 1979), pp. 308–9.

26 *Madkhal*, Vol. II, p. 49; *Badā'i'*, Vol. I, pt 2, p. 364; *Ṣubḥ*, Vol. II, pp. 429–30. According to *Khiṭaṭ*, Vol. I, p. 69, and *Sulūk*, Vol. I, pp. 136–7, the throwing of eggs and slapping were first introduced in the year 1196.

27 *Madkhal*, Vol. II, pp. 51–2.

28 Arabic *mu'annathūn*, which probably has the meaning of *mutakhannithūn*, namely, those imitating women. See, e.g., Shihāb ad-Dīn (Aḥmad b. Ḥamdān al-Adhrū'ī) (d. 1381), *Fatwā*, Berlin MS Landberg 1019 (Ahlwardt, No. 5405), fo. 38a. G. Wiet, in his edition of *Khiṭaṭ* (Cairo, 1911–27), Vol. IV, p. 248, and n. 13, translates "mignons". The rendering in the Būlāq edition of *Khiṭaṭ*, Vol. I, p. 269, *al-mughānūn* ("singers"), is probably erroneous (or is this word a euphemism?). Transvestism in medieval Islam is a phenomenon we know little about, and information seems meagre. Around 865 the prefect of Cairo imprisoned *mu'annathūn*. See *Khiṭaṭ*, Vol. I, p. 313. Ibn Baydakīn at-Turkumānī in his "anti-*bida'*" tract (see Chapter 5

above), written in *ca* 1300, condemned transvestites. See his *Kitāb al-luma' fī'l-ḥawādith wa'l-bida'*, ed. Subhi Labib (Cairo, 1986), Vol. I, p. 93.

29 *Khiṭaṭ*, Vol. I, p. 269, quoting al-Qādī al-Fāḍil.

30 Arabic *samājāt*. See p. 42 above. For *samājāt* as masquerades see Joseph Sadan, "Kings and Craftsmen: A Pattern of Contrast", *Studia Islamica* 56 (1982), 41 n. 77; Shmuel Moreh, "Live Theatre in Medieval Islam", in Moshe Sharon (ed.), *Studies in Islamic History and Civilization in Honour of Professor David Ayalon* (Jerusalem, 1986), p. 572; Moreh, "The Background of Medieval Arabic Theatre: Hellenistic, Roman and Persian Influences", paper read at the Third International Colloquium on "From Jāhiliyya to Islam", Jerusalem, 1985, pp. 16, 35, 37. In a private communication to me Moreh made a distinction between *samājāt*, "masks", and [*arbāb*] *as-samājāt*, "actors".

31 *Khiṭaṭ*, Vol. I, p. 268, has *ḥila* (?). A reading of *khayāl* has been suggested by Paul Casanova in his French translation of *Khiṭaṭ* (Cairo, 1906–20), pt 3, p. 48. It has been questioned by Wiet in his edition of *Khiṭaṭ*, Vol. IV, p. 245, n. 11. However, for the pair *khayāl* and *samājāt* (performance and masquerade (?)) *sub anno* 415 (1024), see Musabbiḥī, *Akhbār Miṣr*, p. 42, quoted also in *Khiṭaṭ*, Vol. I, p. 207. For *khayāl* as a theatrical performance see Moreh, "Live Theatre", esp. pp. 580–2.

32 This is Wiet's suggestion in his edition of *Khiṭaṭ*, Vol. IV, p. 245, n. 8. See the reference cited there, and in Ibn Muyassar, *Akhbār Miṣr*, p. 160.

33 *Madkhal*, Vol. II, pp. 49–50. For students playing (*yal'abūn*) on the day of Nawrūz in Egypt in the first half of the thirteenth century see Udfū'ī, *at-Tālī as-sa'īd* (Cairo, 1966), p. 697. Strikingly enough, there is an identical passage to the one in the *Madkhal* in a book entitled *Kitāb al-hafawāt*, attributed to Ghars an-Ni'ma Muḥammad (1025–1087 or 1088), son of the famous Hilāl aṣ-Ṣābī'ī. It describes the Nawrūz celebration in *Iraq* as follows:

> Colleges were shut and the students played; if a professor came in, he was not treated with respect and might be thrown into the fountain unless he paid a ransom in cash, which the students spent for food. Muslims drank wine in public and ate cleaned lentils like the dhimmis and joined them in throwing water on folk, which was wrong because the clinging garments would reveal the female figure. Respectable people hit each other with water-skins or threw water in their houses or gardens while common folk did this in the streets. A bad man would wait for this feast, put a stone or piece of iron in a skin and hit his enemy in the face and kill him, thus not fearing retaliation since he was one of the crowd.

See A. S. Tritton, "Sketches of Life under the Caliphs (III)", *Muslim World* 62 (1972), 145, quoting from an unspecified manuscript (Istanbul Topkapi Sarayi MS 2631/2? Cf. *GAL* Suppl., Vol. II, p. 922) of the *Kitāb al-hafawāt*. It is unclear whether the striking similarity between the two passages stems from actual similarity in customs between Egypt and Iraq or the two reports are actually one, referring to either Iraq or Egypt.

34 What follows is a composite description, based on reports in *Badā'i'* and *Madkhal*. The pertinent passage in *Badā'i'* is available in three different versions: Būlāq edition (Būlāq, 1311–12/1893–5), Vol. I, pp. 263–4; Cairo and Wiesbaden edition, Vol. I, pt 2, pp. 363–4, considerably more detailed; R. P. A. Dozy, *Dictionnaire détaillé des noms des vêtements* (Amsterdam, 1845), pp. 270–6. *Badā'i'* refers to a report by al-Maqrīzī, *sub anno* AH 787. This would imply a reference to *Sulūk*. A description of the Nawrūz celebrations is missing, however, in the edited text of *Sulūk*. It appears only in *Khiṭaṭ*, Vol. I, pp. 267–9, and is less informative than the text in *Badā'i'*. There

are two French translations of the text in the *Khiṭaṭ*: Coquin, "Fêtes", 72–3; Robert Griveau, "Les Fêtes des Coptes", *Patrologia Orientalis* 10 (1915), 333–43, defective as regards various terms. See also Gaston Wiet, "Fêtes et jeux au Caire", *AI* 8 (1969), 106–7. The passage in *Madkhal*, Vol. II, pp. 52–3, has been translated in Moreh, "Medieval Arabic Theatre", pp. 34–5. Here it is followed with some modification.

35 *Badā'i'* uses the derogatory expression *as-sawād al-a'ẓam min asāfil al-'awāmm*, "the multitude of the lowest commoners".

36 Arabic *khalī'*. Dozy translates "bouffon". For *khalī'* in the sense of "wag, wit and buffoon all in one", see M. M. Badawi, "Medieval Arabic Drama: Ibn Dāniyāl", *Journal of Arabic Literature* 13 (1982), 92. For *khilā'a* as "profligacy" see Franz Rosenthal, *Gambling in Islam* (Leiden, 1975), p. 23.

37 This term appears only in the Cairo and Wiesbaden edition of *Badā'i'*. Its precise meaning eludes me.

38 Arabic *qawī aṭ-ṭibā'*. Dozy, *Dictionnaire détaillé*, translates "de force musculaire".

39 *Madkhal*, Vol. II, p. 52: *damīm fī nafsihi*. See also Langner, *Untersuchungen*, p. 60.

40 For the festive donkey ride as a pagan rite see Le Roy Ladurie, *Carnival*, pp. 308–9.

41 *Ṣubḥ*, Vol. II, p. 429, seems to suggest that not only the name, but the very content, was borrowed from Iran. G. E. von Grunebaum, *Muhammadan Festivals* (London, 1951), p. 54, speaks of an Iranian origin without further information on the precise channel and time of transplantation to Egypt. Cf. Fu'ād 'Abd al-Mu'ṭī as-Sayyād, *Nawrūz wa-āthāruhu fī'l-adab al-'arabī* (Beirut, 1972), pp. 117–19.

42 There is a striking similarity between a report of a special ritual at the court of the "Coptic king" (*Badā'i'*, Būlāq edn, Vol. I, p. 19; the text in the Cairo–Wiesbaden edn, Vol. I, pt 1, p. 87, is less complete) and at the Iranian court (*Ṣubḥ*, Vol. II, pp. 418–19; *Nihāya*, Vol. I, p. 186, quoting Ibn al-Muqaffa'). The almost *verbatim* similarity leads one to suspect that Ibn Iyās erroneously associated information he had about the Iranian court ritual with the ancient Egyptian court. Doubts about the provenance of the text have also been raised by Tah Nidā, cited in as-Sayyād, *Nawrūz*, p. 120 n. 1.

43 In AD 507–11 Ādur's first day appears to have coincided with the spring equinox. Nō Rōz was shifted to the first of Ādur probably around that time. See Boyce, *BSOAS* 33 (1970), 528, 537. For Bahār Jashn as identical with the late Sasanian Nō Rōz, see ibid., 529 (in a private communication to me in 1988, Professor Boyce confirmed this point). In later periods Ādur, with the moving Zoroastrian calendar, slipped back to become a winter month.

44 Metin And, "The Turkish Folk Theatre", *Asian Folklore Studies* 38 (1979), 160–1. The similarity between the Egyptian and Iranian processions has also been pointed out by Moreh, "Medieval Arabic Theatre", p. 17. J. G. Frazer, *The Golden Bough: A Study in Magic and Religion*, pt 6: *The Scapegoat*, 3rd edn (London, 1913), p. 403, quotes al-Bīrūnī's interpretation of the festival: "because the season, which is the beginning of Azur or March, coincides with the sun's entry into Aries, for that day they disport themselves and rejoice because the winter is over".

45 See al-Qazwīnī, *'Ajā'ib al-makhlūqāt*, ed. F. Wüstenfeld (Göttingen, 1849), p. 82.

46 Frazer, *Scapegoat*, pp. 402–3, quoting Thomas Hyde, *Historia Religionis Veterum Persarum* (Oxford, 1700), pp. 183, 249–51. For a much shorter version see al-Qazwīnī (n. 45 above). The subject is briefly treated also in al-Mas'ūdī, *Murūj adh-dhahab wa-ma'ādin al-jawhar*, ed. Barbier de Meynard and Pavet de Courteille (Paris, 1861–77), Vol. III, p. 413; al-Bīrūnī, *Chronology*, p. 211. Frazer speculated that the "abrupt disappearance of the Persian clown at a certain hour of the day,

coupled with the leave given to the populace to thrash him if they found him afterwards, points plainly enough to the harder fate that probably awaited him in former days, when he paid with his life for his brief tenure of a kingly crown".

47 This was confirmed to me by Professor Ariel Shisha-Halevi of the Hebrew University in a private communication in 1988.

48 For Frazer's view see n. 53 below. See more recently Jacques Heers, *Fêtes des fous et carnavals* (Paris, 1983), pp. 26–8.

49 Frazer, *Scapegoat*, pp. 306–9, should be modified by more recent studies, especially his hypothesis about the sacrifice of the Saturnalia king. See, e.g., Nilsson, "Saturnalia", in *Paulys Real-Encyclopädie der klassischen Altertumswissenschaft* (Stuttgart, 1921); H. H. Scullard, *Festivals and Ceremonies of the Roman Republic* (London, 1981), pp. 205–7; Eckard Lefèvre, "Saturnalien und Palliata", *Poetica* 20 (1988), 32–46. I am indebted to my colleague Dr Uri Poznanski for his bibliographical advice. Frazer's discussion of ancient Mesopotamia (*Scapegoat*, pp. 354–411) seems unfounded in the light of more recent research. See, e.g., Walter Burkert, *Structure and History in Greek Mythology and Ritual* (Berkeley, 1979), pp. 68–9 and 172 n. 13. I thank my colleague Professor Mordechai Cogan for advice on this point.

50 For the festival of the Kalends of January and its resemblance to Saturnalia see Michel Meslin, *La Fête des kalendes de janvier dans l'empire romain* (Brussels, 1970), esp. pp. 66–93.

51 Edward Westermarck, *Pagan Survivals in Mohammedan Civilisation* (London, 1933, rep. Amsterdam, 1973), pp. 151–3, 163–4, 166. Westermarck's report finds an interesting parallel in an account of another festival in Fez, Morocco, in the early years of our own century. It deserves to be quoted in full:

> The Mohammedan students of Fez, in Morocco, are allowed to appoint a sultan of their own, who reigns for a few weeks, and is known as *sulṭān ṭ-ṭulba*, "the Sultan of the Scribes". This brief authority is put up for auction and knocked down to the highest bidder. It brings some substantial privileges with it, for the holder is freed from taxes thenceforward, and he has the right of asking a favour from the real sultan. The favour is seldom refused; it usually consists in the release of a prisoner. Moreover, the agents of the student-sultan levy fines on the shopkeepers and householders, against whom they trump up various humorous charges. The temporary sultan is surrounded with the pomp of a real court, and parades the streets in state with music and shouting, while a royal umbrella is held over his head. With the so-called fines and free-will offerings, to which the real sultan adds a liberal supply of provisions, the students have enough to furnish forth a magnificent banquet; and altogether they enjoy themselves thoroughly, indulging in all kinds of games and amusements. For the first seven days the mock sultan remains in the college; then he goes about a mile out of the town and encamps on the bank of the river, attended by the students and not a few of the citizens. On the seventh day of his stay outside the town he is visited by the real sultan, who grants him his request and gives him seven more days to reign, so that the reign of "the Sultan of the Scribes" nominally lasts three weeks. But when six days of the last week have passed the mock sultan runs back to the town by night. This temporary sultanship always falls in spring, about the beginning of April.

J. G. Frazer, *The Golden Bough: A Study in Magic and Religion*, pt 3: *The Dying God*, 3rd edn (London, 1911), pp. 152–3 and the source cited there. According to Eugène Aubin, *Le Maroc d'aujourd'hui* (Paris, 1904), pp. 283–7, the custom goes back to 1665. In that year a local prince granted permission to students, who had assisted him in a political struggle, to elect a "sultan". Frazer, however, is of the opinion that this explanation "has all the air of a fiction devised to explain an old custom, of which the real meaning and origin had been forgotten".

52 A laconic statement on the celebration of Saturnalia in Egypt in AD 80 can be found in Naphtali Lewis, *Life in Egypt under Roman Rule* (Oxford, 1983), p. 24.

53 Samuel Kinser, *Carnival, American Style: Mardi Gras at New Orleans and Mobile* (Chicago, 1990), pp. 3–4. According to Kinser, it was humanists and churchmen who only after 1450 began associating Carnival with Saturnalia and Bacchanalia. Yet five centuries separate the last mention of customs similar to those of Carnival (Lupercalia in AD 494) from the first medieval mention of Carnelevare (in 965). Kinser is far more cautious than Frazer (*Scapegoat*, p. 312), who was inclined to see Saturnalia and Carnival as identical. However, one could still challenge Kinser by asking whether a documentary gap is in itself sufficient proof for a real absence as far as ancient times are concerned.

54 *Khiṭaṭ*, Vol. I, p. 268, quoting Ibn Wāṣif Shāh. For Manāwush (?) or Manāwus (?) as a post-diluvian king see the so-called Pseudo-Mas'ūdī *Akhbār az-zamān*, ed. 'Abd Allāh as-Sāwī (Beirut, 1980), pp. 201–3; *Nihāya*, Vol. XV, pp. 67–9.

55 G. Maspero, "L'Abrégé des merveilles", in Maspero, *Etudes de mythologie et d'archéologie égyptiennes*, Vol. VI (Paris, 1912), pp. 472–5; M. A. Murray, "Nawruz, or the Coptic New Year", *Ancient Egypt* (1921), 79–81; Murray, "Maqrizi's Names of the Pharaohs", *Ancient Egypt* (1924), 52. Murray, an Egyptologist, suggests that "Menaqiush" be identified as king of the XIIIth dynasty. Also Çeres Wissa Wassef, *Pratiques rituelles et alimentaires des coptes* (Cairo, 1971), p. 29, seems to accept the medieval reports.

56 Michael Cook, "Pharaonic History in Medieval Egypt", *Studia Islamica* 57 (1983), 90 n. 1, writes that "most of what he [Maspero] had to say, and particularly his attempt to make sense of the names of the king-list of the Hermetic history, is best forgotten". "Hermetic history" is, according to Cook, the expansive and colourful medieval account of Egyptian history from the earliest antediluvian times through the Flood to the Exodus. This, Cook argues, "is not an embodiment of a solid Coptic tradition, and . . . demonstrably Coptic elements are remarkably hard to find in it". It was not known in the tenth century and, in Cook's view, appeared only in the early eleventh century. See "Pharaonic Egypt", 71, 78–103.

57 F. Petrie, "The Palace Titles", *Ancient Egypt* (1924), 115, does not provide details. He seems to be quite cavalier about the gap of thousands of years.

58 See details in Etienne Driton, *Pages d'egyptologie* (Cairo, 1957), p. 146; François Daumas, *Ägyptische Kultur im Zeitalter der Pharaonen* (Munich, 1969), pp. 451–6.

59 Murray has proposed that the ancient Egyptian name for the New Year festival must have been sufficiently similar in sound to its Persian supplanter to make it possible for the latter to supersede it. See "Nawruz", 79. Wissa Wassef, *Pratiques*, pp. 19, 208, thinks that the Persian name was applied only after the Arab conquest of Egypt. This, however, is dismissed by as-Sayyād, *Nawrūz*, p. 119, on the grounds of a report found in *Badā'i'* (discussed in n. 42 above). Strangely enough, as-Sayyād is not in the least concerned with the close approximation of the texts and the doubts it raises as regards the report in *Badā'i'*.

60 Al-Bīrūnī, *al-Qānūn al-Mas'ūdī* (Hyderabad, 1954), Vol. I, p. 264; *li'ḍ-ḍuḥka*. The same is suggested in al-Qazwīnī, *'Ajā'ib* (n. 45 above), p. 82.

61 Mez, *Renaissance*, p. 425; Peter D. Molan, "Charivari in a Medieval Egyptian Shadow Play", *al-Masāq* 1 (1988), esp. 9–13. For the case of medieval Egypt Molan has used the text in *Khiṭaṭ* only.

62 This view is emphasized by Samuel Kinser, who makes the point that the association

of Carnival with pagan origins was deliberately perpetuated by late medieval church reformers, both Catholic and Protestant, and was carried into modern times by folklorists. See *Carnival*, pp. xvii–xviii, 4–5. For the contrast between Carnival and Lent see also Peter Burke, *Popular Culture in Early Modern Europe* (New York, 1978), p. 188. Burke, however, does not exclude the possibility that "Christian meanings were superimposed on pagan ones without obliterating them", p. 191.

63 Ingvild Salid Gilhus, "Carnival in Religion: The Feast of Fools in France", *Numen* 37 (1990), 47 n. 3. Burke suggests that, in a sense "every festival was a miniature Carnival because it was an excuse for disorder and because it drew from the same repertoire of traditional forms, which included processions, races, mock battles, mock weddings, and mock executions". See *Popular Culture*, p. 199.

64 Burke, *Popular Culture*, pp. 180–3, 186–8, 189. For pupils beating teachers see also Jacques Heers, *Fêtes, jeux et joutes dans les sociétés d'occident à la fin du moyen âge* (Montreal, 1971), pp. 130–1; Westermarck, *Pagan Survivals*, pp. 169–75.

65 Natalie Zemon Davis, "Women on Top", in Davis, *Society and Culture in Early Modern France* (Stanford, 1975), pp. 129–30, 136–7, and specific examples there. Transvestism is still an important feature in the popular belsinckling, a form of Christmas mumming in the La Havre Islands, Nova Scotia, as well as in Java. See Roger D. Abrahams and Richard Bauman, "Ranges of Festival Behavior", in Barbara A. Babcock (ed.), *The Reversible World: Symbolic Inversion in Art and Society* (Ithaca, 1978), p. 196; James L. Peacock, "Symbolic Reversal and Social History: Transvestites and Clowns of Java", ibid., pp. 209–24.

66 For the same opinion see Molan, "Charivari", 6–7.

67 Frazer, *Scapegoat*, pp. 328–9, 338–9. Frazer associated "seasons of unbridled licence" with intercalary days that had been inserted in ancient calendars in order to equalize the lunar with the solar years. For Bakhtin and V. Turner see Natalie Zemon Davis, "The Reasons of Misrule", in Davis, *Society and Culture*, pp. 122–3.

68 Frazer, *Scapegoat*, p. 403. See also Mez, *Renaissance*, p. 426. For the motif of "king for a day" at the New Year in medieval Samarqand see Frazer, *Dying God*, p. 151.

69 Frazer, *Scapegoat*, pp. 313–39; Stuart Clark, "Inversion, Misrule and the Meaning of Witchcraft", *Past & Present* 87 (1980), 101. For the "Lord of Misrule" as a theme which appears in medieval Egypt, not only in Nawrūz festivals but also in literature, see Badawi, "Medieval Arabic Drama", 95. Accordingly, in Ibn Dāniyāl's shadow play *Ṭayf al-khayāl*, written in the latter part of the thirteenth century, we find the figures of the mock prince Wiṣāl and his mock employees, who all stand for a topsy-turvy picture of a princely court. Badawi, significantly, has characterized Wiṣāl as "the Arabic *prince des sots* and the Lord of Misrule". One should combine his view with that of Molan (reference in n. 61 above) that Ibn Dāniyāl's play is an enactment of Nawrūz, and hence of the theme of "misrule".

70 In the Feast of Fools in late medieval and early modern France, which was celebrated between Christmas and Epiphany, young clerics roamed masked through the streets. See Muchembled, *Popular Culture*, p. 140, and most recently Gilhus, "Carnival", for the role of the Feast of Fools within the church structure.

71 In Lille, around 1552 and again in 1556, boys and youths in disguise ran through the streets, throwing ashes at one another, singing dissolute songs, and hitting spectators. See Muchembled, *Popular Culture*, pp. 140–1.

72 As part of the celebration of the Feast of the Magi, on 6 January 1525, in the small

town of Boersch in Lower Alsace, twelve youths in procession, led by a piper and drummer (and therefore known as the *Pfeifferknaben*), elected one of their number as their "king" and went from house to house, as was the custom, begging "a gift for their king". See Bob Scribner, "Reformation, Carnival and the World turned Upside-down", *Social History* 3 (1978), 307. In the carnival in Romans (France), in 1580, youths searched for alms from house to house. See Le Roy Ladurie, *Carnival*, pp. 307, 319. In Provence, as late as 1967, the refusal to contribute to the leaders ("abbots") of groups of youths ("abbeys") on a feast day could result in the enactment of a showy *charivari*, that is, a noisy demonstration, approved by public opinion, to humiliate some wrongdoer in the community. See Lucienne Roubin, "Male and Female Space in the Provençal Community", in Robert Forster and Orest Ranum (eds.), *Rural Society in France: Selections from the Annales* (Baltimore, 1977), pp. 163–5.

73 At Saint Quentin (Aisne), toward the end of the sixteenth century, a winner in a Mardi Gras race was declared *roi de chapels* and received all due pomp, like a true prince. He paraded through the streets, flanked by the kings of the two previous years, and preceded by the captains, lieutenants, and members of the *jeunesse*. The *échevins* of the city invited the new prince to a banquet in the great Council Hall. See Muchembled, *Popular Culture*, pp. 143–4.

74 Burke, *Popular Culture*, pp. 199–200.

75 This question has been raised by Abrahams and Bauman as regards a different cultural context in "Ranges of Festival Behavior", p. 193.

76 *Madkhal*, Vol. II, p. 53: "laysa fīhi ḥaraj wa-lā aḥkām taqaʿ".

77 Burke, *Popular Culture*, pp. 201–2 and 317 n. 49; Babcock (ed.), *Reversible World*, p. 22.

78 Abrahams and Bauman, "Ranges of Festival Behavior", p. 206.

79 Scribner, "Reformation", 319.

80 Clark, "Inversion", 101. See, however, the criticism of the functionalist interpretation in Stuart Clark, "French Historians and Early Modern Popular Culture", *Past & Present* 100 (1983), esp. 91–3.

81 E.g., Max Gluckman, *Rituals of Rebellion in South-East Africa* (Manchester, 1952). For rituals of status reversal as reaffirming social structure see also Victor W. Turner, *The Ritual Process:Structure and Anti-Structure* (London, 1969), pp. 177, 181, 201.

82 Burke, *Popular Culture*, p. 201; Babcock (ed.), *Reversible World*, p. 22.

83 The criticism of Gluckman's thesis is less relevant for the present discussion. See Babcock (ed.), *Reversible World*, pp. 23–4.

84 Maria Julia Goldwasser, "Carnival", in Mirca Eliade (ed.), *Encyclopedia of Religion* (16 vols., New York, 1987), Vol. III.

85 Babcock (ed.), *Reversible World*, p. 235.

86 Davis, *Society and Culture*, pp. 97, 130. For examples of political criticism see pp. 117–19, 131.

87 For this function of carnival see Peter Weidkuhn, "Carnival in Basle: Playing History in Reverse", *Cultures* 3/1 (1976), 45.

88 For criticism of carnival in late medieval Europe see, e.g., Burke, *Popular Culture*, pp. 207–22. For a ban on excessive behaviour in the Nuremberg Carnival of 1469 see Samuel Kinser, "Presentation and Representation: Carnival at Nuremberg 1450–1550", *Representations* 13 (1986), 3.

89 It was banned in the ʿAbbāsid Caliphate in 895. See Ṭabarī, Vol. III, p. 2144 (ref. in Mez, *Renaissance*, p. 424); *Nujūm*, Vol. III, pp. 86–7. Two years later, a ban on

bonfires and on the spraying of water was announced in Baghdad. Yet, as soon as the ban was removed, "celebrators trespassed all barriers". See Ṭabarī, Vol. III, p. 2163 (ref. in R. Levy, "Nawrūz", *EI*[1]).

90 For Mihrajān see J. Calmard, "Mihragān", *EI*[2]; Ahsan, *Social Life*, pp. 187–90.

91 Abū 'Umar Muḥammad al-Kindī, *Kitāb al-wulāt wa-kitāb al-qudāt*, ed. R. Guest (Leiden, 1912), p. 269. For dressing in clothes of the opposite sex in the European carnival see Scribner, "Reformation", 326.

92 Kindī, *Wulāt*, p. 294 (ref in Mez, *Renaissance*, p. 425).

93 *Khiṭaṭ*, Vol. I, p. 268, quoting Ibn Zūlāq; Ibn Muyassar, *Akhbār Miṣr*, p. 166; *Badā'i'*, Vol. I, pt 1, p. 190.

94 *Khiṭaṭ*, Vol. I, p. 268, quoting Ibn Zūlāq.

95 Musabbiḥī, *Akhbār Miṣr*, p. 46.

96 *Sulūk*, Vol. I, p. 142.

97 Ibid., Vol. III, p. 394; *Inbā'*, Vol. I, p. 217.

98 *Khiṭaṭ*, Vol. I, p. 269; *Badā'i'*, Vol. I, pt 2, p. 365; Mez, *Renaissance*, p. 425.

99 *Ṣubḥ*, Vol. II, pp. 429–30.

100 *Inbā'*, Hyderabad edition, Vol. VII, p. 369.

101 Faraj, Barqūq's immediate successor, who abdicated in 1405, is reported to have become drunk in the company of his close associates on Nawrūz of that year. See *Nujūm*, Vol. XII, p. 329.

102 See p. 42 and n. 18 above for collecting dates in Egypt in September.

103 J. J. Rifaud, *Voyage en Egypte en Nubie et lieux circonvoisins depuis 1805 jusqu' en 1827* (Paris, 1830), pl. 46. For details on the author see Warren R. Dawson and Eric P. Uphill, *Who was Who in Egyptology*, 2nd edn (London, 1972), p. 249.

104 Murray, "Nawruz", 80.

105 According to *Biographisches Lexikon hervorragender Ärzte 1880–1930*, Vol. I (Munich, 1962), p. 776, Carl Benjamin Klunzinger (1834–1924) studied in Tübingen and other places, practised medicine for one year at Liebenzell, then studied zoology in Stuttgart and Munich. In the 1860s and 1870s he served as medical advisor to the Egyptian government. I owe this information to Professor Shula Volkov and Ms Adina Stern of Tel-Aviv University. For biographical information see also Hermann A. L. Degener, *Unsere Zeitgenossen, Wer ist's?*, 7th edn (Leipzig, 1914), p. 856; D. Henze, *Enzyklopädie der Entdecker und Erforscher der Erde* (Graz, 1986), pp. 43–4. I am indebted to Mr Kai Baumbach of Freiburg University and Professor Thomas Philipp of Erlangen respectively for the two references.

106 For the parodic take-over of the city hall in the Bavarian town of Hirschau in the 1520s, and parallel examples in Switzerland and Austria, see Hans Moser, "Archivalisches zu Jahreslaufbrauchen der Oberpfalz", *Bayerisches Jahrbuch für Volkskunde* (1955), 169–70. For the case of Romans (France) in 1579, see Le Roy Ladurie, *Carnival*. These references appear in Kinser, *Carnival*, p. 392 n. 48.

107 C. B. Klunzinger, *Upper Egypt: Its People and its Products* (English trans., New York, 1878), pp. 184–5. This report with slight changes is cited also under the title "The King of All the Nobles", *Ancient Egypt* (1924), 97. See also Frazer, *Dying God*, pp. 151–2.

108 S. H. Leeder, *Modern Sons of the Pharaohs: A Study of the Manners and Customs of the Copts of Egypt* (London, 1918), pp. 66–7. This bears close similarity to Klunzinger's report. I have insufficient information to state whether Leeder actually copied from Klunzinger.

109 For this custom, see e.g., Frazer, *Scapegoat*, pp. 388–94; Frazer, *Dying God*, pp. 322–33. For burning the old woman personifying Epiphany in Italy, see Burke, *Popular Culture*, p. 193. For burning effigies in connection with Carnival see the general statement ibid., pp. 199, 202.

4 The politics and "moral economy" of the Cairene crowd

1 This chapter is a substantial expansion of my article "Grain Riots and the 'Moral Economy': Cairo, 1350–1517", *Journal of Interdisciplinary History* 10 (1980), 459–78.

2 Nāṣir was the regnal title of Muḥammad b. Qalāwūn (r. 1294–5, 1299–1309). Manṣūr was the regnal title of Qalāwūn (r. 1279–90).

3 *Nujūm*, Vol. VIII, pp. 170–6.

4 For the text of this letter (*'ahd*) see ibid., p. 263.

5 For opening the dam see further pp. 72–3 above.

6 This particular rhyme is termed *balīqa* in Muḥammad Zaghlūl Salām, *al-Adab fī'l-'aṣr al-mamlūkī* (Cairo, 1971), p. 316.

7 Arabic *rukayn*, the diminutive of *rukn*, is in this case apparently a pun on Rukn ad-Dīn, the regnal title of Baybars II.

8 This, apparently, was one of Salār's features.

9 *Sulūk*, Vol. II, p. 55; *Nujūm*, Vol. VIII, pp. 242–4; *Badā'i'*, Vol. I, pt 1, pp. 424–5, quoting Ibn Duqmāq. There are slight differences among the three sources with regard to this rhyme.

10 See W. M. Brinner, "Ḥarfūsh", *EI*².

11 *Sulūk*, Vol. II, pp. 55, 69–70, 71; *Nujūm*, Vol. VIII, pp. 268–71; Dawādārī, Vol. IX, pp. 187–8; *Badā'i'*, Vol. I, pt 1, p. 425.

12 For his biography see, e.g., *Nujūm*, Vol. X, pp. 46–7; Robert Irwin, *The Middle East in the Middle Ages: The Early Mamluk Sultanate 1250–1382* (London, 1986), pp. 125–8.

13 For this *khānqāh* see L. A. Ibrahim, "The Great Ḫānqāh of the Amir Qawṣūn in Cairo", *Mitteilungen des Deutschen Archäologischen Institut* 30 (1974), 37–64.

14 *Khiṭaṭ*, Vol. II, p. 100, tells that *'allāqa* (pl. *'alālīq*), was a lollipop in human or animal shape, with a string at the end, made especially for children.

15 *Sulūk*, Vol. II, pp. 574–7, 579, 586–95; *Nujūm*, Vol. X, pp. 24–30, 38–48, 51–2, 60–1. For a shorter version see *Badā'i'*, Vol. I, pt 1, pp. 491–4.

16 Most likely al-Manṣūr Abū Bakr (mentioned above), third ruler of the Qalāwūnids, who was deposed after a short reign in 1341, sent to Upper Egypt, and murdered there. See Irwin, *Middle East*, p. 127.

17 *Sulūk*, Vol. II, pp. 595, 599; *Nujūm*, Vol. X, pp. 52, 55–6.

18 For the medieval case see, e.g., Jacob Lassner, *Islamic Revolution and Historical Memory: An Inquiry into the Art of 'Abbāsid Apologetics* (New Haven, 1986).

19 For a brief description of the circumstances see Irwin, *Middle East*, p. 26.

20 For *fiṭra* as a theological concept see D. B. Macdonald, "Fiṭra", *EI*².

21 *Badā'i'*, Vol. I, pt 1, p. 289, quoting Abū Shāma. One wonders which text by the latter was in front of Ibn Iyās. In Abū Shāma's *Tarājim rijāl al-qarnayn* (Beirut, 1974), *sub anno* AH 648, there is no such information.

22 *Badā'i'*, Vol. I, pt 1, p. 289; Irwin, *Middle East*, p. 27.

23 A modern classic on the subject is George Rudé, *The Crowd in History* (New York, 1964).
24 André Raymond, "Quartiers et mouvements populaires au Caire au XVIIIème siècle", in P. M. Holt (ed.), *Political and Social Change in Modern Egypt* (London, 1968), pp. 104–16; Ervand Abrahamian, "The Crowd in Iranian Politics 1905–1953", *Past & Present* 41 (1968), 184–210; Abrahamian, "The Crowd in the Persian Revolution", *Iranian Studies* 2 (1969), 128–50; Gabriel Baer, "Popular Revolt in Ottoman Cairo", *Islam* 54 (1977), 213–42; Stephen L. McFarland, "Anatomy of an Iranian Political Crowd: The Tehran Bread Riot of December 1942", *IJMES* 17 (1985), 51–65; Juan R. I. Cole and Moojan Momen, "Mafia, Mob and Shiism in Iraq: The Rebellion of Ottoman Karbala 1824–1843", *Past & Present* 112 (1986), 112–43.
25 Lapidus, *Muslim Cities*, p. 143.
26 Ibid., p. 165.
27 Ibid., pp. 170, 183–4.
28 Lapidus deals mainly with Syrian towns, where violent protest, chiefly in the context of economic hardship, was likely to turn into attacks on provincial governors. See ibid., pp. 149–52, 166–7. See also A. N. Poliak, "Les Révoltes populaires en Egypte à l'époque des mamelouks et leurs causes économiques", *REI* 8 (1934), 268–9; William M. Brinner, "The Murder of Ibn An-Našu: Social Tensions in Fourteenth-Century Damascus", *JAOS* 77 (1957), 207–10. The case of Cairo is treated to some extent in Lapidus, *Muslim Cities*, pp. 148–9, 165.
29 Lapidus lists mob activity for the years 1341–2, 1342–3, 1366–9, 1379–81, 1388, 1389–90, and 1397–8, as well as some undated cases (see *Muslim Cities*, pp. 148–9 and the references on pp. 289, 291). Poliak, "Révoltes", 267–8, adds riots in 1401 and 1480. To these one can still add protests, looting, and riots which occurred in 1377 (*Sulūk*, Vol. III, p. 314); 1398–9 (ibid., p. 965); 1399–1400 (ibid., p. 1011); 1419 (*Sulūk*, Vol. IV, p. 484); 1468 (*Nujūm*, Vol. XVI, p. 375).
30 Lapidus, *Muslim Cities*, p. 165.
31 There is an almost stereotypic description of the "riff-raff" (*ghawghā'*) waiting below the Citadel in 1342 to see who of two fighting emirs would lose, so that his property could be looted. See *Sulūk*, Vol. II, p. 598; *Nujūm*, Vol. X, p. 55. For examples of crowds attacking disgraced Mamluks and looting their property see, e.g., *Sulūk*, Vol. III, pp. 41–2 (year 1358); *Nujūm*, Vol. XII, pp. 85, 86 (year 1398); *Badā'iʿ*, Vol. II, pp. 201, 202–3 (year 1438); *Badā'iʿ*, Vol. IV, p. 138 (year 1508).
32 *Badā'iʿ*, Vol. I, pt 1, pp. 383–4.
33 Arabic *ʿalālīq*. See pp. 54–5 and n. 14 above. In *Nahj*, p. 78 of the Arabic text, the word is rendered erroneously as *ʿalā'iq*. The German translation (p. 210) "Foltergeräten", "instruments of torture", is incomprehensible in the context of the entire passage.
34 Arabic *rusul*. See *Nahj*, p. 78 of the Arabic text and the German "Scharfrichtern" on p. 210.
35 *Nujūm*, Vol. IX, pp. 135, 137–9 (*sub anno* AH 739); *Sulūk*, Vol. II, pp. 479, 480–1, 482 (*sub anno* AH 740); *Nahj*, p. 78.
36 In 1341 the people "would have killed" the disgraced emir Āqbughā had he not been saved by the prefect of Cairo. See *Nujūm*, Vol. X, p. 10. When a leading emir, Shujāʿ ad-Dīn Ghurlū, was murdered in 1346 or the following year, and his hand was found stretching out of his grave, the people came in large numbers, uncovered the corpse,

and dragged it to be burnt at the foot of the Citadel. This was averted only after the sultan intervened. See *Sulūk*, Vol. II, p. 737; *Nujūm*, Vol. X, p. 167; *Badā'i'*, Vol. I, pt 1, p. 515 (they actually burnt the corpse). In 1149, a group of commoners attacked the *muḥtasib* and pelted him with stones. They also attacked a qadi who served in the sultan's administration, dragging him off his horse, tearing his headgear, and taking away his rings. He was barely saved by a Mamluk. About a year later the same qadi also lost favour with the sultan; his property was confiscated and he went on trial. When he was being taken to prison, the crowd almost killed him. Another attempt to take his life was repeated when he was sent into exile in Tarsus. See *Badā'i'*, Vol. II, pp. 275, 279–80, 281.

37 *Badā'i'*, Vol. IV, pp. 274–5.

38 Lapidus, *Muslim Cities*, p. 147.

39 Edward P. Thompson, "The Moral Economy of the English Crowd in the Eighteenth Century", *Past & Present* 50 (1971), esp. 83.

40 For a general statement concerning this fact see *Sulūk*, Vol. IV, p. 345.

41 *Passages de la chronique d'Egypte d'ibn al-Ma'mūn*, ed. Ayman F. Sayyid (Cairo, 1983), pp. 95–6. Of the total, 120,000 *irdabb*s was shipped to frontier towns in Palestine. The *irdabb* in medieval Egypt equalled 69.6 kg. See E. Ashtor, *Histoire des prix et des salaires dans l'Orient médiéval* (Paris, 1969), p. 124 n. 1.

42 Ira M. Lapidus, "The Grain Economy of Mamluk Egypt", *JESHO* 12 (1969), 3.

43 For *ahrā'*, *makhāzin sulṭāniyya*, and *shuwan*, see, e.g., *Itti'āẓ*, Vol. II, pp. 224, 226; Vol. III, pp. 72, 86, 165–6, 341; *Khiṭaṭ*, Vol. I, pp. 264–5; *Sulūk*, Vol. III, p. 147; *Ḥawādith*, pp. 314–15. For the administration of these granaries see *Khiṭaṭ*, Vol. I, p. 465; *Nihāya*, Vol. VIII, pp. 219–21.

44 For the Fāṭimid period see *Khiṭaṭ*, Vol. I, pp. 464–5. For the years 1367 and 1387 see *Sulūk*, Vol. III, pp. 147, 569. For the sultan's personal grain (*al-ghilāl as-sulṭāniyya*) see *Ḥawādith*, p. 539.

45 *Itti'āẓ*, Vol. III, p. 72.

46 According to al-Asadī, a fifteenth-century chronicler, Cairo's populace (about 150,000 to 300,000; see Introduction above) consumed 1,000 *irdabb*s daily; that is, about 25,000 tons a year. See *at-Taysīr wa'l-i'tibār wat-taḥrīr wa'l-ikhtiyār* (Cairo, 1967), p. 142. These figures suggest an annual *per capita* consumption of about 80 to 160 kg. By comparison, annual *per capita* consumption of grain in fourteenth-century Europe is assumed to have been 150 to 200 kg. See Wilhelm Abel, *Agricultural Fluctuations in Europe from the Thirteenth to the Twentieth Centuries* (London, 1980), p. 41. For a figure of 200 kg in the sixteenth century see Fernand Braudel, *The Mediterranean and the Mediterranean World in the Age of Philip II* (New York, 1972), Vol. I, p. 420. E. W. Lane estimated the annual grain consumption of an average Cairene "middle-class" family in the first half of the nineteenth century to be 8 *irdabb*s, that is 560 kg. See *Manners and Customs of the Modern Egyptians* (London, 1966), p. 581.

47 The granary of the officer Baktamūr contained 36,000 *irdabb*s, that is, 2,500 tons, at the time of his death in 1332. See *Sulūk*, Vol. II, p. 357. The vizier Ibn Zunbūr had 20,000 *irdabb*s, or 1,400 tons upon the confiscation of his property in 1352. See ibid., p. 881; *Nujūm*, Vol. X, p. 282. For other examples see *Sulūk*, Vol. II, p. 565; *Ḥawādith*, p. 230. Emir Bashtak (d. 1341 or 1342) received from his *iqṭā'* 135,000 *irdabb*s (annually). See Shujā'ī, p. 219. For a general treatment of the Mamluk "fief" see Cl. Cahen, "Iḳṭā'", *EI*[2]; Lapidus, "Grain Economy", 5. A truly exceptional amount, in fact

one that equalled the sultans' normal reserves, was found in the possession of Emir Salār after his death in 1310 or 1311. See *Sulūk*, Vol. II, p. 98; *Nujūm*, Vol. IX, p. 19; Lapidus, *Muslim Cities*, p. 51. For Salār see above, this chapter.

48 *Nujūm*, Vol. VII, p. 198.

49 *Nujūm*, Vol. X, p. 120.

50 Ibid., p. 218. For a general remark on grain allowances see *Khiṭaṭ*, Vol. I, p. 465.

51 *Sulūk*, Vol. IV, p. 690. These were terminated in 1425 (for how long is unclear).

52 *Itti'āẓ*, Vol. II, p. 226; *Ighātha*, pp. 20–1; Boaz Shoshan, "Fāṭimid Grain Policy and the Post of the Muḥtasib", *IJMES* 13 (1981), 184. In that case, however, the vizier al-Yazūrī bought the grain from the merchants and stored it in the central granaries in order to regulate the market.

53 In the Mamluk period there were boats with a capacity of 1,000 *irdabb*s each, and some could carry as much as 5,000, or about 350 tons. See *Khiṭaṭ*, Vol. II, p. 167; Khalīl b. Shāhīn aẓ-Ẓāhirī, *Zubdat kashf al-Mamālīk*, ed. Paul Ravaisse (Paris, 1894), p. 123. For transportation on the Nile see also *Ḥawādith*, p. 252. The Ottomans required all boats licensed for trafficking on the Nile to serve as grain carriers after the harvest. See Lapidus, "Grain Economy", 7.

54 *Khiṭaṭ*, Vol. I, pp. 88–9; *Sulūk*, Vol. II, p. 159; *Nujūm*, Vol. IX, p. 45.

55 Lapidus, "Grain Economy", 8, n. 1. For grain prices around 1300 see Ashtor, *Prix*, pp. 283–5.

56 *Khiṭaṭ*, Vol. II, p. 124.

57 Lapidus, "Grain Economy", 9–10.

58 For grain shops at Bāb ash-Sha'riyya in the latter part of the fifteenth century see *Ḥawādith*, p. 685.

59 *Sulūk*, Vol. II, pp. 394, 395.

60 At the beginning of the fourteenth century these amounted to 10–20 per cent. See *Nujūm*, Vol. IX, pp. 45–6. In 1398–9 they were half a *dirham* per *irdabb*. See *Khiṭaṭ*, Vol. II, p. 292; *Badā'i'*, Vol. I, pt 2, p. 548, apparently quoting al-Maqrīzī.

61 In 1404 the price of 1 *irdabb* was 400 (copper) *dirham*s, to which the following were added (all figures in copper *dirhams*): brokerage – 10, transport – 7, sifting – 2, milling – 30. See *Sulūk*, Vol. III, p. 1134; *Badā'i'*, Vol. I, pt 2, p. 696. In 1415 the price of 1 *irdabb* was 300 and fees were as follows: brokerage – 10, transport – 15, sifting and milling – 100. Total fees amounted to 200 copper *dirham*s. See *Sulūk*, Vol. IV, p. 333. For fees in 1426 see ibid., p. 712. In 1450, or in the year after, fees for milling were so high (120 copper *dirham*s) that most people mobilized hand mills to operate at home. See *Tibr*, p. 313; *Ḥawādith*, pp. 100–1.

62 See Raymond de Roover, "The Concept of the Just Price: Theory and Economic Policy", *Journal of Economic History* 18 (1958), 428–9; Thompson, "Moral Economy", 83; Louise A. Tilly, "The Food Riots as a Form of Political Conflict in France", *Journal of Interdisciplinary History* 2 (1971), 25, 27. In France, the fatherly monarch was, by his own proclamation and by universal anticipation, the supreme victualler. See Steven L. Kaplan, *Bread, Politics, and Political Economy in the Reign of Louis XV* (The Hague, 1976), p. 5.

63 Contrast what follows with Lapidus, that "In general, the Mamluk government had no grain policy apart from taking measures necessary to facilitate taxation." See "Grain Economy", 8–9. Elsewhere, however (p. 10), Lapidus makes a distinction between the self-interested emirs and the "more complex" policy of sultans. As we shall shortly see, at least as regards the institution of state granaries, Egyptian regimes had been

more paternalistic than, say, early modern French regimes, which did not establish granaries. See also Kaplan, *Bread*, p. 9.

64 *Itti'āẓ*, Vol. III, p. 140. Al-Maqrīzī's remark that the act was intended "to enhance the vizier's prestige" does not detract from the relevance of this example for our purpose.

65 Ibid., pp. 165–6. It should be noted, however, that his vizier did not abide by the order.

66 *Sulūk*, Vol. I, pp. 717–18; Lapidus, *Muslim Cities*, p. 54.

67 *Nujūm*, Vol. VIII, p. 243.

68 For 1320 see *Nahj*, pp. 61–2. For 1336 see *Ighātha*, pp. 39–40. For 1382 see *Sulūk*, Vol. III, p. 457; *Badā'i'*, Vol. I, pt 2, p. 298. For 1394 see *Sulūk*, Vol. III, p. 818. For 1416 see *Inbā'*, Vol. III, p. 85. For 1428 see ibid., p. 405. For 1449 see *Ḥawādith*, p. 51. For 1450 see ibid., p. 89. For 1451 see *Tibr*, p. 346. For 1467–8 see *Badā'i'*, Vol. III, pp. 16–17; *Ḥawādith*, p. 617. For 1470 see *Badā'i'*, Vol. III, p. 43; *Inbā' al-haṣr*, p. 162. For 1487 see *Badā'i'*, Vol. III, p. 238. In 1449 Sultan Jaqmaq punished an officer who had refused to sell in a situation of shortage. See *Nujūm*, Vol. XV, p. 395; *Tibr*, pp. 259–60.

69 For sultanic mills (*ṭawāḥīn sulṭāniyya*) see *Ṣubḥ*, Vol. III, p. 479; Ibn Furāt, Vol. IX, p. 41. Prior to *ca* 1400 there were over eighty mills in the Cairene suburb of Minyat ash-Shīraj. After the calamity of 1403 only one remained. See *Khiṭaṭ*, Vol. II, p. 130. For mills in Būlāq in 1458 see *Ḥawādith*, pp. 313–15.

70 For 996 see *Itti'āẓ*, Vol. I, p. 291. For 1004–5 see *Ighātha*, p. 16. For 1054 see *Itti'āẓ*, Vol. II, p. 226. For al-Fā'iz's reign (1154–60) see *Ighātha*, pp. 28–9. For 1416 see *Sulūk*, Vol. IV, p. 344.

71 Opposition to price control in medieval Islam was grounded in the conviction (expressed in a *ḥadīth*) that Muḥammad himself objected to price regulation, which, in his opinion, was a right reserved for God only. See at-Tirmidhī, *al-Jāmi' aṣ-ṣaḥīḥ* (Cairo, 1937), Vol. III, pp. 605–6. For the opinion of al-Māwardī, the eleventh-century jurist, see his *al-Aḥkām as-sulṭāniyya* (Paris, 1853), p. 428. Sultan al- Mu'ayyad Shaykh proclaimed in 1415 that the "level of prices is in God's hand" (*al-as'ār bi-yad Allāh*), presumably implying his objection to price control. See *Nujūm*, Vol. XIV, p. 39. The assumption was that God would keep prices at a just level. See *Sulūk*, Vol. III, p. 818; Ibn Furāt, Vol. IX, p. 387. There were, however, opinions in favour of price fixing whenever public order was at stake. See, for example, Henri Laoust, *Essai sur les doctrines sociales et politiques de Takī-D-Dīn Aḥmad b. Taymiya* (Cairo, 1935), pp. 437, 460. In medieval Europe the "just price" actually meant the market price. However, in cases of collusion or emergency, the authorities retained the right to interfere. See de Roover, "Just Price", and Herlihy's comment which follows on pp. 437–8. For the adverse attitude toward price regulation in late medieval and early modern France see Tilly, "Food Riots", 31–2.

72 For 1006 see *Itti'āẓ*, Vol. II, p. 69; *Ighātha*, pp. 15–16. For 1024 see *Itti'āẓ*, Vol. II, pp. 151, 165; Bianquis, "Crise", p. 84. For 1264 see *Sulūk*, Vol. I, p. 506. For 1427 see *Sulūk*, Vol. IV, pp. 750–1.

73 For 1455 see *Ḥawādith*, p. 230. For 1467 see ibid., p. 617. For 1468 see *Inbā' al-haṣr*, pp. 13–14, 28. For 1470 see ibid., p. 162. For 1471 see ibid., p. 243. For 1472 see ibid., p. 477. For 1486 see *Badā'i'*, Vol. III, p. 233. In 1416 the sultan took upon himself to "study" (*naẓar*) the prices, and it appears that he indeed fixed them. See *Sulūk*, Vol. IV, p. 337; *Nujūm*, Vol. XIV, p. 39; Badr ad-Dīn al-'Aynī, *as-Sayf al-muhannad fī sīrat al-Malik al-Mu'ayyad*, ed. Fahīm M. Shaltūt (Cairo, 1967), pp. 341–2. Ash-

tor's assertion (*A Social and Economic History of the Near East in the Middle Ages* (Berkeley, 1976), p. 315) that the Mamluks "had the utmost interest in keeping prices high", needs modification in the light of details provided below. For the fifteenth-century inflation see Boaz Shoshan, "Money Supply and Grain Prices in Fifteenth-Century Egypt", *Economic History Review* 36 (1983), 46–67.

74 For 1204 see *Itti'āẓ*, Vol. II, p. 151. For 1264 see *Sulūk*, Vol. I, p. 507. For 1374 see *Sulūk*, Vol. III, p. 233. For 1468 see *Inbā' al-haṣr*, pp. 13–14; *Ḥawādith*, pp. 676, 685. For 1486 see *Badā'i'*, Vol. III, p. 233. See on this problem also Lapidus, "Grain Economy", 11–12.

75 *Itti'āẓ*, Vol. III, p. 86.

76 *Ighātha*, p. 31.

77 The term *fuqarā'*, which in the Mamluk period came to denote Sufis, should be understood here in its primary meaning ("poor"). For the decreasing number of *fuqarā'*, following the fall in grain prices, see *Sulūk*, Vol. I, p. 508. For *fuqarā'* including women and children see, e.g., *Nujūm*, Vol. XII, p. 91.

78 *Nujūm*, Vol. VII, p. 180; *Dhayl*, Vol. III, p. 252.

79 *Sulūk*, Vol. I, pp. 507–8; *Khiṭaṭ*, Vol. II, pp. 205–6; *Dhayl*, Vol. I, pp. 554–5; Vol. II, p. 662. There is a short version in *Badā'i'*, Vol. I, pt 1, p. 319, *sub anno* AH 661 (the term used for the poor is *ḥarāfīsh*).

80 For 1295 see *Sulūk*, Vol. I, p. 810; Lapidus, *Muslim Cities*, p. 55. For 1374 see *Ighātha*, p. 40. For 1416 see *Sulūk*, Vol. IV, p. 347; *Inbā'*, Vol. III, p. 85. For 1426 see *Sulūk*, Vol. IV, p. 712.

81 *Sulūk*, Vol. III, p. 856; Ibn Furāt, Vol. IX, pp. 432, 434; Lapidus, *Muslim Cities*, p. 55.

82 *Nujūm*, Vol. XII, p. 109.

83 In 1054 or 1055 the Fāṭimid al-Mustanṣir requested from Constantine IX, the Byzantine emperor, 400,000 *irdabb*s of grain, but the Christian ruler died before the transport left. See Ibn Muyassar, *Akhbār Miṣr*, p. 13. From Italian archives we learn of the export of grain from Italian and Catalan cities to Egypt in years of shortage in the last decades of the thirteenth and early decades of the fourteenth century, then in the crisis which Egypt suffered in 1403–6, and once again in the 1470s and 1480s. See Eliyahu Ashtor, "The Wheat Supply of the Mamluk Kingdom", *Asian and African Studies* (Haifa) 18 (1984), 283–4, 286, 287–90; Ashtor, *Levant Trade in the Later Middle Ages* (Princeton, 1983), pp. 222, 236, 242, 466, 503. Less convincing is Ashtor's argument ("Wheat Supply", 285, 286–7) that wheat from the Christian West was bought also in regular years. Was it financially worth while for Egyptians to buy imported grain? Ashtor (ibid., 295) does not ponder the problem. He also assumes that importing was exclusively undertaken by the regime, but it need not have been.

84 This is provided we accept Ashtor's figure of 1 dinar as the "normal" price of 100 kg of wheat at the beginning of the eleventh century. See *Prix*, p. 124.

85 Shoshan, "Fāṭimid Grain", 187 n. 9; Bianquis, "Crise", 91–2. Only following one qadi's advice in 1052 or 1053 was grain replaced by another commodity as a monopoly. See *Itti'āẓ*, Vol. II, p. 225; *Khiṭaṭ*, Vol. I, p. 109; Hassanein Rabie, *The Financial System of Egypt A.H. 564–741/A.D. 1169–1341* (London, 1972), p. 92.

86 For a detailed explanation of this practice see, e.g., Lapidus, *Muslim Cities*, pp. 56–9. For 1336 see *Sulūk*, Vol. II, p. 414. For 1386 see *Sulūk*, Vol. III, p. 553; *Badā'i'*, Vol. I, pt 2, p. 379. For 1396 see Ibn Furāt, Vol. IX, pp. 427–8, 439; Lapidus, *Muslim Cities*, p. 53. For 1389 see Ibn Furāt, Vol. IX, p. 144; Lapidus, *Muslim Cities*, p. 53.

87 *Sulūk*, Vol. IV, pp. 801, 820, 872, 933, 934; Ahmad Darrag, *L'Egypte sous le règne de Barsbay 825–841/1422–1438* (Damascus, 1961), pp. 152–3; Lapidus, *Muslim Cities*, pp. 52–3, with slight inaccuracies. See also ibid., pp. 36, 57, 126–8.

88 *Sulūk*, Vol. II, pp. 394–6; *'Iqd*, Istanbul, Topkapi Sarayi MS 2911/C 34, fos. 8b–11b; Lapidus, *Muslim Cities*, p. 54. In 1416, a year of exceptionally high prices, one emir arrived from Upper Egypt with large supplies of grain, presumably intending to sell them in Cairo at a high price. However, he was forced to sell at the market price. See *Inbā'*, Vol. III, p. 86. In 1470 it was rumoured that the cause of a price increase was the hoarding of grain by the *dawādār* Yashbek and the obstacles he put on supplies from Upper Egypt to Cairo. See *Badā'i'*, Vol. III, p. 42. A poem critical of him was written for that reason.

89 Speculation with grain was considered sinful by Muslim jurists, and, according to the contemporary Ibn Taymiyya, the qadi had the duty to imprison speculators. See Ibn Taymiyya, *al-Ḥisba fī'l-Islām* (Damascus, 1967), pp. 23, 47–8.

90 E.g., in 1415. See *Sulūk*, Vol. IV, pp. 330–1. For 1419 see *Sulūk*, Vol. IV, p. 503. For 1425 see ibid., pp. 710, 711. For 1427 see ibid., p. 750. The manipulatory actions of grain owners are noted in a general statement in *Khiṭaṭ*, Vol. I, p. 61.

91 For 1374 see *Sulūk*, Vol. III, p. 233. For 1383 see *Badā'i'*, Vol. I, pt 2, p. 298. For 1396 see Ibn Furāt, Vol. IX, pp. 434–5. For 1415 see *Sulūk*, Vol. IV, pp. 331, 332, 334; *Badā'i'*, Vol. II, p. 24. For 1416 see *Inbā'*, Vol. III, p. 85. For 1426 see *Sulūk*, Vol. IV, p. 710; *Badā'i'*, Vol. II, p. 104. For 1427 see *Sulūk*, Vol. IV, p. 750. For 1449 see *Ḥawādith*, pp. 47–8; *Tibr*, pp. 259–60. For 1450 see *Ḥawādith*, p. 88; *Tibr*, p. 311. For 1451 see *Tibr*, p. 346. For 1462 see *Ḥawādith*, p. 429; *Badā'i'*, Vol. II, p. 394. For 1467 see *Badā'i'*, Vol. II, p. 449. For 1468 see *Ḥawādith*, p. 685; *Inbā' al-haṣr*, p. 28.

92 In 1427 the gathering of Egyptians at the bank of the Nile to wait there for the plenitude was banned. See *Sulūk*, Vol. IV, pp. 748–9. In 1462 Sultan Khushqadām contemplated the destruction of the Nilometer. See *Badā'i'*, Vol. II, p. 394.

93 For *khushkār* and *huwwārī* see E. Ashtor, "The Diet of Salaried Classes in the Medieval Near East", in Robert Forster and Orest Ranum (eds.), *Biology of Man in History* (Baltimore, 1975), pp. 127, 128.

94 There is the interesting report on a bakery situated in the "Little Market of the Arabs" (*suwayqat al-'arab*) outside Bāb Zuwayla, which, around the mid fourteenth century, produced 7,000 loaves daily for the neighbourhood. See *Khiṭaṭ*, Vol. II, p. 106.

95 It remains unclear whether the people of Cairo bought baked bread, or rather bought grain, took it to the millers, and then took the dough to the bakers. The occurrence of bread riots, as we shall soon see, suggests that many Cairenes obtained their loaves from bakeries. For the opinion that in the Cairo of the eighteenth century most people still baked their own bread see André Raymond, *Artisans et commerçants au Caire au XVIIIe siècle* (Damascus, 1972), p. 55 n. 1. For the same in contemporary London and Paris see Thompson, "Moral Economy", 83–4; Tilly, "Food Riots", 27. In seventeenth-century Geneva everyone used to bake their own bread, and there was much anxiety in 1673 when the possibility of forbidding domestic baking was raised. See Fernand Braudel, *Capitalism and Material Life 1400–1800* (New York, 1973), p. 76. However, in Venice around the middle of the sixteenth century, only about 22 per cent of the populace baked their own bread. See Brian Pullan, *Rich and Poor in Renaissance Venice* (Cambridge, Mass., 1971), p. 294.

96 *Itti'āẓ*, Vol. II, p. 151; Bianquis, "Crise", 81. For another case in the same year see *Itti'āẓ*, Vol. II, p. 165. For 1006 see ibid., p. 69; *Ighātha*, pp. 15–16. Incidentally,

bakers, at least around the mid eleventh century, were organized under their own "head" (*'arīf*). See *Itti'āẓ*, Vol. II, pp. 224–5; *Ighātha*, p. 18. For *'arīf* see Goitein, *Economic Foundations*, p. 84.

97 *'Iqd*, Istanbul, Topkapi Sarayi MS Ahmed III 2911/a 19, fo. 114b. For 1420 see *Inbā'*, Vol. III, p. 215.

98 *Itti'āẓ*, Vol. II, p. 74; Shoshan, "Fāṭimid Grain", 183, where some misinterpretation occurs.

99 *Itti'āẓ*, Vol. II, pp. 134–5.

100 Ibid., pp. 164–5. The man was 'Abd Allāh Muḥammad b. Jaysh b. Ṣamṣama al-Kutāmī. His father was one of the first Fāṭimid governors of Damascus. See Ibn Qalānisī, *Dhayl ta'rīkh Dimashq* (Leiden, 1908), passim.

101 *Badā'i'*, Vol. I, pt 2, p. 126; Lapidus, *Muslim Cities*, p. 145.

102 *Sulūk*, Vol. III, p. 818; *Nuzha*, Vol. I, p. 391; Ibn Furāt, Vol. IX, p. 387; Lapidus, *Muslim Cities*, p. 54.

103 *Sulūk*, Vol. III, pp. 859–60, 871; *Nuzha*, Vol. I, pp. 429–30; Ibn Furāt, Vol. IX, pp. 439–40, 455.

104 *Sulūk*, Vol. IV, pp. 330–6, 343–4. For a confrontation with bakers in 1341 see Shujā'ī, p. 103. In that case the prefect punished them.

105 *Sulūk*, Vol. IV, p. 964.

106 For 1452 see *Tibr*, p. 353. For 1468 see *Badā'i'*, Vol. III, p. 11.

107 *Inbā' al-haṣr*, pp. 476–7.

108 'Abd al-Bāsiṭ, *Ḥawādith*, fo. 303a.

109 *Badā'i'*, Vol. IV, pp. 302–3.

110 *Sulūk*, Vol. IV, pp. 698, 706; *Inbā'*, Vol. III, p. 350; *Nujūm*, Vol. XIV, pp. 281–2, quoting al-Maqrīzī. Ibn Taghrī Birdī was aware of the animosity between his source and al-'Aynī, the main "villain" in this incident.

111 For 1348 see *Sulūk*, Vol. II, p. 758. For 1377 see ibid., p. 210. For 1380 see *Sulūk*, Vol. III, p. 395. For 1382 see *Sulūk*, Vol. III, p. 457; *Badā'i'*, Vol. I, pt 2, p. 298. For 1394 see *Nuzha*, Vol. I, p. 391. For 1397 see ibid., pp. 459–60. For 1449 see *Nujūm*, Vol. XV, pp. 397–401; *Tibr*, pp. 260–1; *Badā'i'*, Vol. II, pp. 275–6. For 1480 see *Badā'i'*, Vol. III, p. 165. For 1489 see ibid., p. 263. For 1509 see *Badā'i'*, Vol. IV, p. 116. See also Lapidus, *Muslim Cities*, p. 146.

112 *Badā'i'*, Vol. II, p. 104.

113 In contradistinction, in medieval Normandy it was believed that "no miller can enter Heaven". See H. E. Jacob, *Six Thousand Years of Bread: Its Holy and Unholy History* (New York, 1945), p. 129. For the attitude toward millers in eighteenth-century England see Thompson, "Moral Economy", 103–7.

114 Thompson, "Moral Economy", 79. For studies employing Thompson's model see Andrew Charlesworth and Adrian J. Randall, "Morals, Markets and the English Crowd in 1766", *Past & Present* 114 (1987), 200 n. 2. Thompson has been challenged by Dale Edward Williams, "Morals, Markets and the English Crowd in 1766", *Past & Present* 104 (1984), 56–73. See also the rejoinder by Charlesworth and Randall, "Morals".

115 Tilly, "Food Riots", 46–7.

116 For the slogan "Prices are in God's hand" (*as-si'r bi-yad Allāh*) in 1394 see *Nuzha*, Vol. I, p. 391.

117 During the shortage in 1513 people in Cairo protested against the shipment of grain to Syria. See *Badā'i'*, Vol. IV, pp. 302–3.

118 Thompson, "Moral Economy", 89–94.

119 Tilly, "Food Riots", 23, 25–6, 35–45. For the liberal ideology of grain marketing, which in France emerged around the middle of the eighteenth century, see Kaplan, *Bread*, pp. 97–163.

120 Tilly, "Food Riots", 23–4, 46–7. For this point see also Charles Tilly, "Food Supply and Public Order in Modern Europe", in Charles Tilly (ed.), *The Formation of National States in Western Europe* (Princeton, 1975), pp. 385–8.

121 In Egypt, there was an inflationary decade in 1370–80 and prolonged inflation in the second half of the fifteenth century. This could account for grain riots during these periods. Between *ca* 1400 and 1450, however, grain prices were generally stable, and still some riots occurred. For price data see Shoshan, "Money Supply", 50 n. 21 and p. 54.

122 It is possible, of course, that for earlier periods similar incidents simply went unrecorded. Cf. Tilly's remark ("Food Riots", 24 n. 4) that in France there are few documented grain riots before the mid seventeenth century, and only sparse information on such riots before the end of that century. She assumes that either there were few of them, or they were not considered worth mentioning.

123 For the same argument as regards France see Tilly, "Food Riots", 24.

5 Popular culture and high culture in medieval Cairo

1 These cultural blocks are briefly suggested in the Introduction. For a general outline of the socio-cultural system in medieval Islam see Boaz Shoshan, "High Culture and Popular Culture in Medieval Islam", *Studia Islamica* 83 (1991), 67–107.

2 Popular culture is obviously a modern concept which first emerged at the end of the eighteenth century. See, e.g., Burke, *Popular Culture*, pp. 3–22.

3 H. Laoust, "Ibn Taymiyya", *EI*². For Ibn Taymiyya's complex relationship with the Mamluk elite see Memon, *Ibn Taimiya*, pp. 46–57.

4 See Chapter 1 above.

5 Memon, *Ibn Taimiya*, p. 54.

6 Laoust, "Ibn Taymiyya", *EI*². On one occasion Ibn Taymiyya was released from prison by Ḥusām ad-Dīn Muhannā' b. 'Īsā. See Memon, *Ibn Taimiya*, p. 54. For this dignitary see *Badā'i'*, Vol. I, pt 1, p. 467. For other Mamluk admirers of Ibn Taymiyya see *JSS* 33 (1988), 96 and n. 68. I owe this reference to Professor U. Haarmann of Freiburg University.

7 *Iqtiḍā' ṣirāṭ al-mustaqīm mukhālafat aṣḥāb al-jaḥīm*. Memon's *Ibn Taimiya* is a translation of most of the Arabic text with a valuable introduction to some of Ibn Taymiyya's doctrines.

8 Memon, *Ibn Taimiya*, pp. 210–12, 221–2. For an attack on popular festivals and their description see pp. 241–331.

9 A Yale University manuscript of this work was published by Charles D. Matthews, "A Muslim Iconoclast (Ibn Taymiyyeh) on the 'Merits of Jerusalem and Palestine'", *JAOS* 56 (1936), 1–21. For a more recent edition see *Kitāb az-ziyāra*, ed. Sayf ad-Dīn al-Kātib (Beirut, 1980).

10 Memon, *Ibn Taimiya*, pp. 77–8, 86.

11 Donald P. Little, "Did Ibn Taymiyya Have a Screw Loose?", *Studia Islamica* 41 (1975), 107.

12 *Madkhal*, Vol. I, pp. 255–313; Vol. II, pp. 46–68. See further information on him in

J. C. Vadet, "Ibn al-Ḥādjdj", *EI*[2], Vol. III, p. 779; C. Brockelmann, "Al-ʿAbdarī", *EI*[1]; Langner, *Untersuchungen*, pp. 20–3. On pp. 24–62 Langner draws on the *Madkhal* for her discussion of various customs and festivals.

13 *Madkhal*, Vol. II, pp. 47–8.

14 Ed. Subhi Labib (2 vols., Wiesbaden, 1986). Labib's German and Arabic introductions in Vol. I supersede his earlier discussion of that book in "The Problem of the *Bidʿa* in the Light of an Arabic Manuscript of the 14th Century", *JESHO* 7 (1964), 191–6. For the approximate date of the composition of the work see also *Lumaʿ*, Vol. I, p. 497; P. M. Holt, *BSOAS* 51 (1988), 331–2.

15 *Lumaʿ*, Vol. I, pp. 76–100, 214–29, 287–316.

16 Donald P. Little, "The Historical and Historiographical Significance of the Detention of Ibn Taymiyya", *IJMES* 4 (1973), 312. Cf. Memon, *Ibn Taimiya*, pp. 49–50. For a detailed account of the trial, following the discovery in 1326 of Ibn Taymiyya's *fatwā* against *ziyāras*, see Hasan Qasim Murad, "Ibn Taymiya on Trial: A Narrative Account of his *Miḥan*", *Islamic Studies* 18 (1979), 23–5.

17 The chief Mālikite qadi of Cairo, who brought Ibn Taymiyya to trial, wrote a rebuttal on the question of *ziyāra*. See Murad, "Ibn Taymiya on Trial", 25. Taqī ad-Dīn as-Subkī (d. 1355) wrote *Shifāʾ as-saqām fī ziyārat khayr al-anām*, subtitled *The Waging of War against those Rejecting the Ziyāra* (*Shann al-ghāra ʿalā man ankara safar az-ziyāra*) (Hyderabad, 1897). For the third scholar see *Nujūm*, Vol. IX, p. 270.

18 Murad, "Ibn Taymiya on Trial", 24.

19 Johs. Pedersen, "Masdjid", *EI*[1], sec. B/4. For early controversies as regards the subject see Yūsuf Rāġib, "Les Premiers Monuments funéraires de l'Islam", *AI* 9 (1970), 21–2.

20 Jalāl ad-Dīn as-Suyūṭī, *Ḥusn al-maqāṣid fī ʿamal al-mawlid*, Berlin MS (Ahlwardt, No. 9541), fo. 28b. Suyūṭī quotes also from the *Madkhal*'s chapter on the *mawlid* to buttress his argument. His short treatise is essentially a polemic against the Mālikite Tāj ad-Dīn b. ʿUmar b. ʿAlī al-Lakhm al-Iskandarī, known as al-Fakhānī, who, in his *al-Mawrid fīʾl-kalām ʿalā ʿamal al-mawlid*, considered the celebrations to be a "condemned innovation" (*bidʿa madhmūma*). See also von Grunebaum, *Muhammadan Festivals*, p. 76; Memon, *Ibn Taymiya*, p. 5; H. Fuchs, "Mawlid", *EI*[1]; Schimmel, "Religious Life", 370.

21 See Chapter 3 above.

22 *Khiṭaṭ*, Vol. I, p. 313.

23 *Khiṭaṭ*, Vol. II, p. 287; Ignaz Goldziher, "Veneration of Saints in Islam", in Goldziher, *Muslim Studies*, Vol. II (London, 1971), pp. 320–1.

24 Musabbiḥī, *Akhbār Miṣr*, pp. 14–15.

25 *Madkhal*, Vol. I, p. 253.

26 *Nujūm*, Vol. VIII, p. 230.

27 *Sulūk*, Vol. III, p. 749; *Inbāʾ*, Vol. I, p. 318; Ibn Furāt, Vol. IX, p. 266.

28 The connection between plagues and immorality is a theme recurring in Mamluk sources.

29 *Sulūk*, Vol. IV, pp. 486, 594, 619; *Badāʾiʿ*, Vol. II, p. 147; *Inbāʾ*, Vol. III, p. 470.

30 *Badāʾiʿ*, Vol. IV, p. 76.

31 *Ṣubḥ*, Vol. IV, pp. 7–8; Fr. Buhl and J. Jomier, "Maḥmal", *EI*[2], informative especially on processions in the modern era. The political significance of the *maḥmil* and its role in establishing Egyptian hegemony, mainly *vis-à-vis* the province of Iraq in the pre-Ottoman period, are discussed in Jacques Jomier, *Le Maḥmal et la caravane*

égyptienne des pèlerins de la Mecque (XIIIe–XXe siècles) (Cairo, 1953), pp. 27–34, 42–56.

32 Buhl and Jomier, "Maḥmal", *EI*². Lane provides a particularly vivid description of the procession in 1834. See *Manners*, pp. 440–8.

33 *Ṣubḥ*, Vol. IV, p. 57.

34 E.g., *Badā'i'*, Vol. II, pp. 145, 456. In 1467 a firecracket (*ṣārūkh*, pl. *ṣawārīkh*; see R. Dozy, "Sārūkh", in *Supplément aux dictionnaire arabe*, 3rd edn (Leiden, 1967)) flew over the Citadel and set the sultan's stable on fire. The people, we are told, considered this event a bad omen, and indeed the sultan died the following year. See *Badā'i'*, Vol. II, p. 447.

35 This is Gibb's translation (see n. 36 below) of the term *umanā' ar-ru'asā'*. As scholars have argued that there were no corporations in Mamluk Egypt (e.g., Lapidus, *Muslim Cities*, p. 96), a preferable rendering would be "heads of professions". See Goitein, *Economic Foundations*, p. 84.

36 *Travels of Ibn Baṭṭūṭa*, Vol. I, p. 59; Arabic text, *Riḥla*, pp. 46–7. See also Jomier, *Maḥmal*, p. 37; Langner, *Untersuchungen*, pp. 39–41. Gibb notes that it is scarcely possible that Ibn Baṭṭūṭa could have witnessed this particular procession himself, since during the months of Rajab and Shawwāl of AH 726 he was on the move, and on his next visit to Cairo in 749 (1348–9), the caravan had already left. See *Travels of Ibn Baṭṭūṭa*, Vol. I, pp. 58–9 n. 181.

37 Jomier, *Maḥmal*, p. 42, translates "cortège d'accompagnement". In 1450 it was dropped because of the small number of Mamluks participating in the Pilgrimage, and because of high prices. See *Ḥawādith*, pp. 95–6. It was later reintroduced, and then once again abolished under Sultan Qāyit Bāy (1468–96). See *Badā'i'*, Vol. III, p. 330.

38 *Ṣubḥ*, Vol. IV, p. 58; Jomier, *Maḥmal*, p. 42.

39 *Khiṭaṭ*, Vol. II, p. 23.

40 *Ḥawādith*, pp. 303–5; *Badā'i'*, Vol. II, p. 341.

41 *Nujūm*, Vol. XIV, pp. 86–7; Schimmel, "Religious Life", p. 367, for the first quarter of the fifteenth century.

42 *Badā'i'*, Vol. IV, pp. 409–12. Part of a *maḥmal* designed for Sultan Qānṣawh al-Ghawrī, the oldest *maḥmal* known to have been preserved, is now at the Topkapi Sarayi museum in Istanbul. For a study of its inscription see Jacques Jomier, "Le Maḥmal du sultan Qānṣūh al-Ghūri (début XVIe siècle)", *AI* 11 (1972), 183–8. For other descriptions of splendid processions see *Badā'i'*, Vol. III, pp. 104, 106–7 (year 1474); ibid., pp. 161–2 (year 1480).

43 *Ṣubḥ*, Vol. IV, p. 58; Jomier, *Maḥmal*, p. 37. For 1383 see *Badā'i'*, Vol. I, pt 2, p. 334. For 1432 see *Badā'i'*, Vol. II, p. 141. For 1435 see ibid., p. 161. For 1438 see ibid., p. 179.

44 *Badā'i'*, Vol. IV, p. 145. For a military show in 1504 or 1505 see a relatively detailed description in ibid., p. 72.

45 *Badā'i'*, Vol. II, p. 243; *Ḥawādith*, p. 15.

46 *Ḥawādith*, p. 180. It was abolished for an unspecified reason under Qāyit Bāy (1468–96). See *Badā'i'*, Vol. III, p. 330.

47 *Ṣubḥ*, Vol. IV, p. 57.

48 For *turjumān* as interpreter see *Sulūk*, Vol. III, p. 379; *Badā'i'*, Vol. I, pt 2, p. 255. According to Doris Behrens-Abuseif, *Azbakiyya and its Environs from Azbak to Ismail 1476–1879* (Cairo, 1985), p. 41, a *turjumān* was an official in charge of foreign merchants.

49 Arabic *surriyāqāt*. See Dozy, *Supplément*, s.v.

50 *Nujūm*, Vol. XV, p. 128; *Ḍaw'*, Vol. III, p. 303; Schimmel, "Religious Life", 367. The poet Zayn ad-Dīn Sha'bān b. Muḥammad al-Āthārī (or al-Miṣrī) (d. 1425; see further information on him in *Ḍaw'*, Vol. III, pp. 301–3; *Inbā'*, Vol. III, pp. 353–5) composed a short poem on that occasion in which he pointed out that the action of the Interpreter symbolized an age when donkeys were exalted above the truly worthy. It is noteworthy that about 200 years later the Ottoman writer Muṣṭafā 'Alī of Gallipoli, who visited Cairo in 1599, reported of the "nice custom . . . that one of the relatives of the person that undertakes the pilgrimage . . . has the Koran verse on the pilgrimage inscribed with large letters on the wall of his door. Some even decorate it with various embellishments, and colors. Those who pass through that street will know for sure that the owner of that house has gone on the pilgrimage that year." See *Muṣṭafā 'Alī's Description*, p. 33. This phenomenon has been retained. "The custom in [modern] Egypt was for the façade of the pilgrims' houses, in the popular quarters, to be decorated around the door with naive frescos recalling their journey. These frescos, painted at the time of their return, might stay in place for several years before being worn away by time." See Buhl and Jomier, "Maḥmal", *EI*²; Jomier, *Maḥmal*, pl. VI. For this sort of graffiti see Giovanni Canova, "Nota sulle raffigurazioni populari del pellegrinaggio in Egitto", *Annali della Facoltà di lingue e letterature straniere di Cá Foscari* 14/3 (1975), 83–94; Jean Michot, "Les Fresques du pèlerinage au Caire", *Art and Archeology Research Papers* 13 (1978), 7–21.

51 *Badā'i'*, Vol. II, p. 243; *Ḥawādith*, p. 15.

52 *Ḥawādith*, p. 189.

53 *Sulūk*, Vol. IV, p. 614.

54 The reporter is al-'Asqalānī himself. See *Inbā'*, Vol. III, pp. 402–3.

55 For the earliest possible occurrence of all this, in Rajab 840 (1437), see *Sulūk*, Vol. IV, p. 1006. For the following year see ibid., p. 1027.

56 Compare this to the custom associated with the Emir of Nawrūz in Chapter 3 above.

57 *Ḥawādith*, pp. 189, 300, 316, 493, 538–9; *Nujūm*, Vol. XVI, p. 123; 'Abd al-Bāsiṭ, *Ḥawādith*, fo. 121a. For a "funny man" (*shakhṣ muḍḥik*) playing the role of a "demon" in 1512 see *Badā'i'*, Vol. IV, pp. 254–5.

58 The intriguing information above raises the question of the role of both masks and demons in late medieval Islam. It appears that the only sources utilized thus far for studying these are popular works such as *Thousand and One Nights* and *Sīrat Sayf b. Dhī Yazan*. See J. Chelhod, "'Ifrīt", *EI*². For demon-stories in the *Nights* see Mia I. Gerhardt, *The Art of Story-Telling: A Literary Study of the Thousand and One Nights* (Leiden, 1963), pp. 280–1. Humans masked as demons featured, of course, in medieval European carnivals such as the German Fastnacht. See, e.g., Dietz-Rüdiger Moser, *Fastnacht-Fasching-Karneval, Das Fest der "Verkehrten Welt"* (Graz, 1986), p. 205; Anthony Caputi, *Buffo: The Genius of Vulgar Comedy* (Detroit, 1978), pp. 56–8.

59 A detailed description of the ceremonies in the years AH 516–18, based on al-Maqrīzī and his earlier sources, is given in Paula A. Sanders, "The Court Ceremonial of the Fatimid Caliphate in Egypt", unpublished doctoral dissertation, Princeton University (1984), 182–205. Her study, however, treats the subject from an exclusively royal point of view. For modern time we have the description for the year 1834 in Lane, *Manners*, Ch. XXVI.

60 For the precise itinerary of the caliph in the Fāṭimid period see *Ṣubḥ*, Vol. III, pp. 516–17. According to one of our sources, of the early Mamluk sultans only Baybars participated in person, and it was not until the days of Barqūq at the end of the fourteenth century that a sultan participated again. See *Nuzha*, Vol. I, p. 67; *Inbā'*, Vol. I, p. 273. For the participation of sultans in the later Mamluk period see, e.g., *Nujūm*, Vol. XI, p. 233 (year 1383); Ibn Furāt, Vol. IX, p. 306 (year 1392); ibid., p. 342 (year 1393); ibid., p. 442 (year 1396); ibid., p. 468 (year 1397); *Badā'i'*, Vol. I, pt 2, pp. 502–3 (year 1397); *Inbā'*, Vol. III, p. 436 (year 1429); *Badā'i'*, Vol. II, p. 431 (year 1465).

61 *Sulūk*, Vol. IV, pp. 501–2; *Nujūm*, Vol. XIV, pp. 86–7; *Badā'i'*, Vol. III, p. 330 (the latter part of the fifteenth century).

62 E.g., *Sulūk*, Vol. I, p. 73; William Popper, *The Cairo Nilometer: Studies in Ibn Taghrī Birdī's Chronicle of Egypt* (Berkeley, 1951), pp. 71–2, quoting Ibn Duqmāq. For *takhlīq al-miqyās* in 1280 and 1281 see Ibn Furāt, Vol. VII, pp. 181–2. For 1383 see *Badā'i'*, Vol. I, pt 2, p. 330. For 1384 see ibid., p. 348.

63 *Ḥawādith*, p. 111.

64 For the sultan participating in the ceremony in person, see, e.g., *Badā'i'*, Vol. I, pt 2, pp. 453–4 (year 1392); pp. 502–3 (year 1397); *Badā'i'*, Vol. II, p. 7 (year 1413); p. 22 (year 1414); p. 39 (year 1418); p. 49 (year 1419); p. 55 (year 1420); p. 135 (year 1430). See also Popper, *Nilometer*, pp. 82, 85–6. Leo Africanus reported in the first half of the sixteenth century about the Mamluk sultan himself taking an axe and breaking into the wall. The leading persons of his entourage did the same in order to demolish the part of the wall retaining the water. See Wiet, *Cairo*, p. 118.

65 *Intiṣār*, Vol. IV, pt 1, pp. 114–15.

66 *Sulūk*, Vol. IV, pp. 501–2.

67 E.g., *Sulūk*, Vol. I, p. 136 (year 1196); *Nuzha*, Vol. II, p. 448 (year 1419).

68 *Itti'āẓ*, Vol. III, p. 232; *Badā'i'*, Vol. I, pt 1, p. 251. The latter has the name Ibn Maqshar (?).

69 Ibn Muyassar, *Akhbār Miṣr*, p. 97; *Itti'āẓ*, Vol. III, p. 107.

70 For a general statement see *Sulūk*, Vol. IV, p. 748. In 1416, and later in 1458, shacks erected for people waiting for the plenitude were turned into a place of "abominations", prostitution, and wine drinking, and therefore were removed. See *Sulūk*, Vol. IV, p. 358; *Inbā'*, Vol. III, p. 93; *Badā'i'*, Vol. II, p. 27; 'Abd al-Bāsiṭ, *Ḥawādith*, fo. 120b. For a similar case in 1469 see *Inbā' al-haṣr*, p. 203.

71 *Badā'i'*, Vol. III, p. 363. For this complex see also Vol. III, pp. 280–1. For the Qadi Ibn al-Ji'ān see *Ḍaw'*, Vol. XI, pp. 8–10.

72 *Ṣubḥ*, Vol. III, p. 517, speaks of "about 1,000 boats" sailing on such occasions in the Fāṭimid period. In 1421 a boat full of spectators sank during the festival; on board also was a high-ranking emir. See *Nuzha*, Vol. II, p. 520.

73 Wiet, *Cairo*, p. 118.

74 For 1400 see *Sulūk*, Vol. III, p. 1021; *Badā'i'*, Vol. I, pt 2, p. 589. For 1416 see *Sulūk*, Vol. IV, p. 358; *Inbā'*, Vol. III, p. 93. For 1426–7 see *Sulūk*, Vol. IV, pp. 748–9. For 1466 see *Badā'i'*, Vol. II, p. 440. For 1511 see *Badā'i'*, Vol. IV, p. 231.

75 For royal processions in the Fāṭimid period see M. Canard, "Cérémonial fatimide et cérémonial byzantin", *Byzantion* 21 (1951), esp. 396–404; Canard, "La Procession du nouvel an chez les Fatimides", *Annales de l'Institute d'Etudes Orientales de la Faculté des Lettres d'Alger* 10 (1952), 364–98. For New Year processions in Muḥarram see also most recently Sanders, "Court Ceremonial", 146–69.

However, according to Sanders (p. 161) "the audience for this elaborate display seems primarily to have been the participants themselves".

76 In the fourteenth and fifteenth centuries processions in Cairo, most of which were "royal" – that is, in which the Mamluk sultan featured – were almost an annual event. This is a phenomenon which deserves a detailed study.

77 E.g., *Khiṭaṭ*, Vol. II, pp. 107–8 (years 1172 and 1261); *Sulūk*, Vol. I, p. 87 (year 1296); P. M. Holt, "The Structure of Government in the Mamluk Sultanate", in P. M. Holt (ed.), *The Eastern Mediterranean Lands in the Period of the Crusades* (Warminster, 1977), p. 47.

78 For the sultan's annual (at least in the second half of the fourteenth century) procession from the Hippodrome to the Citadel, upon concluding the polo tournament, see *Badā'i'*, Vol. I, pt 2, p. 136. In 'Īd al-Fiṭr, the feast concluding the Ramaḍān fast, there was the Procession of the Vizier (*mawkib al-wazīr*), from the Citadel to his residence, riding a *baznārī* (?) (Schimmel: "whitish"; Wiet: "with a large saddle-cloth") mule and wearing a special costume. Mamluk troops (*'ujāqiyya*) and incense burners led the procession. See *Badā'i'*, Vol. IV, p. 104; Schimmel, "Religious Life", 364; G. Wiet, *Journal d'un bourgeois au Caire* (Paris, 1955–60), Vol. I, p. 101. The last vizier who conducted that procession was deposed in 1462 or 1463. See *Badā'i'*, Vol. II, p. 405.

79 *Sulūk*, Vol. I, pp. 377, 701, 939; Vol. IV, pp. 507, 963; *Nujūm*, Vol. VIII, p. 167; Vol. XIV, pp. 89–90; Vol. XV, p. 70; *Badā'i'*, Vol. III, p. 228; Vol. IV, p. 105. For a detailed description of the procession in 1426, following the successful raid of Cyprus, see *Sulūk*, Vol. IV, pp. 724–5.

80 This appears to be a decoration used also on other occasions, e.g., in 1390, following another victory. See *Sulūk*, Vol. III, p. 715.

81 *Sulūk*, Vol. I, pp. 938–40; *Nujūm*, Vol. VIII, pp. 165–8.

82 *Badā'i'*, Vol. IV, pp. 478–9, French trans. Wiet, *Journal*, pp. 442–3.

83 E.g., *Sulūk*, Vol. I, p. 780; Vol. II, pp. 211, 241, 335, 392, 469, 882; Vol. III, pp. 354–5, 482; Vol. IV, pp. 528, 746–7; *Nujūm*, Vol. XI, p. 183; Vol. XII, p. 3; Vol. XIV, pp. 60–1; Vol. XV, p. 342; *Badā'i'*, Vol. IV, pp. 212, 336, 397.

84 E.g., *Sulūk*, Vol. I, p. 457; Vol. II, pp. 356, 876; Vol. III, pp. 52, 704, 705, 825; *Nujūm*, Vol. VIII, p. 167; Vol. IX, p. 107; Vol. XII, p. 3; *Badā'i'*, Vol. III, pp. 34, 139, 162.

85 E.g., *Sulūk*, Vol. I, p. 444; Vol. II, p. 211; Vol. III, p. 705; *Nujūm*, Vol. IX, p. 99; Vol. XII, p. 3; *Badā'i'*, Vol. III, pp. 34, 106, 139.

86 E.g., *Sulūk*, Vol. I, p. 832; Vol. II, pp. 211, 241.

87 E.g., *Sulūk*, Vol. I, p. 290; *Badā'i'*, Vol. III, p. 55.

88 *Sulūk*, Vol. II, pp. 211, 241, 335; *Nujūm*, Vol. VIII, p. 165; vol. IX, p. 61; vol. XIV, p. 60; *Badā'i'*, Vol. III, pp. 34, 55, 77, 106, 162, 271; Vol. IV, pp. 274, 333–4, 336, 367.

89 *Sulūk*, Vol. I, p. 939. See also pp. 831–2; Vol. II, p. 83; *Nujūm*, Vol. VIII, p. 166.

90 E.g., *Sulūk*, Vol. II, p. 356; Vol. III, p. 705; *Nujūm*, Vol. XII, p. 3; *Badā'i'*, Vol. IV, pp. 202, 212, 236, 333; vol. V, p. 41.

91 *Nujūm*, Vol. XIV, p. 299; *Badā'i'*, Vol. III, pp. 186, 460; Vol. IV, pp. 202, 212, 213, 236, 274, 333, 336; Vol. V, p. 41.

92 E.g., in 1420. See *Nujūm*, Vol. XIV, p. 105: "li-qaḍā' ḥawā'ijihim".

93 *Badā'i'*, Vol. V, pp. 35–7.

94 For a similar argument see Lawrence M. Bryant, *The King and the City in the Parisian Royal Entry Ceremony: Politics, Ritual, and Art in the Renaissance* (Geneva, 1986), pp. 15–16.

95 Roger Chartier, *The Cultural Uses of Print in Early Modern France* (Princeton, 1987), p. 22.

96 Stuart Hall, "Notes on Deconstructing 'the Popular'", in Raphael Samuel (ed.), *People's History and Socialist Theory* (London, 1981), p. 234. For a general statement about mutual influence among subcultures see also Robert Mandrou, "Cultures populaire et savante: rapport et contacts", in Jacques Beauroy *et al.* (eds.), *The Wolf and the Lamb: Popular Culture in France from the Old Regime to the Twentieth Century* (Saratoga, 1976), p. 18. For the interaction between learned and popular cultures in medieval Christendom see briefly Le Goff, "Learned and Popular Dimensions", p. 29. Mikhail Bakhtin, in his work on Rabelais, written in 1940 (English trans. *Rabelais and his World* (Cambridge, Mass., 1968)), introduced the notion of "circularity" between the cultures of the dominant and subordinate classes in pre-industrial Europe. For a brief appreciation of Bakhtin's contribution see Carlo Ginzburg, *The Cheese and the Worms: The Cosmos of a Sixteenth-Century Miller* (Baltimore, 1980), p. xii.

97 For the Christian case see the general remarks in Stephen Wilson (ed.), *Saints and their Cults: Studies in Religious Sociology, Folklore and History* (Cambridge, 1983), pp. 29–40; Weinstein and Bell, *Saints & Society*, p. 4. For Islam see Goldziher, "Veneration".

98 *Nujūm*, Vol. XV, pp. 176–7.

99 *Badā'i'*, Vol. III, p. 156. See further information on him in W. Khalidi, "al-Dasūḳī, Burhān al-Dīn Ibrāhīm", *EI*².

100 On 'Abd al-Qādir ad-Dashṭūṭī (or Tashṭūṭī) see *Ḍaw'*, Vol. IV, pp. 300–1; Najm ad-Dīn al-Ghāzzī, *al-Kawākib as-sā'ira bi-a'yān al-mi'a al-'āshira* (Beirut, 1945–59), Vol. I, pp. 246–50; J.-C. Garcin, "Deux saints populaires du Caire au début du XVIe siècle", *BEO* 29 (1977), esp. 137–42.

101 *Badā'i'*, Vol. III, pp. 259–60; Schimmel, "Religious Life", 373. There is an ironical sequel to this story: it was later discovered that the man was actually not the renowned Sufi. The humiliated sultan took severe measures against those deceiving him (or who may themselves have been deceived).

102 E. M. Sartain, *Jalāl al-Dīn al-Suyūṭī* (Cambridge, 1975), Vol. I, p. 24; Vol. II, p. 235. Cf. Vol. II, pp. 20–2.

103 Ibn Ẓāfir, *Risāla*, p. 76 of Arabic text, pp. 174–5 of French trans.

104 Ibn Baṭṭūṭa, *Riḥla*, pp. 28, 29, 30; *Travels of Ibn Baṭṭūṭa*, Vol. I, pp. 28–9, 30, 32; *Durar*, Vol. IV, pp. 82–4 (No. 3766); *Nahj*, pp. 67–8. For Yalmalāk see *Durar*, Vol. I, p. 411; A. L. Mayer, *Saracenic Heraldry* (Oxford, 1933), pp. 59–62. In *Travels of Ibn Baṭṭūṭa*, Vol. I, p. 31 n. 79, Gibb dismisses Mayer's doubts concerning the identification.

105 Arabic: "wa-naẓara fi'l-nujūm wa-fī 'ilm al-ḥiraf wa-bari'a fī ma'rifat manāfi' an-nabāt".

106 *Tuḥfa*, pp. 50–1.

107 See p. 17 above.

108 *Badā'i'*, Vol. II, p. 393; *Nujūm*, Vol. XVI, p. 269; Schimmel, "Religious Life", 371.

109 *Badā'i'*, Vol. III, pp. 199, 330; Vollers, "Aḥmed al-Badawī", *EI*¹.

110 *Badā'i'*, Vol. III, p. 393; Schimmel, "Religious Life", 372.

111 Ibn al-Ḥimṣī, *Ta'rīkh*, fo. 21b. For Sīdī Ismā'īl see p. 17 above.

112 Such a list would include Shaykh Ḥasan b. 'Abd Allāh as-Sabbān (d. 1379), who lived by the Succour Gate. Among those venerating him was the father of Ibn Ḥajar

al-ʿAsqalānī. See *Inbāʾ*, Vol. I, p. 203. Other venerated *shaykhs* were Muḥammad b. ʿAbd Allāh az-Zawharī (d. 1398), see *Nujūm*, Vol. XIII, p. 10; *Ḍawʾ*, Vol. VIII, pp. 120–1 (No. 280); Saʿīd b. ʿAbd Allāh al-Maghribī (d. 1428), see *Nujūm*, Vol. XV, pp. 149–50; *Ḍawʾ*, Vol. IV, p. 255 (No. 952); Muḥammad Abū ʿAbd Allāh al-Hiwī, known as as-Safārī (d. 1451), see *Tibr*, p. 375; Muḥammad al-Maghribī (d. 1455), see *Nujūm*, Vol. XVI, pp. 177–8; *Ḍawʾ*, Vol. X, p. 125 (No. 523); ʿUmar b. Ibrāhīm al-Bābānī (al-Bānyāsī), known as ʿUmar al-Kurdī (d. 1458), see *Ḍawʾ*, Vol. VI, p. 64 (No. 219); Ibrāhīm al-Ghannām (d. 1465), see *Nujūm*, Vol. XVI, p. 344; *Ḍawʾ*, Vol. I, pp. 188–9; Ibrāhīm al-Matbūlī (d. 1472), see *Ḍawʾ*, Vol. I, pp. 85–6.

113 Marilyn R. Waldman, "Primitive Mind/Modern Mind, New Approaches to an Old Problem Applied to Islam", in Richard C. Martin (ed.), *Approaches to Islam in Religious Studies* (Tucson, 1985), esp. pp. 94, 100. Waldman, relying on Jack Goody's work, also provides a subtle criticism of the latter.

Select bibliography

Primary sources

'Abd al-Bāsiṭ, *Ḥawādith ad-duhūr fī maḍā'l-ayyām wash-shuhūr*, Oxford, Bodleian Library MS Huntington No. 610.

al-'Abdarī, *see* Ibn al-Ḥājj.

al-'Aynī, Badr ad-Dīn, *'Iqd al-jumān fī ta'rīkh ahl az-zamān*, ed. Muḥammad M. Amīn, Cairo, 1408/1988; Istanbul, Topkapi Sarayi MS Ahmed III No. A2911/a 19.

as-Sayf al-muhannad fī sīrat al-Malik al-Mu'ayyad, ed. Fahīm M. Shaltūt, Cairo, 1967.

al-Bakrī, Abū'l-Ḥasan Aḥmad b. 'Abd Allāh, *al-Anwār wa-miṣbāḥ* (or *miftāḥ*) *as-surūr* (or *al-asrār*) *wa'l-afkār fī dhikr* (*sayyidinā*) *Muḥammad al-muṣṭafā al-mukhtār*, Cairo, 1330/1919; Cairo, 1959; Vatican Library MS Borg No. 125.

Beiträge zur Geschichte der Mamlukensultane in dem Jahren 690–741 der Hiǵra nach arabischen Handschriften, ed. K. V. Zetterstéen, Leiden, 1919.

al-Bīrūnī, *al-Āthār al-bāqiya*, English trans. *The Chronology of Ancient Nations* by C. Edward Sachau, London, 1879.

Ibn 'Arabshāh, *at-T'alīf aṭ-ṭāhir fī shiyam al-Malik aẓ-Ẓāhir*, London, British Library MS BM Or. 3026.

Ibn 'Aṭā' Allāh, *Ibn 'Aṭā'illāh's Sufi Aphorisms* (*Kitāb al-Ḥikam*), trans. with intr. and notes by Victor Danner, Leiden, 1973.

Tāj al-'arūs al-ḥāwī li-tahdhīb an-nufūs, on the margins of Ibn 'Aṭā' Allāh, *Kitāb at-tanwīr fī isqāṭ at-tadbīr*, Cairo, 1321/1903–4.

Ibn Baṭṭūṭa, *Riḥla*, Beirut, 1379/1960; English trans. *The Travels of Ibn Baṭṭūṭa A.D. 1325–54* by H. A. R. Gibb, 3 vols., Cambridge, 1958–71.

Ibn ad-Dawādārī, *Kanz ad-durar wa-jāmi'l-ghurar*, Vol. IX: *ad-Durr al-fākhir fī sīrat al-Malik an-Nāṣir*, ed. Hans R. Roemer, Cairo, 1960.

Ibn Duqmāq, *al-Intiṣār li-wāsiṭat 'iqd al-amṣār*, Vols. IV and V, Cairo, 1309/1891–2.

Ibn Furāt, *Ta'rīkh Ibn al-Furāt*, Vols. VII–IX, ed. Costi K. Zurayk, Beirut, 1936–42.

Ibn Ḥajar al-'Asqalānī, *ad-Durar al-kāmina fī a'yān al-mi'a ath-thāmina*, 5 vols., Cairo, 1385/1966.

Inbā' al-ghumr bi-anbā' al-'umr, 3 vols., Cairo, 1969–72; 9 vols., Hyderabad, 1967–76.

Ibn al-Ḥājj al-'Abdarī, *al-Madkhal*, 2 vols., Cairo, 1348/1929.

Ibn al-Ḥimṣī, *Ḥawādith az-zamān wa-wafayāt ash-shuyūkh wa'l-aqrān*, Vol. II, Cambridge University Library MS Dd.11.2[7].

Ibn Hishām, *as-Sīra an-nabawiyya*, 2 vols., Cairo, 1375/1955.

Ibn Iyās, *Badā'i' az-zuhūr fī waqā'i' ad-duhūr*, 2 vols., Būlāq, 1311–12/1893–5; 5 vols., Cairo and Wiesbaden, 1960–75.
Ibn Kathīr, *al-Bidāya wa'n-nihāya fi't-ta'rīkh*, 14 vols., Cairo, 1351/1932.
Ibn Ma'mūn al-Baṭā'iḥī, *Passages de la chronique d'Egypte*, ed. Ayman F. Sayyid, Cairo, 1983.
Ibn Muyassar, *Akhbār Miṣr* (*Choix de passages de la chronique d'Egypte d'Ibn Muyassar*), ed. Ayman Fuad Sayyid, Cairo, 1981.
Ibn Sa'd, *aṭ-Ṭabaqāt al-kubrā*, 8 vols., Beirut, 1376/1957–1380/1960.
Ibn Taghrī Birdī, *Ḥawādith ad-duhūr fī maḍā'l-ayyām wash-shuhūr*, ed. William Popper, University of California Publications in Semitic Philology, Vol. 8, Berkeley, 1942.
al-Manhal aṣ-ṣāfī wa'l-mustawfī ba'da'l-wāfī, 4 vols., Cairo, 1984–6.
an-Nujūm az-zāhira fī mulūk Miṣr wa'l-Qāhira, 16 vols., Cairo, 1929–72; English trans. *History of Egypt 1392–1469 A.D.* by William Popper, University of California Publications in Semitic Philology, Vols. 13–19, 22–4, Berkeley, 1953–63.
Ibn Ẓāfir, Ṣafī ad-Dīn Ibn Abī'l-Manṣūr, *La Risāla: biographies des maîtres spirituels connus par un cheikh égyptien du VIIe/XIIIe siècle*, ed. and trans. Denis Gril, Cairo, 1986.
al-Jawharī, *Inbā' al-haṣr bi-abnā' al-'aṣr*, Cairo, 1970.
Nuzhat an-nufūs wa'l-abdān fī tawārīkh az-zamān, 3 vols., Cairo, 1970–4.
al-Kisā'ī, *The Tales of the Prophets of al-Kisā'ī*, trans. W. M. Thackston, Jr, Boston, 1978.
al-Majlisī, *Biḥār al-anwār*, 2nd edn, 110 vols., Tehran, 1965–72.
al-Maqrīzī, *Ighāthat al-umma bi-kashf al-ghumma*, Cairo, 1957.
Itti'āẓ al-ḥunafā' bi-akhbār al-a'imma al-Fāṭimiyyīn al-khulafā', 3 vols., Cairo, 1967–73.
al-Mawā'iẓ wa'l-i'tibār bi-dhikr al-khiṭaṭ wa'l-āthār, 2 vols., Būlāq, 1854; partly ed. Gaston Wiet, 5 vols., Cairo, 1911–27; French trans. Paul Casanova, 2 pts, Cairo, 1906–20.
as-Sulūk li-ma'rifat duwal al-mulūk, 4 vols., Cairo, 1934–73.
al-Mas'ūdī, Abū'l-Ḥasan 'Alī, attributed, *Ithbāt al-waṣiyya li'l-imām 'Alī b. Abī Ṭālib*, Najaf, 1374/1955.
Mufaḍḍal b. Abī'l-Faḍā'il, *an-Nahj as-sadīd wa'd-durr al-farīd fī mā ba'da ta'rīkh Ibn al-'Amīd* (*Ägypten und Syrien zwischen 1317 und 1341 in der Chronik des Mufaḍḍal b. Abī l-Faḍā'il*), ed. Samira Kortantamer, Freiburg i. B., 1973.
Musabbiḥī, *Akhbār Miṣr* (*Chronique d'Egypte*), ed. Ayman F. Sayyid and Thierry Bianquis, Cairo, 1978.
Muṣṭafā 'Alī's Description of Cairo of 1599, ed., trans., and annot. Andreas Tietze, Vienna, 1975.
an-Nuwayrī, *Nihāyat al-arab fī funūn al-adab*, 30 vols., Cairo, 1923–90; Leiden University Library MS OR–2N.
al-Qalqashandī, *Ṣubḥ al-a'shā*, 14 vols., Cairo, 1914–28.
as-Sakhāwī, *aḍ-Ḍaw' al-lāmi' fī a'yān al-qarn at-tāsi'*, 12 vols., Cairo, 1353–5/1934–6.
at-Tibr al-masbūk fī dhayl as-sulūk, Būlāq, 1896.
Tuḥfat al-aḥbāb wa-bughyat aṭ-ṭullāb, Cairo, 1356/1937.
aṣ-Ṣāliḥī, Muḥammad b. Yūsuf, *Subul al-hudā war-rashād fī sīrat khayr al-'ibād* (= *as-Sīra ash-shāmiyya*), 6 vols., Cairo, 1392/1972–1402/1982.
ash-Sha'rānī, 'Abd al-Wahhāb b. Aḥmad, *aṭ-Ṭabaqāt al-kubrā*, Cairo, 1316/1898.
aṭ-Ṭabaqāt aṣ-ṣughrā, Cairo, 1390/1970.

ash-Shujā'ī, *Ta'rīkh al-Malik an-Nāṣir Muḥammad b. Qalāwūn aṣ-Ṣāliḥī wa-awlādihi*, ed. Barbara Schäfer, Wiesbaden, 1977.
as-Suyūṭī, *Ḥusn al-muḥāḍara fī ta'rīkh Miṣr wa'l-Qāhira*, 2 vols., Cairo, 1904.
aṭ-Ṭabarī, *Ta'rīkh ar-rusul wa'l-mulūk*, 3 vols., Leiden, 1964.
Tha'labī, Abū Isḥāq Aḥmad, *Qiṣaṣ al-anbiyā'* or *'Arā'is al-majālis*, Cairo, 1950.
Travels of Ibn Baṭṭūṭa, see Ibn Baṭṭūṭa.
at-Turkumānī, Idrīs b. Baydākīn, *Kitāb al-luma' fi'l-ḥawādith wa'l-bida'*, ed. Subhi Labib, 2 vols., Wiesbaden, 1986.
al-Yūnīnī, Quṭb ad-Dīn, *Dhayl mir'āt az-zamān*, 4 vols., Hyderabad, 1954–61.
Zurqānī, Muḥammad b. 'Abd al-Bāqī, *Sharḥ 'alā'l-mawāhib al-laduniyya*, Vol. I, Cairo, 1325/1907.

Secondary works

Abrahams, Roger D., and Richard Bauman, "Ranges of Festival Behavior", in Barbara A. Babcock (ed.), *The Reversible World: Symbolic Inversion in Art and Society*, Ithaca, 1978.
Abu Lughod, Janet L., *Cairo: 1001 Years of the City Victorious*, Princeton, 1971.
Ahlwardt, W., *Die Handschriften-Verzeichnisse der königlichen Bibliothek zu Berlin, arabische Handschriften*, 10 vols., Berlin, 1887–99.
Ashtor, E., *Histoire des prix et des salaires dans l'Orient médiéval*, Paris, 1969.
'Ashūr, Sa'īd 'Abd al-Fattāḥ, *al-Mujtama' al-miṣrī fī 'aṣr salātīn al-mamālīk*, Cairo, 1962.
Aston, Margaret, "Popular Religious Movements in the Middle Ages", in Geoffrey Barraclough (ed.), *The Christian World: A Social and Cultural History*, New York, 1981, pp. 157–70.
Babcock, Barbara A. (ed.), *The Reversible World: Symbolic Inversion in Art and Society*, Ithaca, 1978.
Badawi, M. M., "Medieval Arabic Drama: Ibn Dāniyāl", *Journal of Arabic Literature* 13 (1982), 83–107.
Bannerth, Ernst, "La Rifā'iyya en Egypte", *Mélanges de l'Institut dominicain d'études orientales du Caire* 10 (1970), 1–35.
Bianquis, Thierry, "Une crise frumentaire dans l'Egypte fatimide", *JESHO* 23 (1980), 67–101.
Boglioni, Pierre, "La Culture populaire au moyen âge: thèmes et problèmes", in *La Culture populaire au moyen âge*, Montreal, 1979, pp. 13–37.
Boyce, Mary, "Iranian Festivals", in Ehsan Yarshater (ed.), *The Cambridge History of Iran*, Vol. III, pt 2: *The Seleucid, Parthian and Sasanian Periods*, Cambridge, 1983, pp. 792–815.
Brinner, W. M., "Ḥarfūsh", *EI*².
Brockelmann, Carl, *Geschichte der arabischen Litteratur*, 2nd edn, 2 vols., Leiden, 1943–9; 3 supplementary vols., Leiden, 1937–42.
Buhl, Fr. and J. Jomier, "Maḥmal", *EI*².
Burke, Peter, *Popular Culture in Early Modern Europe*, New York, 1978.
"Popular Culture between History and Ethnology", *Ethnologia Europaea* 14 (1984), 5–13.
Chartier, Roger, "Culture as Appropriation: Popular Cultural Uses in Early Modern France", in Steven L. Kaplan (ed.), *Understanding Popular Culture: Europe from the Middle Ages to the Nineteenth Century*, Berlin, 1984, pp. 229–53.

Clark, Stuart, "Inversion, Misrule and the Meaning of Witchcraft", *Past & Present* 87 (1980), 98–127.
"French Historians and Early Modern Popular Culture", *Past & Present* 100 (1983), 62–99.
Coquin, R. G., "Les Fêtes coptes vues par les Musulmans", *Nouvelle revue du Caire* 2 (1978), 57–76.
Davis, Natalie Zemon, *Society and Culture in Early Modern France*, Stanford, 1975.
"From 'Popular Religion' to Religious Cultures", in Steven Ozment (ed.), *Reformation Europe: A Guide to Research*, St Louis, 1982, pp. 321–41.
Dols, Michael W., *The Black Death in the Middle East*, Princeton, 1977.
Duri, A. A., "The Iraq School of History to the Ninth Century – A Sketch", in Bernard Lewis and P. M. Holt (eds.), *Historians of the Middle East*, London, 1962, pp. 46–53.
The Rise of Historical Writing among the Arabs, Princeton, 1983.
Fernandes, Leonor, "Some Aspects of the *zāwiya* in Egypt at the Eve of thc Ottoman Conquest", *AI* 19 (1983), 9–17.
The Evolution of a Sufi Institution in Mamluk Egypt: The Khanqah, Berlin, 1988.
Frazer, J. G., *The Golden Bough: A Study in Magic and Religion*, pt 3: *The Dying God*, 3rd edn, London, 1911; pt 6: *The Scapegoat*, 3rd edn, London, 1913.
Fuchs, H., "Mawlid", *EI*[1].
Fuchs, H. and F. de Jong, "Mawlid", *EI*[2].
Garcin, Jean-Claude, "Histoire et hagiographie de l'Egypte musulmane à la fin de l'époque mamelouke et au début de l'époque ottomane", in *Hommages à la mémoire de Serge Souneron 1927–1976*, Vol. II: *Egypte post-pharaonique*, Cairo, 1979, rep. in Jean-Claude Garcin, *Espaces, pouvoirs et idéologies de l'Egypte médiévale*, London, 1987.
Gardet, L., "Dhikr", *EI*[2].
Gilhus, Ingvild Salid, "Carnival in Religion: The Feast of Fools in France", *Numen* 37 (1990), 24–52.
Gluckman, Max, *Rituals of Rebellion in South-East Africa*, Manchester, 1952.
Goitein, S. D., *A Mediterranean Society*, Vol. I: *Economic Foundations*, Berkeley, 1967.
Goldwasser, Maria Julia, "Carnival", in Mirca Eliade (ed.), *Encyclopedia of Religion*, 16 vols., New York, 1987, Vol. III.
Goldziher, Ignaz, "Veneration of Saints in Islam", in Ignaz Goldziher, *Muslim Studies*, Vol. II, London, 1971, pp. 255–341.
Griveau, Robert, "Les Fêtes des Coptes", *Patrologia Orientalis* 10 (1915), 333–43.
Grunebaum, G. E. von, *Muhammadan Festivals*, London, 1951.
Gurevich, Aron, *Medieval Popular Culture: Problems of Belief and Perception*, Cambridge, 1988.
Hall, David, Introduction to Steven L. Kaplan (ed.), *Understanding Popular Culture: Europe from the Middle Ages to the Nineteenth Century*, Berlin, 1984, pp. 5–18.
Hall, Stuart, "Notes on Deconstructing 'the Popular'", in Raphael Samuel (ed.), *People's History and Socialist Theory*, London, 1981, pp. 227–40.
Heers, Jacques, *Fêtes des fous et carnavals*, Paris, 1983.
Irwin, Robert, *The Middle East in the Middle Ages: The Early Mamluk Sultanate 1250–1382*, London, 1986.
Jomier, Jacques, *Le Maḥmal et la caravane égyptienne des pèlerins de la Mecque (XIIIe–XXe siècles)*, Cairo, 1953.

Jong, F. de, "Cairene *Ziyāra*-Days: A Contribution to the Study of Saint Veneration in Islam", *Welt des Islams* NS 17 (1976–7), 26–43.

Kinser, Samuel, "Presentation and Representation: Carnival at Nuremberg 1450–1550", *Representations* 13 (1986), 1–41.

Carnival American Style: Mardi Gras at New Orleans and Mobile, Chicago, 1990.

Kister, M. J., "Some Reports concerning Mecca from Jāhiliyya to Islam", *JESHO* 15 (1972), 61–93, rep. in M. J. Kister, *Studies in Jāhiliyya and Early Islam*, London, 1980.

"The *Sīrah* Literature", in A. F. L. Beeston *et al.* (eds.), *Arabic Literature to the End of the Umayyad Period*, Cambridge, 1983, pp. 352–67.

Klunzinger, C. B., *Upper Egypt: Its People and its Products*, English trans., New York, 1878.

Ladurie, Emmanuel Le Roy, *Carnival in Romans*, New York, 1979.

Lane, E. W., *Manners and Customs of the Modern Egyptians*, London, 1966.

Langner, Barbara, *Untersuchungen zur historischen Volkskunde Ägyptens nach mamlukischen Quellen*, Berlin, 1983.

Lapidus, Ira Marvin, *Muslim Cities in the Later Middle Ages*, Cambridge, Mass., 1967.

"The Grain Economy of Mamluk Egypt", *JESHO* 12 (1969), 1–15.

Leeder, S. H., *Modern Sons of the Pharaohs: A Study of the Manners and Customs of the Copts of Egypt*, London, 1918.

Le Goff, Jacques, "The Learned and Popular Dimensions of Journeys in the Otherworld in the Middle Ages", in Steven L. Kaplan (ed.), *Understanding Popular Culture: Europe from the Middle Ages to the Nineteenth Century*, Berlin, 1984, pp. 16–37.

Levy, R., "Nawrūz", *EI*[1].

Little, Donald P., "The Nature of *Khānqāh*s, *Ribāṭ*s, and *Zāwiya*s under the Mamlūks", in Wael B. Hallaq and Donald P. Little (eds.), *Islamic Studies Presented to Charles J. Adams* (Leiden, 1991), pp. 91–105.

McPherson, J. W., *The Moulids of Egypt*, Cairo, 1941.

Makdisi, G., "Ibn ʿAṭāʾ Allāh", *EI*[2].

Mandrou, Robert, "Cultures populaire et savante: rapport et contacts", in Jacques Beauroy *et al.* (eds.), *The Wolf and the Lamb: Popular Culture in France from the Old Regime to the Twentieth Century*, Saratoga, 1976.

Massignon, L., "Nūr Muḥammadī", *EI*[1].

Memon, Muhammad Umar, *Ibn Taimiya's Struggle against Popular Religion*, Mouton, 1976.

Mez, Adam, *The Renaissance of Islam*, London, 1937.

Molan, Peter D., "Charivari in a Medieval Egyptian Shadow Play", *Al-Masāq* 1 (1988), 5–24.

Muchembled, Robert, *Popular Culture and Elite Culture in France, 1400–1750*, Baton Rouge, 1985.

Murray, Alexander, "Religion among the Poor in Thirteenth-Century France: The Testimony of Humbert of Romans", *Traditio* 30 (1974), 285–324.

Murray, M. A., "Nawruz: or the Coptic New Year", *Ancient Egypt* (1921), 79–81.

"Maqrizi's Names of the Pharaohs", *Ancient Egypt* (1924), 51–5.

an-Najjār, Muḥammad Rajab, *Hikāyāt ash-shuṭṭār wa'l-ʿayyārīn fi't-turāth al-ʿarabī*, Kuwait, 1981.

Newby, Gordon Darnell, *The Making of the Last Prophet: A Reconstruction of the Earliest Biography of Muḥammad*, Columbia, S.C., 1989.

Nwyia, Paul, *Ibn 'Aṭā' Allāh (m. 709/1309) et la naissance de la confrérie Šāḏilite*, Beirut, 1972.

Paret, Rudi, *Die legendäre Maghāzi–Literatur, arabische Dichtungen über die muslimischen Kriegszüge zu Mohammeds Zeit*, Tübingen, 1930.

Petry, Carl F., *The Civilian Elite of Cairo in the Later Middle Ages*, Princeton, 1981.

Poliak, A. N., "Les Révoltes populaires en Egypte à l'époque des mamelouks et leurs causes économiques", *REI* 8 (1934), 251–73.

Raymond, André, "La Population du Caire de Maqrīzī à la Description de l'Egypte", *BEO* 28 (1975), 201–15.

"La Population du Caire et de l'Egypte a l'époque ottomane et sous Muḥammad 'Alī", in *Mémorial Ömer Lûtfi Barkan*, Paris, 1980, pp. 169–78.

Rosenthal, F., "al-Bakrī, Abū'l-Ḥasan", *EI*².

Rubin, U., "Pre-existence and Light, Aspects of the Concept of Nūr Muḥammad", *Israel Oriental Studies* 5 (1975), 62–119.

Sanders, Paula A., "The Court Ceremonial of the Fatimid Caliphate in Egypt", unpublished doctoral dissertation, Princeton University, 1984.

as-Sayyād, Fu'ād 'Abd al-Mu'ṭī, *Nawrūz wa-āthāruhu fi' l-adab al-'arabī*, Beirut, 1972.

Schimmel, Annemarie, "Some Glimpses of the Religious Life in Egypt during the Later Mamlūk Period", *Islamic Studies* 4 (1965), 353–92.

"Sufismus und Heiligenverehrung im Spätmittelalterlichen Ägypten", in E. Gräf (ed.), *Festschrift Werner Caskel*, Leiden, 1968, pp. 274–89.

Scribner, R. W. (Bob), "Reformation, Carnival and the World turned Upside-down", *Social History* 3 (1978), 303–29.

"Ritual and Popular Religion in Catholic Germany at the Time of the Reformation", *Journal of Ecclesiastical History* 35 (1984), 47–77, rep. in R. W. Scribner, *Popular Culture and Popular Movements in Reformation Germany*, London, 1987, pp. 17–47.

Shaked, Shaul, "Aspekte von Noruz, dem iranischen Neujahrsfest", in Jan Assmann and Theo Sundermeier (eds.), *Studien zum Verstehen fremder Religionen*, Vol. I: *Das Fest und das Heilige*, Gütersloh, 1991, pp. 88–102.

Shoshan, Boaz, "Fāṭimid Grain Policy and the Post of the Muḥtasib", *IJMES* 13 (1981), 181–9.

"High Culture and Popular Culture in Medieval Islam", *Studia Islamica* 83 (1991), 67–107.

Somerville, John C., *Popular Religion in Restoration England*, Gainesville 1977.

Spufford, Margaret, *Small Books and Pleasant Histories: Popular Fiction and its Readership in Seventeenth-Century England*, Athens, Ga., 1982.

Staffa, Susan Jane, *Conquest and Fusion: The Social Evolution of Cairo A.D. 642–1850*, Leiden, 1977.

at-Taftazānī, Abū'l-Wafā', *Ibn 'Aṭā' Allāh al-Iskandarī wa-taṣawwufuhu*, 2nd edn, Cairo, 1969.

Taylor, Christopher S., "The Cult of Saints in Late Medieval Egypt", *Newsletter of the American Research Center in Egypt* 139 (1987), 13–16.

Thompson, Edward P., "The Moral Economy of the English Crowd in the Eighteenth Century", *Past & Present* 50 (1971), 76–136.

Tilly, Louise A., "The Food Riots as a Form of Political Conflict in France", *Journal of Interdisciplinary History* 2 (1971), 23–57.

Trimingham, J. Spencer, *The Sufi Orders in Islam*, Oxford, 1971.

Turner, Victor W., *The Ritual Process: Structure and Anti-Structure*, London, 1969.

Vollers, K., "Aḥmed al-Badawī", *EI*[1].

Vollers, K. and E. Littmann, "Aḥmad al-Badawī", *EI*[2].

Watt, W. Montgomery, *Muhammad at Mecca*, Oxford, 1953.

"The Materials Used by Ibn Isḥāq", in Bernard Lewis and P. M. Holt (eds.), *Historians of the Middle East*, London, 1962, pp. 23–34.

Weidkuhn, Peter, "Carnival in Basle: Playing History in Reverse", *Cultures* 3/1 (1976), 29–53.

Weinstein, Donald and Rudolph M. Bell, *Saints & Society: The Two Worlds of Western Christendom, 1000–1700*, Chicago, 1982.

Westermarck, Edward, *Pagan Survivals in Mohammedan Civilisation*, London, 1933, rep. Amsterdam, 1973.

Wiet, Gaston, *Cairo: City of Art and Commerce*, Norman, 1964.

Wilson, Stephen (ed.), *Saints and their Cults: Studies in Religious Sociology, Folklore and History*, Cambridge, 1983.

Winter, Michael, *Society and Religion in Early Ottoman Egypt: Studies in the Writings of 'Abd al-Wahhāb al-Sha'rānī*, New Brunswick, 1982.

Yarshater, Ehsan, "Nawrūz", in Mirca Eliade (ed.), *Encyclopedia of Religion*, 16 vols., New York, 1987, vol. x.

Yaziçi, Tahsin, "Ḳalandāriyya", *EI*[2].

Index